D0128697

GWYNETH PALTROW

GWYNETH PALTROW

Valerie Milano

The publication of *Gwyneth Paltrow* has been generously supported by the Government of Canada through the Book Publishing Industry Development Program.

CANADIAN CATALOGUING IN PUBLICATION DATA

Milano, Valerie
Gwyneth Paltrow

ISBN 1-55022-407-7

1. Paltrow, Gwyneth. 2. Motion picture actors and actresses – United States – Biography. I. Title.
PN2287.P227M54 2000 791.43'028'092 C00-930436-3

Front cover photo by Tammy Calder / Shooting Star.
Back cover photo by Paul Jasmin / Visages.
Cover design by Guylaine Régimbald.
Interior design by Yolande Martel.
This book is set in Electra and Fairfield.

Printed by Printcrafters Inc., Winnipeg, Manitoba, Canada.
Distributed in Canada by General Distribution Services,
325 Humber College Blvd., Etobicoke, Ontario M9W 7C3.
Distributed in the United States by LPC Group,
1436 West Randolph Street, Chicago, Illinois, 60607. U.S.A.

Published by ECW PRESS,
2120 Queen Street East, Suite 200,
Toronto, Ontario M4E 1E2.
ecwpress.com

PRINTED AND BOUND IN CANADA

Contents

Introduction

WELL BEFORE CELEBRATING HER 30TH BIRTHDAY, Gwyneth Paltrow has lived what by all appearances is a charmed, fairy-tale existence. By the time she turned 26, she had appeared in 20 feature films and won an Academy Award for Best Actress. Her personal life seems just as rich as her professional one, with highly publicized romances with perennial heartthrob Brad Pitt and movie-star-of-the-near-future Ben Affleck. And if those relationships didn't endure, well, Paltrow always exudes that particular kind of confidence that leaves the lasting impression that these dalliances were mere learning experiences, necessary emotional interludes before finding the person who will inevitably be the true great love of her life. Because, after all, isn't that what happens to a princess?

And make no mistake, as Hollywood peeks around the corner at the brave new millennial world, Paltrow is first among the vanguard of actors on whom the hopes of Hollywood Future lie. Certainly, she has the pedigree — as the daughter of actress Blythe Danner and director/producer Bruce Paltrow, Gwyneth is seen by many as Hollywood royalty, the scion of artistic and literate parents who are not only respected by their peers but admired for successfully balancing their professional and personal lives while raising unusually gifted, cultured, and responsible children. Neither Gwyneth nor her brother Jake are likely to ever make headlines bouncing in and out of rehab centers or getting arrested for trashing hotel rooms.

But at the same time, the very values that keep Gwyneth Paltrow grounded also keep her at a wary distance from the celebrity machine. No doubt because she was literally raised around a movie set, Paltrow tends to project an intriguing air of aloofness toward her fans and the media, making her a bit of an enigma. Thus, it's more than just her fair complexion and patrician looks that have prompted others to dub her the new Grace Kelly of her generation.

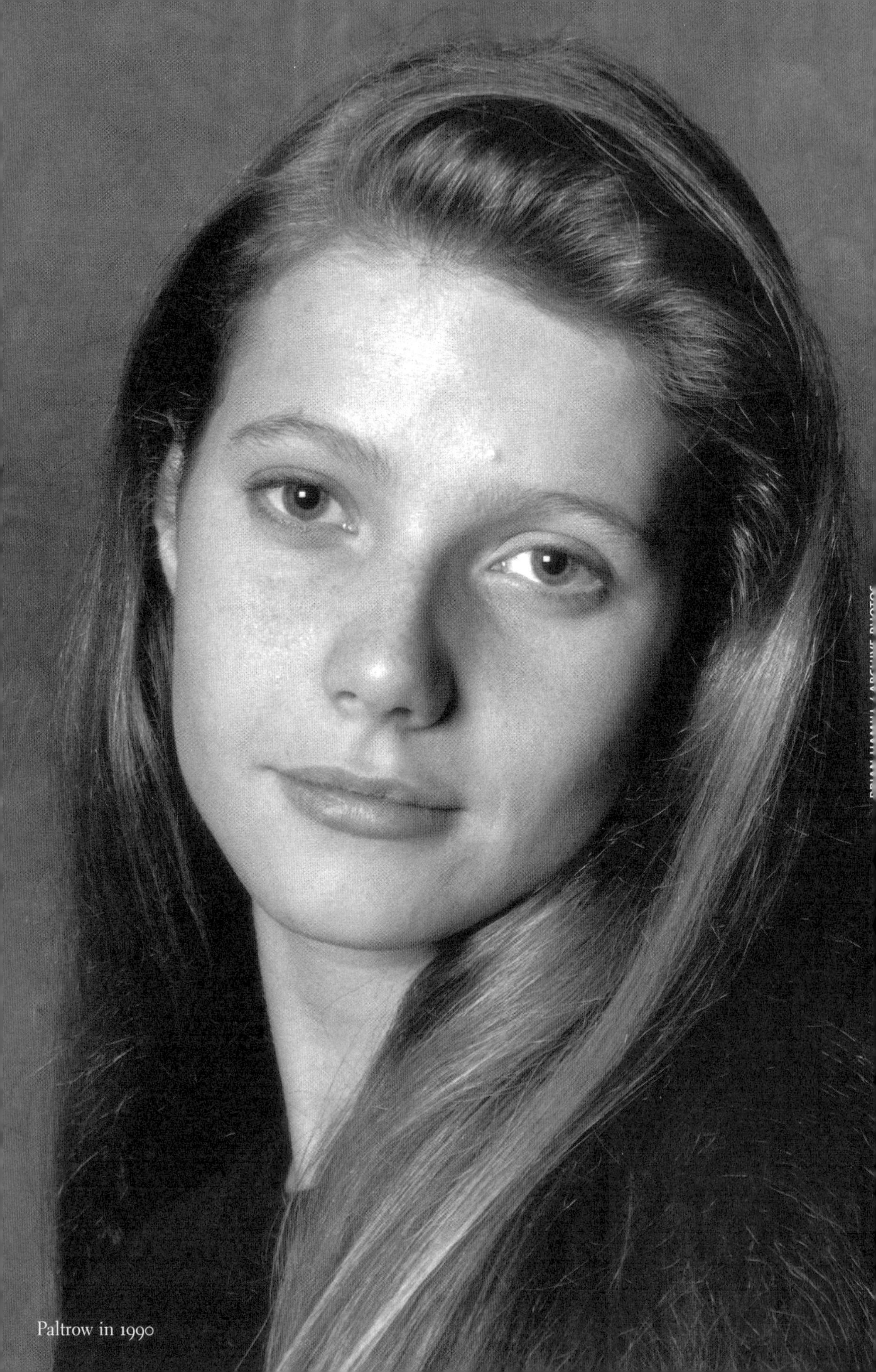

Paltrow in 1990

From the earliest days of her career, Paltrow has been known to ooze an ever-so-slight reserve that has been interpreted as coolness by some and self-protection by others. More than likely, Paltrow is simply trying to follow the example set by wise parents who never let the glamour of show business intrude upon their private lives and who kept *what* they did in proper perspective in relation to *who* they were as people.

That said, not even the most sage of parents can completely prepare their children for life away from the nest — especially when said child becomes romantically involved with one of the most desired men in the world. Paltrow's relationship with and engagement to Brad Pitt thrust her into the white-hot glare of the media in a way that could have embittered the most amiable of souls. But again, Paltrow's breeding won out, and she not only survived the experience but also seemed to emerge the better for it: not only more mature but with her humor and dignity more deeply honed.

Perhaps more than anything, it is Paltrow's ability to maintain grace under pressure that sets this Hollywood princess apart from her peers. Her maturity, combined with obvious talent and proven screen presence, puts her squarely at the head of the Hollywood class of 2000 and makes her someone worth getting to know beyond the press releases and sound bites.

1

The Stuff of Which Dreams Are Made

IT'S MARCH 21, 1999, and the stage is set for the 71st Annual Academy Awards. When Gwyneth Paltrow steps out of her limousine, she pauses for the briefest of moments to look at the scene taking place outside the Dorothy Chandler Pavilion, one of Los Angeles's grandest theater showplaces. Rolled out at her feet is the red carpet, which at the moment is filled with the movie world's best and brightest. On one side of the carpet, stardust-glazed fans, compressed together on bleachers, seem to shriek louder with each new famous face who walks past. On the other side, the photographers and press are lined up, desperately calling out to the stars and beseeching them to strike a pose in their direction so that they can obtain the money shot their publications expect.

There are so many celebrities flowing past, it's hard for the fans and media to know whom to call out to first. Anne Heche and Ellen DeGeneres, who are celebrating their one-year anniversary, are there, and so is Geoffrey Rush and Paltrow's fellow Best Actress nominee, Cate Blanchett. Liam Neeson, Uma Thurman, and power couple Warren Beatty and Annette Benning can be spotted, too. But even in the overflow of arrivals, Paltrow seems to move as though backlit by an aura of expectation.

Accompanying Paltrow, one of Hollywood's most eligible bachelorettes, is her father, Bruce Paltrow, who follows a step or two behind his daughter, soaking in each step she takes with poignantly apparent parental pride. At one point, Bruce gallantly steps forward to shield Gwyneth from a potentially embarrassing photo op when one of her bra pads abruptly slips. Papa Paltrow acts as a human screen while his daughter hastily rearranges the undergarments of her flowing pink gown.

As she moves slowly down the carpet, waving to fans, being bathed in bursts of flashbulbs, and graciously answering questions for a dozen broadcast reporters, Paltrow refuses to acknowledge her position as front-

Paltrow's father escorts her to the 1999 Academy Awards
ALEC MICHAEL / GLOBE PHOTOS

runner for the Best Actress Award, saying over and over how honored she is just to be there.

A half hour before the Academy Awards are to begin, all those wanting to make a fashionably almost-late entrance converge on the carpet, creating a mob of sequins and tuxes. Nervous network staffers, anxious to get everyone in their seats by the start of the live telecast, plead with those still outside to *please* get inside. At one point, a loudspeaker squawks insistently, "Mr. Nolte, the doors are closing. Please enter the theater."

As Paltrow and her father leave the deafening noise and disconcerting chaos of the red carpet area behind them, the atmosphere subtly changes. As the telecast begins, a mist of anxious excitement is suddenly felt; over the next few hours, the lives of a lucky few in the audience will be changed forever. And in the case of Gwyneth Paltrow, it seems inevitable that the night will ultimately belong to her, because no other actor, male or female, has come so far so fast. In fact, Paltrow's life has been so charmed that, had it been a movie, she probably would have turned down the part for lack of believability. Indeed, the story of Paltrow's life really is the stuff of which dreams are made.

FROM THE VERY BEGINNING of her life, Gwyneth Paltrow was truly extraordinary. That fact first became apparent to her mother, Blythe Danner, in the summer of 1974, when she was appearing in a production of *The Seagull* at the Williamstown Theater in Massachusetts. Danner recalls rehearsing at the theater one day when Gwyneth was still a toddler.

"She didn't have anything on except her golden curls," Danner says. "She could barely talk, yet she knew the whole speech better than I did." She recalls Gwyneth starting to recite lines of dialogue, Chekhov's words being spoken in the lisping voice of a child. "'The men, the lions, the eagles, the part-widges,'" Danner recalls to *Time* magazine's Richard Corliss, imitating her daughter. "That was the beginning. We should have known then, I guess."

It actually should have come as no surprise to Danner and her husband, Bruce Paltrow, that both of their children, Gwyneth and her younger brother Jake, would end up following in their parents' artistic footsteps, since show business is literally in their blood. Paltrow's mom is considered one of the premiere actresses of her generation. Born in Philadelphia in 1943 to a banker father and housewife mother, Danner was raised with an emphasis on manners and decorum. After attending Bard College, she served notice on the American theater scene in 1968 with her performance in the off-Broadway play, *Summertree*. A year later, she earned a Best Supporting Actress Tony for *Butterflies Are Free*, her Broadway debut. That same year, 1969, she met an up-and-coming director and producer named Bruce Paltrow, and the two were married.

After more theater roles, including the musical *1776* in which Danner played Thomas Jefferson's wife, she and Paltrow moved to Los Angeles, and it wasn't long before Hollywood came a-calling, dubbing her "the new goddess in town." Danner costarred with Ken Howard in the 1973 series, *Adam's Rib*. The sitcom, based on the 1949 Katharine Hepburn–Spencer Tracy vehicle about newly wedded attorneys who find themselves representing opposing clients, was yanked after only a few months. Danner would later star in another series, *Tattinger's*, which was produced by her husband but which would suffer the same undistinguished end as *Adam's Rib*.

However, Danner fared much better on the big screen. After a role in *Hearts of the West*, she was cast as Robert Duvall's wife in *The Great Santini*, which became the sleeper hit of 1979 and further cemented her reputation as an actress of unusually high quality. After *The Great Santini*, it seemed as though Danner was poised for a major film career, but her true ambitions lay elsewhere.

"My mother probably could have been a bigger movie star than any woman of her generation," Paltrow says proudly. "She's a brilliant woman. But she chose to stay home and be with the family. For my mom, the family always came first. I can't believe the movies my mother turned down. Think of all the great women's roles in the early '80s and late '70s. But she didn't want to leave us. She's not ambitious like that, and I just respect her so much for that." As for Danner, it was no big deal. "I've had a fantastic life, a full life. I enjoyed motherhood and acting and trying to balance them," she tells Luaine Lee in August 1997.

Paltrow's senior year at Spence School, 1990

CLASSMATES.COM YEARBOOK ARCHIVES

Instead of pursuing a film career, Danner worked mostly in the theater, which allowed her to stay close to her young children — Gwyneth, born September 28, 1972, and Jake, born two years later. During the summer, the family would accompany Danner to Williamstown, Massachusetts, where she'd perform at the Williamstown Theater Festival, of which she has been a part for more than two decades. And it was during those long, lazy summer days of watching her mom work on stage that Paltrow's desire to act started taking root.

"I always knew I wanted to act. And I know I am an actress because my mother was an actress," Paltrow says. "My mom is a brilliant actress. I used to sit and watch her in the theater, just rehearsing, and it seemed so magical to me," she tells Demetrios Mattheou from the *Independent on Sunday*.

Paltrow says watching her mother dress up and become other people made her seem so "empowered." "I always knew that I wanted to do what my mom did, but my parents never encouraged me," she admits, explaining that "they didn't want their child to be heartbroken; they didn't know if I had no talent."

However, her brother Jake says Gwyneth, who as a youngster he named Gunny, "has always been creative and a little dramatic." "When I was 5, Gwyneth developed something called Pickleonial Tours. It was a very elaborate Universal Studios-type tour. She'd tie a Radio Flyer wagon to a Big Wheel and give kids tours of the neighborhood. She also developed an entire language with her friends. That was really impressive. She's always been a very together person," he tells David Hochman in *US* magazine.

While Paltrow's mom certainly had a most recognizable name and face, her dad, who also set an example of how to be uncompromising in one's work, was just as great an influence in her life. As a television writer and producer, Bruce Paltrow has earned a reputation for creating quality programs. Some, such as *St. Elsewhere* and *The White Shadow*, have been enormously successful; others, such as *Home Fires* and *Road Home*, less so. But through it all, Paltrow has stayed on course, regardless of ratings.

"Maybe it's because I'm getting older or because my children are getting bigger," Bruce Paltrow once commented, "but I just find the amount of violence in the world and the amount of dirt in the world and the aggressive nature of urban life — I just find it harder and harder and harder." Which is why he was among the first vanguard of producers in the 1990s to develop family dramas. In addition to not wanting to be part of the problem, Paltrow also believes "that our country is rooted in a fundamental love of family and love of home, and it just seems to me there is a better life out there and maybe we should examine it."

As is often the case of parents who make their living in the entertainment business, both Paltrow and Danner hoped their children would follow a different path, if for no other reason than their firsthand knowledge of how difficult a business it can be. But early on, Danner knew where her daughter's heart was. She recalls Gwyneth's performance of a cabaret number in first or second grade. "And during the applause, I saw this look in her eye," she tells critic Richard Corliss, "and I said to my husband, 'Oh, she's discovered it. Now she knows the thrill.'"

Thrill or no, Paltrow and Danner weren't about to unduly encourage Gwyneth at such an early age. "I worked with many child actors who unfortunately didn't have childhoods," Danner adds. "So the last thing we wanted to do was push our children into acting. We felt that if Gwyneth had talent and wanted a career, eventually it would find her and she would find it."

At the same time, however, the very nature of their parents' work was such that Gwyneth and Jake were frequently surrounded by people who were working in front of and behind the camera — two of their father's closest friends were Michael Douglas and Steven Spielberg, who Gwyneth calls Uncle Morty. "I've always loved films and always loved theater. Growing up and being exposed to all of it in that way is very productive for a child," Gwyneth opines.

Although Paltrow and Danner were well settled in Los Angeles, they made the surprising decision to relocate to New York. While the move meant that Danner would be better able to pursue opportunities in the theater, the uprooting was made primarily for the benefit of the children. As parents, Paltrow and Danner simply believed that New York was a more culturally rich environment in which to raise Gwyneth and Jake. Plus, it wasn't as though their children were unfamiliar with New York. Gwyneth had spent the better part of second and third grade there while Danner was appearing on Broadway, and they had several relatives who lived near the city.

"It was very important to my mother that we be raised for the latter part [of our childhoods] here," Gwyneth says. "I think she found so many aspects of LA superficial. There's so much culture in New York, the museums and the theater. Just walking down the street here you're exposed to everything."

So in 1984, Paltrow and Danner packed up the kids and moved east. It was a decision none of the Paltrows would ever regret.

Blythe Danner and Bruce Paltrow have always kept their children's best interests in mind

2

Destination Hollywood

PALTROW AND DANNER moved their family into a townhouse on 92nd Street, and Gwyneth found that life in Manhattan was a vast world apart from the beaches and casual environs of Los Angeles. This fact was made ever so clear at her new Upper East Side private all-girls prep school, the ultra chichi and academically demanding Spence, which had its students studying philosophy and law by the seventh grade.

Although the school is noted for its high standard of education, Paltrow didn't exactly seem to take advantage of her academic opportunities, finding the rigors of Spence so hard, she "would have found it easier to translate Hebrew." "You cannot believe the classes — law and physics in the seventh grade!" she says. "I was at sea."

Part of her difficulties might have stemmed from a heart that wasn't completely dedicated to her studies. "I'd have spurts of diligence, spurts of sloth," Paltrow acknowledges to *Buzz* magazine's Jesse Kornbluth, adding, "The move to New York itself was wonderful for me. No American education I know of compares to what you get in a New York private school — you get fed so well. And then you add what you learn just walking down the street."

However unique her education at Spence might have been, her teenage angst was typical. Gangly and awkward, Paltrow says she was not a youthful beauty. "I was an ugly duckling," she admits. "I had braces, and I was skinny and little, and I had a bad haircut."

Interestingly, after moving east, Paltrow temporarily seemed to lose a little of her performance fire, taking but one acting class. But it wasn't because her passion for acting was waning, it was simply because she was more focused on adjusting to such a different environment and lifestyle.

Then, when Paltrow was 13, she had what she considers an epiphany. "I was always with my mom on sets and in theaters, but I didn't really get it," she says, referring to what it really means to act. "I didn't say,

Smiling through senior year, 1990
CLASSMATES.COM YEARBOOK ARCHIVES

'Oh my mother's an actress,' I think because she put her kids so forward."

When she was in her early teens, however, Paltrow saw her mom play Blanche DuBois in the Williamstown Theater production of Tennessee Williams's classic, *A Streetcar Named Desire*, which costarred Christopher Walken and Sigourney Weaver.

"I had just returned from camp in Burlington, Vermont," Paltrow recalls to Sherryl Connelly of the *New York Daily News*. "I had never read the play or seen a rehearsal. I went to the opening night and sat with my father, and Mom was too much. I just saw her come completely apart in front of me. It was the most profound experience. It was the most powerful, moving thing I'd ever seen in my entire life. She was so extraordinary, so gifted. Afterward, when I went backstage in her dressing room, all I could do was weep. I held on to her and I cried and cried and cried."

From that point on, the summers in Williamstown took on a different meaning for Paltrow. "It was really an exceptional way to grow up," she reveals to David Hochman in *US* magazine, "because I was both in the realm of the acceptable world and also a carnie kid or a gypsy. On one hand, I had this great East Coast private-girls-school education. On the other, I would go to rehearsals with my mother and sit barefoot and cross-legged watching her work." She would also help her mother run her lines and do makeup.

Occasionally, Paltrow got the opportunity to enjoy the sensation of performing, kind of. "I believe the first play I was in, when I was about seven, was *The Greeks*," she recalls. "I played a dead child."

No matter what the role, the impression made upon Paltrow watching her mother emote on stage was indelible. "When you're growing up around someone who always chooses their work very carefully, and works with great people, and is unbelievably brilliant as an actress, you grow up seeing only the good side of show business — complete with morals, values, and concerns for decency," she reveals.

At school, Gwyneth played Titania, Queen of the Fairies, in a production of Shakespeare's *A Midsummer Night's Dream*. But even though their daughter's ambitions were starting to become more focused on show business, Paltrow and Danner still offered no overt support to her or, for that matter, to Jake, who was eyeing a career behind the camera *à la* dad. No matter how much Gwyneth pleaded to be allowed to go on some auditions, it was reiterated that school always had to come first.

"My parents wanted us to wait," Paltrow says. "There was never a sense that we needed to rush into this business." In fact, Danner admits that she harbored hopes that her daughter would ultimately pursue a more academic career. "I thought she was too bright," she admits. "I wanted her to be the next Margaret Mead."

But fate seemed to conspire against that hope, and when Paltrow was 16 years old, the first crack in her parents' armor appeared. One night, she and her dad went to see the movie *Silence of the Lambs* with family friends Kate Capshaw and Steven Spielberg. Paltrow recalls, "While we were standing in line, Steven just turned around and asked me if I'd like

CLASSMATES.COM YEARBOOK ARCHIVES

Paltrow and her parents have always been close
CLASSMATES.COM YEARBOOK ARCHIVES

to play Wendy in *Hook*. And I said, 'Certainly.'" Unfortunately, though, the movie was only in the preproduction stage, and it would be awhile before Paltrow would get her first taste of moviemaking.

Even though Danner had no intention of encouraging her daughter's thespian aspirations, she was adamant about exposing both of her children to as much theater as possible — whether they always liked it or not. "I saw Shakespeare in the Berkshires all the time," notes Paltrow. "But I mean, when I was 13, I'd rather have been watching *The Cosby Show*."

As she matured and reached high school age, Paltrow's youthful awkwardness gave way to a burgeoning beauty of which she wasn't particularly aware. Sometimes her regal good looks caused benign griping from her classmates, one of whom remembers standing in the locker room next to an unclothed Paltrow, who said, "Isn't it interesting how different people's bodies are?" "Like, she was comparing my body to hers," Paltrow's former classmate recalls, "and I just wanted to hit her." It was in high school, then, that people not only began seeing Paltrow as beautiful, but also as somewhat emotionally distant.

While in high school, Paltrow also had the opportunity to see some of the world, spending part of one school year as a foreign exchange student in Spain. And as time went on, Paltrow occasionally found herself falling into an Upper East Side stereotype, hanging out with friends and arguing the merits of Russian literature while drinking coffee and self-consciously smoking cigarettes. "It doesn't make any sense," Paltrow says now of this phase. "It's mental posturing."

Although every parent likes to hope that their child will be the exceptional teenager who won't rebel or cause gray hairs, Paltrow went through what Danner now refers to as the "tumultuous" years, although Gwyneth is quick to point out that now, "My mother and I are pretty good friends." Not only did her academic diligence wax and wane, but Paltrow was also prone to late nights out partying with friends, often not leaving the house until after her parents had gone to bed. However, Paltrow wasn't totally insensitive to her parents. She would leave notes under the assumption that it would spare them unnecessary worry, even though they knew she was hanging out at Upper East Side bars.

Dear Mom and Dad,
I didn't run away. I haven't been kidnapped. I'm out at the clubs. You can punish me in the morning.

By the time Paltrow graduated from Spence, it was abundantly clear that her parents' dreams of higher education for their daughter needed to be tempered. Her somewhat casual approach to school had earned her grades that weren't good enough to get Paltrow accepted into any of the top schools to which she had applied. She was finally accepted at the University of California at Santa Barbara, which had been made possible in large part by Michael Douglas, an alumni of UCSB, who had lobbied on her behalf.

"I chose the University of California at Santa Barbara because I had a romantic picture of a quiet school in a quaint beach town. Wrong!" Paltrow says, referring to the university's reputation as a party school.

Although she set out for college with the best of intentions, prepared to finish with a degree in art history, Paltrow's heart simply wasn't in the classroom, and she was forced to really ponder her future. "It was such an inappropriate place for me to be," she would later say. "I just felt something bigger out there waiting. I didn't know what it was. I didn't know if it had something to do with acting or love or, as it turned out, both of these things."

However, if you have to go to college, the University of Santa Barbara is a lovely place to spend four years. Located about an hour north of Los Angeles and nestled between the ocean and the mountains, you couldn't ask for a more beautiful setting to study and learn. But if your heart is elsewhere, even the best surroundings can become an emotional prison. Despite the opportunity to further her education, Paltrow's heart and mind would never be on the college's campus, because compared to acting, art history paled.

"I kept missing classes to drive to LA to audition," Paltrow would later admit. "I remember my father saying, 'You really have to do one thing or the other; either you should go to college or not. This middle ground is not productive, because neither is going to be productive when you're doing both half.'"

Even so, Paltrow was still torn between what she wanted to do and her natural desire to avoid disappointing her parents, who, she says, "had dreams of me being an anthropologist, something more academic." For as independent as she was, she craved her parents' blessing and couldn't move forward until she had it. That moment came during the summer after her first year of college.

As she always did, Danner was heading to Williamstown for the summer theater season. However, this particular year was special, because Danner, who was to star in a production of *Picnic*, had arranged for her daughter to also appear in the drama as the young female lead.

Throughout the summer, Paltrow had been engaged in an ongoing

Paltrow and a friend at NYC's Jet Lounge

© AZZARA / LIAISON AGENCY

discussion with her parents about her education. She had suggested that perhaps she take a hiatus from school, but her father was against it — he wanted her to make a definitive decision one way or the other.

Finally, it was her father's words that made her come to a decision. After watching a dress rehearsal, Paltrow's father went backstage and spoke the words his daughter had been waiting to hear. "He was being very effusive about my performance," Paltrow recalls, "and he said, 'I don't think you should go back.' It was this incredible moment in my life, because I never thought I would hear him say that. I knew then that he thought I had it." Later, in a discussion with John Clark of *Newsday*, Paltrow adds, "It's probably the one moment in my life that was truly one of the most amazing things and at the same time was really a definitive thing."

However, Paltrow does admit that she could have taken a different path. "I could have been something else," she muses to Jesse Kornbluth. "I would have loved to study art history, and then get an internship at the Guggenheim collection in Venice. But this is what I'm supposed to do." Like artisans of the past, Paltrow says, "I sort of feel like I'm doing my parents' trade."

Danner also came to accept that, once she saw "where [Gwyneth's] heart was and how talented she was," there was really no choice but to let her follow her personal muse. "I think [children] come into the world as they're going to be," Danner says, "and [Gwyneth] does have an extraordinary instrument, a fantastic talent."

While Paltrow's path may have been determined in the womb, Danner wanted to make sure that her daughter was clear about what really mattered, and she impressed upon her the idea that "work is the most important thing." As she recounts to journalist Luaine Lee in August 1997, Danner told Gwyneth, "You must work very hard, don't ever coast. You're incredibly talented, you're very, very beautiful, and don't be seduced by all the extraneous stuff. Remember, it's the work that's first."

But more than Danner's words, it was a lifetime of parental example, both professional and personal, that made the biggest impression on Paltrow. "I saw my parents do quality work, and I think that just forces you to push for a higher standard," Paltrow says. And it was that desire to live up to the quality of her parents' creative ethic that would most inform the direction that her career would ultimately take.

But before she could have a career, Paltrow needed a job or two. She moved herself to Los Angeles in the latter part of the summer of 1990, and her first order of business once she settled in was to find an agent and obtain her Screen Actor's Guild Union card.

Getting representation is always the biggest hurdle for up-and-coming actors, and it would be disingenuous not to suggest that, in this pursuit, Gwyneth did have a bit of an advantage having the Paltrow name. Even though she had only limited professional experience, including working

PATRICK MCMULLAN / LIAISON AGENCY

on a television pilot that her dad was shooting, Paltrow quickly found an agent willing to sign her; Hollywood is one place that openly acknowledges its nepotistic ways.

"Rick Kurtzman took me on," Paltrow says. "Everyone thought he was crazy. You know how it is in LA. No one gets excited until everyone gets excited; it's like sheep. But Rick signed me although I'd only done Williamstown and a pilot of my dad's — little nepotistic things. So I'll never leave him."

Although Paltrow's parents had given her full approval to pursue an acting career, they offered no other help. The family was obviously financially comfortable, but Paltrow was expected to support herself. If she wanted to be an actress, her parents wanted her to understand from the very start the possible financial hardships that might accompany such an endeavor.

Undaunted, Paltrow joined thousands of other would-be actors in getting the most flexible job available — waitressing. She worked at DC3, an expensive and then-trendy restaurant located on the property of Santa Monica Airport, which is an airport of a different kind. Used primarily for private planes, Santa Monica Airport plays host to several celebrity events every year and is also the home of Jerry Seinfeld's private car collection, which is stored in two leased hangars. "I would work in the restaurant, making $11 a night in tips, and buy a pack of cigarettes and coffee and toilet paper and stuff," Paltrow says of her early days in LA.

Home at the time was a small apartment not far from her job — not that she stayed home all that often. Just as she had done in New York, Paltrow became intimately familiar with the Los Angeles bar and club scene. One of her closer friends in those early struggling-actress days was Emily Lloyd, who had become film's latest teen sensation after starring in *Wish You Were Here*. Siskel and Ebert gave Lloyd their ultimate double thumbs up and called her work in the film, in which she plays a 1950s suburban English teenager desperate to lose her virginity, "one of the great debut performances of recent years." It was also a slightly controversial role, in that Lloyd's character, Lynda, ends up having an affair with a 52-year-old friend of her father.

Lloyd and Paltrow seemed inseparable for awhile, hanging out at then-hot spots like the Trinity and Tryst. "These clubs, they're so posey," Lloyd observes. "Everyone tries to look important. It's ridiculous, isn't it? Unless you're incredibly good-looking you don't get in. It's not fair."

That said, it didn't keep Lloyd at home. Although she was just a year older, Lloyd seemed eons wiser than Paltrow and was living a life her friend could only dream of. Lloyd had moved to Los Angeles while riding the crest of attention brought on by *Wish You Were Here* and immediately made another name for herself as one of the more social young stars. If there was a party going on, Lloyd was there.

"I'm not mature," she admits during an interview with John Stark of *People* magazine. "I like being slightly crazy. Like I walked into a train and pretended to have an epileptic fit just to see the reaction. I'm quite loud and open, and I speak before I think, so in that way, I guess I'm quite American."

Lloyd also made it clear that traditional theater training left her cold. "I can't believe what they got us to do, like pretend to be a chocolate in a chocolate box," she once recounted. "One day I got annoyed with the teacher and said, 'Look, I'm stale,' and I walked out of class."

Initially, it was that kind of candor and apparent lack of cynicism that made Lloyd a critical favorite and one of the most sought-after young actresses around. Directors all over town, including Steven Spielberg, put in requests to meet her. And she had her pick of films. She costarred with Peter Falk in *Cookie*, then played opposite Bruce Willis in *In Country*. Paltrow would listen with tugs of envy as Lloyd recounted preparing for her roles. For *Cookie*, she moved in with an Italian family in Brooklyn for two weeks to learn the nuances of the accent she would have to adopt for the part, then for *In Country*, she spent time in Paducah, Kentucky, in order to perfect a Southern drawl.

However, Lloyd was also the kind of child actor that Paltrow's parents had gone to great lengths to prevent their daughter from becoming. By the time she was 16, Lloyd had already dropped out of school, and by 17, she was living half a world away from her family. Like Paltrow, Lloyd also came from a theatrical family: her grandfather, Charles Lloyd Pack, was an actor; her father, Roger Lloyd Pack, is a leading member of London's National Theater Company; and her mother, Sheila, is a theatrical agent.

For the audition for *Wish You Were Here*, Lloyd says she went on pure instinct and won the role over 200 other actresses. But by the time Paltrow was ready to devote her full attention to acting, Lloyd was already becoming worn down by both the business and her own indulgent behavior. In 1990, Lloyd returned to her home in England, complaining of "nervous exhaustion." Unfortunately, in the ensuing years, she gained the kind of "rash and brash" reputation that can kill a career.

But ultimately, it was an apparent lack of grounding that had undermined Lloyd. Having watched up-close and personally her friend professionally self-destruct, Paltrow gleaned an important lesson on how not to handle a career. More than ever, Paltrow began to fully appreciate the tenacity her parents had shown in making sure that she was ready to meet the challenges offered by Hollywood, both on and off the sound stages.

3

The Big Screen

ALTHOUGH HER SCREEN TIME was minimal, *Hook*, which was released in 1991, provided Paltrow with her first taste of what working on a major Hollywood production is like. Considering that she would later become one of the queens of independent films, it's ironic that one of her inaugural film experiences would be on such a big-budget, convoluted Hollywood production that was typical of the way the major studios did business.

In 1985, composer John Williams and lyricist Leslie Bricusse worked on *Hook* as a stage musical, but the project was scrapped after about 10 songs were written. Then in 1988, director Nick Castle helped develop a script for TriStar Pictures that was meant to update the Peter Pan story. That script eventually became *Hook*, but Castle, who was supposed to direct the movie, was dumped and replaced by Steven Spielberg.

TriStar was supposed to make it up to Castle by signing him to direct *Sleepless in Seattle*, which the studio hoped would star Kim Basinger and Dennis Quaid. Eventually, Nora Ephron would direct Tom Hanks and Meg Ryan in the film, and Castle would go on to helm another film, *Tap*, starring Gregory Hines.

Some critics were of the opinion that the producers should have stuck with Castle. Roger Ebert spoke for many when he wrote, "The ads for Steven Spielberg's *Hook* ask the question, 'What if Peter Pan grew up?' But the answer, alas, is that then he would probably star in a lugubrious retread of a once-magical idea. A movie very much like this one. . . . The sad thing about the screenplay for *Hook* is that it's so correctly titled: This whole construction is really nothing more than a hook on which to hang a new version of the Peter Pan story."

Hal Hinson of the *Washington Post* added, "What it doesn't do . . . is instantly take a place in your heart. For all its pomp and color, for all the talent of its contributors, it's not a movie for which you can build a deep affection. The movie is about happy thoughts, but it takes a somewhat mechanical approach to happiness. It's hard to be elated about a machine, and that's what *Hook* is — an $80 million Happy Thought machine."

At 18, Paltrow won her first film role that hadn't come from the benefit of family ties when she was cast in 1991's *Shout* alongside John Travolta. Because it was released before *Hook*, *Shout* is considered Paltrow's official, not to mention inauspicious, movie debut. Directed by Jeffrey Hornaday, the choreographer of *Flashdance* and *A Chorus Line*, *Shout* was on the opposite end of the cinematic spectrum from *Hook*; it was a small film, featuring a relatively unknown cast and starring an actor who had appeared to get his career back on track with *Look Who's Talking*. Fortunately, so few people saw *Shout* that it didn't cause Travolta's career any lasting harm.

In the film, Travolta plays a 1950s teacher who gets a job at the Benedict Home for Boys, an orphanage and repository for what used to be called wayward young men. In an effort to reach his distant pupils, Travolta turns to that sound of the devil, rock and roll — a move that goes against the grain of the bullish headmaster. Naturally, the headmaster's daughter, played by then-newcomer Heather Graham, falls in love with Travolta's most rebellious student, played by heartthrob-in-the making, James Walters.

Rita Kempley of the *Washington Post* said of the film: "It's the standard underdeveloped stuff of adolescent movies, but with an Oliverian twist: All the kids are orphans as Dickens meets *Footloose*." And that was one of the kinder reviews. Leonard Maltin deemed it a bomb: "*Wheeze* would have been a better title for this turkey." And *Entertainment Weekly* noted that "When Travolta is stuck in the wrong role, there isn't an actor alive who can seem at once so ingenuous and so ridiculous. Also starring James Walters as the 'brooding' hero — he's James Dean meets Calvin Klein." Finally, Melissa Pierson, in her review of new video releases for 1997, gave the movie a D rating, calling it "*Footloose* goes to prison camp."

Again, because *Shout* came and went so quickly, few noticed that James Walters changed his name to Jamie and later popped up in prime time. After appearing in the short-lived series, *The Heights*, Walters scored a coup when he joined the cast of *Beverly Hills 90210* as Ray Pruitt, Tori Spelling's abusive, wrong-side-of-the-tracks boyfriend. Walters also spent a moment in pop music heaven with two top-10 singles, "How Do You Talk to an Angel" and "Hold On."

But like Emily Lloyd and so many other young stars before them, Walters wasn't able to sustain his momentum — in this case, he was simply too interchangeable with the hordes of other would-be singer/actor hunks — and he disappeared into the shadows of Hollywood as quickly as he had emerged.

As her parents had so correctly warned her, to truly succeed Paltrow knew she must keep the work first, maintain her integrity, both personal and professional, and find the roles that would set her apart. And so, Paltrow's next role after the one-two punch of *Hook* and *Shout* was in the 1992 television miniseries, *Cruel Doubt*. As if divined by the Fates, NBC cast Danner to play Paltrow's on-screen mom. It was an intriguing choice — not from a talent standpoint, because Danner's reputation was sterling, but from a sheer commercial one. As Danner herself notes, "I'm a semi-anonymous person in the television business. I don't think I have any TV-Q at all — *whatever* that is."

What she did know was that she was thrilled to be playing opposite her then-19-year-old daughter, and she took the opportunity to brag a little about her child. "I was cast because of her," Danner says. "She got the part first, and I guess they thought I looked right as her mother."

Paltrow was able to show much more of her range as an actor in the miniseries than she had been able to in either of the feature films that she had under her belt. The mini was based on the true story of Chris Pritchard, a North Carolina teen who in 1988 had conspired with some friends to kill his stepfather and mother, Leith and Bonnie Von Stein. Two books had been written on the case — *Cruel Doubt* by Joe McGinniss and *Blood Games* by Jerry Bledsoe — and CBS had also aired a telefilm on the story called *Honor Thy Mother*.

The basic facts of the case were never in question. Shortly after Leith Von Stein came into a $2 million inheritance, he was bludgeoned and stabbed to death while in bed. However, the attack on Bonnie failed, and she survived. It didn't take police long to focus their attention on Bonnie's son from a previous marriage, Pritchard, who was the picture of disconnected youth. An ineffectual student, when Pritchard wasn't busy dropping LSD with his friends, he'd spend the majority of his time obsessed with the fantasy role-playing game, Dungeons and Dragons.

The detectives working on the case theorized that Pritchard's motive was simple greed — if Leith and his mother were dead, he and his younger sister Angela would inherit the money. Pritchard, along with two of his close friends, James Upchurch and Neal Henderson, were eventually tried for the murder and attack. The jury found that while Upchurch had physically done the deed, Pritchard and Henderson had conspired with him.

What made *Cruel Doubt* stand apart from the usual crime-of-the-week movie was that the real focus wasn't on the crime itself but on Bonnie being forced to come to grips with the reality that her son had wanted her dead. Even after Pritchard admitted his role in the crime, Bonnie refused to accept his confession. Danner shone in the role as Bonnie Von Stein, and she showed her daughter firsthand how it's done. As Ken Tucker notes in *Entertainment Weekly*: "*Cruel Doubt* is much more absorbing than *Honor Thy Mother* was, and one big reason is that Danner's interpretation of Bonnie is more detailed than Sharon Gless's in the same role: Where Gless played Bonnie as a drab, confused victim, Danner goes deeper. . . . It is Danner's nuanced portrayal of Bonnie's conflicted character that gives the story its moral and emotional complexity."

Ken Tucker also observed that "In the far smaller role of Chris's sister, Paltrow is a minor revelation. The actress, who happens to be the daughter of Danner and TV producer Bruce Paltrow (*St. Elsewhere*), summons up her own brand of sour-faced teen alienation, and does it so convincingly that when Angela briefly becomes a suspect, we feel it would be perfectly possible for this glowering girl to off her parents."

For the first time, Paltrow had managed to draw positive attention to herself and get others within the industry to take notice of her ability as an actor. Now the question was, what would come of it? "You really don't know until you begin," Paltrow says. "I was sort of waiting. I knew it was just a matter of time, I knew it *was* going to happen," she says, although at the same time admitting, "When I was starting, I thought, 'Well, when is it going to happen?'"

The answer was sooner rather than later. Her next role, in the 1993 film *Flesh and Bone*, allowed Paltrow to finally prove that she was much more than merely the daughter of two famous, well-connected parents. Rather, she was now an actress to be reckoned with on her own terms.

Flesh and Bone is the kind of movie that frequently acts as a springboard for a performer hoping to make a name for themselves. Serious in nature, with a character-driven plot, dramas such as this one give an actor the opportunity to showcase themselves in a meaty role. And although she really didn't have any reason to be overly confident, Paltrow says she instinctively knew the role of Ginnie was hers.

In this, Paltrow's first costarring film role of consequence, she joined an A-list cast that included Dennis Quaid, Meg Ryan, and James Caan. The writer and director of the film, Steve Kloves, was fresh off his critically acclaimed box office hit, *The Fabulous Baker Boys*, and the movie was being produced by industry heavyweight Sydney Pollack. Like *Cruel Doubt, Flesh and Bone* dealt with the darker side of human nature.

Kloves vividly remembers Paltrow's audition for the role, for which she arrived wearing Lolita sunglasses. "She had tons of spontaneity and raw nerve. You could feel the confidence. If you're another actor, you're a fool if you don't take her seriously, because she'll smoke you," Kloves tells Richard Corliss of *Time* magazine. "Gwynny is very American," he continues, "but the interesting part of American — dark and dangerous. Her appeal is her mystery and unpredictability. It's what people liked about Steve McQueen."

Flesh and Bone is set in the desolate and vast spaces of West Texas and opens with a flashback in which a mute, apparently lost little boy shows up on a family's doorstep and is taken in and given a place to sleep. It turns out to be a scam. During the night, the youngster lets in his father, Roy (played by James Caan), whose intent is to rob the family while they sleep. But the plan goes awry, and the boy's dad ends up slaughtering the entire family — except for an infant.

Thirty years later, the little boy, named Arlis, has grown up and become a melancholy man who has never been able to assuage himself of his guilt over the killings. Arlis becomes involved with Kay, an equally lost soul, and thinks he might finally have a chance at happiness, until old pappy comes back to town, toting a petty thief and con artist named Ginnie (played by Paltrow), who blithely steals jewelry off of corpses. As it turns out, Arlis discovers that Kay is the baby that was spared during the botched robbery 30 years earlier, which prompts the revelation that he cannot hide from his past anymore. And Roy's return foreshadows the inevitable confrontation between father and son.

Not exactly the happiest of plots, which in Hollywood is still an iffy venture in the best of dark films. By most accounts, *Flesh and Bone* lacked the focus of character depth to overcome its relentless bleakness. As *People* film critic Leah Rozen noted, "There's so much to like and admire about *Flesh and Bone*, beginning with its quirky characters and lively dialogue, that the fact that it ultimately disappoints is doubly disappointing. The problem here is that although there's abundant flesh, as in atmosphere and personality, there's too little bone, in the form of ideas. . . . The weak link is Quaid's real-life wife, Ryan: She tries hard, but the effort shows."

According to *USA Today* reviewer Mike Clark, the film is a "sins-of-the-father drama that is merely two-hours-plus of portent." "Yet," Clark adds, "it's not impossible to see why a few first-rank film critics got enthused. Philippe Rousselot's photography of rural Texas is a model of mood; as the foxy thief who hooks up with Quaid's bad-daddy Caan, Gwyneth Paltrow (Blythe Danner's real-life daughter) might have gotten a supporting-Oscar nomination had the film not flopped."

That the movie failed to ignite the box office was disappointing to Paltrow, but even more distressing was the constant reference to her familial ties as being the daughter of Blythe Danner and Bruce Paltrow. She found it interesting that although her parents were well regarded within the industry, her link to them wasn't necessarily fodder for the masses. "It's funny," Paltrow tells *Newsday*'s John Clark, "like you read articles on Ben Stiller, and I think they say less about his parents, that he's the son of Anne Meara and Jerry Stiller, and I think people would know more who they are. Why don't they do it with Ben?"

Although Paltrow acknowledges that her parents are well known, which "certainly gets you in the door," she does point out that they aren't the ones going on the auditions. "It helps you in that it sets you apart when you're auditioning," Paltrow says. "People say, 'Oh, this is Blythe Danner's daughter, let's see if she's any good,' but it doesn't keep you in the room, and it certainly doesn't give you the part. People want to see if the progeny can perform. Whoever says that I get work because of my relations hasn't done their homework."

But not all reviewers honed in on Paltrow's parentage when evaluating *Flesh and Bone*. Some actually singled out her performance, such as Harper Barnes of the *St. Louis Post-Dispatch*: "Most of the interest so far seems to be in the on-screen teaming of offscreen spouses Quaid and Ryan, and they work well together. However, someday *Flesh and Bone* may be remembered more for the strong performance of Gwyneth Paltrow as a survivor we never quite know how to read. This young actress, in one of her first feature-film roles, steals the movie when she's on screen. There's something in her quiet eyes that suggests inner depths we'd like to know a whole lot more about. That's the secret to successful under-acting."

In an otherwise disappointing film, Leonard Maltin believed the "undeniable standouts are Philippe Rousselot's photography and the performance of newcomer Paltrow as a sexy con woman." And, in a thoughtful critique, Desson Howe of the *Washington Post* saw *Flesh and Bone* as an opportunity missed: "There's a faintly perceptible grinding sound in *Flesh and Bone*. It's the friction between stars and subject matter. What we have is a film-noir homage starring Dennis Quaid and Meg Ryan. Quaid and Ryan are multi-talented performers individually but, as a couple, they're Dennis and Meg. This 'In Cold Blood'-style fable demands a darker credibility. . . . It remains for us to enjoy *Flesh* for its passing qualities, its atmosphere and Caan's and Paltrow's performances."

Roger Ebert was equally effusive in his review of *Flesh and Bone* in the *Chicago Sun-Times*: "The real eye-opener . . . is Gwyneth Paltrow, who more than holds her own playing opposite three established stars. Her performance as the sexy, cynical Ginnie is fresh and unaffected, and it doesn't take long for us to get into the character's head to understand her motives and crushed dreams."

Although nobody will ever know for sure whether or not having the Paltrow name helped open doors for Gwyneth, both director Kloves and producer Pollack say that what drew them to the young actress was her own unique qualities and inherent screen presence and magnetism. "There's a kind of hypnotic thing that happens with real movie stars that makes it difficult not to watch them," Pollack explains, "and she has that quality. You could say it in a million different ways. You could say she's waiflike. You could say she's gamine. You could say she's gorgeous. You could say all those things, and they would be true, but it's the particular mixture — and the non-specificness — that makes her fascinating. We saw that in *Flesh and Bone*. As soon as she came on the screen, you thought, 'who the hell is *that*?'"

Kloves says Paltrow first caught his attention when he saw her in *Cruel Doubt*. When he called her in to audition, he says that he immediately "had a gut feeling she was the one." "She walked in wearing this little sundress," he explains, "and she's all sunshine, and then we started to read, and it was like a veil came down over her face and she was Ginnie. And it was chilling, because Ginnie was a chilling character." But Kloves admits that there was another intriguing aspect to Paltrow: "She had this almost Holly Golightly thing. She used to say this one thing that would just kill you. She'd be in the middle of a conversation and she'd say, 'I'm just a girl.' It used to slay people: 'But then, I'm just a girl.'"

Kloves says the irony is that Paltrow is anything but superficial, and her efforts to portray herself as just a waif belie her urban street smarts and business savvy. "You feel it with Gwynny," he says. "She was a remarkable 19-year-old, and I think some of that had to do with the fact that she'd spent an enormous amount of time in New York. There was sophistication and an intelligence that came from that. She could have had a real Beverly Hills lifestyle."

Despite its dark subject matter, for Paltrow, working on *Flesh and Bone* had been a lot of fun, especially hanging out with Caan, who is never one to pass up the opportunity to flirt with a pretty young costar. "Jimmy was incredible. Crazy, but great," Paltrow enthuses. On the other hand, as she tells *Cosmopolitan*'s David Ragan in April 1996, "Having an actress for a mother, I was well educated about the manipulative behavior you might experience from another actor. While making *Flesh and Bone*, I discovered [James Caan] could be really mean. Some mornings he wouldn't talk to me. And when it was my close-up, he'd call me a fucking bitch, just to get reactions. But I was ahead of him — I knew what he was doing."

Flesh and Bone was released in November 1993, and while Paltrow's performance created an industry buzz, it didn't have the immediate impact she had hoped it would. And despite the positive reception and solid reviews, Paltrow hit a dry spell that all actors must learn to navigate, and she began having doubts that she would be able to climb to the next level. Of course, Paltrow's desert lasted a mere three months — that's the kind of "suffering" that can make your peers want to strangle you.

But within Paltrow's period of discontent, she did lose several good roles that would have made her stock rise considerably. One of them was in *Legends of the Fall*, starring future love interest Brad Pitt, which went to Julia Ormond, and another was in Woody Allen's *Husbands and Wives*, which went to Juliette Lewis. "I was really getting frustrated," Paltrow admits. "I was thinking, 'I'm *never* going to get anywhere.'"

But Kloves tells John Clark that he understands why some directors may have been hesitant to cast Paltrow. "She's strong. If you cast her, you're really making a choice. There's nothing generic about Gwynny. The other problem was that she was 20 years old, and she was reading for parts sometimes for 25- to 30-year-olds. I mean, 20 *is* 20. How many interesting parts are there for 20-year-old women?"

Ultimately, Paltrow managed not to lose her actor's faith by turning to her parents for support and guidance. And they told her, "Don't worry. If you're getting this close, then it's just a matter of time." They were right.

4

Reaching for the Stars

FOR PALTROW, 1993 was a banner year. In addition to the critical notice she received for *Flesh and Bone*, her personal life was on an upswing. Earlier in the year she had started dating actor Robert Sean Leonard. Although Leonard was "Hollywood handsome," he wasn't a flavor-of-the-month type, and he seemed typical of someone Paltrow would date.

Leonard was born in 1969 in Westwood, New Jersey. Bobby, as Paltrow calls him, was a history major at Fordham University for five years and then later attended Columbia University. In 1993, during the time he and Paltrow were seeing each other, he received a Tony nomination for Best Featured Actor in a Play for his role in *Candida*.

At this point in her career, Paltrow had begun working steadily enough that her days of waitressing were already a faded memory. In May 1993, she appeared in her second major television production, a movie called *Deadly Relations*, in which she costarred as Robert Urich's daughter in yet another ripped-from-the-headlines tale of family dysfunction.

Deadly Relations is the story of Leonard Fagot, a man who took the concept of disciplinarian to dizzying heights. An ex-marine, Fagot did not like being disobeyed, and when his daughters went against his wishes and married men he considered undesirables, he took out large insurance policies on his new sons-in-law. Fagot eventually murdered one of his daughter's husbands and was convicted of the crime, and two of his daughters went on to write a book upon which the movie was based.

Another film of Paltrow's released in 1993 was the thriller *Malice*, starring Alec Baldwin, Nicole Kidman, and Bill Pullman. Despite the top-drawer cast, *Malice* failed to ignite much interest among critics or moviegoers. The convoluted plot has Baldwin playing an egomaniacal surgeon who rents a room from an old school chum, Andy, after moving to a new town. Andy's wife, Tracy, is none too pleased to have a boarder, especially after he performs emergency surgery on her. The ensuing malpractice suit is only one of many red herrings that the movie tosses out like so many hulled peanut shells.

Roger Ebert called *Malice* "one of the busiest movies I've ever seen, a film jam-packed with characters and incidents and blind alleys and red herrings. Offhand, this is the only movie I can recall in which an entire subplot about a serial killer is thrown in simply for atmosphere."

Another reviewer noted that "Things are never what they seem — even when it would make more sense if they were. Revelation follows revelation, one of them laid out at excessive length in a crotchety cameo by Anne Bancroft. We're asked to accept a conspiracy of shocking audacity, puzzling complexity and highly dubious motivation. No, there's no asking about it. The moviemakers simply assume our willingness to dispense with the whys and wherefores and concentrate on the, *What's next?*" Or, as Leonard Maltin succinctly put it, *Malice* is "Overheated and fairly absurd."

Fortunately for Paltrow, her screen time in the film was minimal, and once again, she was able to avoid any professional taint. In fact, her name was now being bandied about as a possible casting coup for several then-high-profile projects. One movie in development that was generating *beaucoup de* buzz at the time was the planned remake of *Sabrina*, which already had Harrison Ford cast as the male lead.

Ford didn't seem overly concerned about casting, nor was he anxious about taking on a part popularized by one of the great screen legends, Humphrey Bogart. Rather, what he was most interested in was taking a step away from the action-movie genre. "I wanted to do something light, where I didn't have to hit anybody or have anybody hit me," Ford says.

While it wasn't difficult to accept the casting of Ford as the male lead in the film, industry trade papers openly pondered who would possibly fill the shoes of the original Sabrina, and the film's producer, Scott Rudin, rode the wave of publicity generated by the search for the "new Audrey Hepburn." At one point in the film's development, it was rumored that Whitney Houston had expressed interest in the title role, but Rudin wanted to go with someone younger and more waifish.

Rudin and the film's director, Sydney Pollack, scoured young Hollywood for the right actress. They pursued Winona Ryder, only to find that her acting dance card was full. They mulled over the possibility of casting Meg Ryan or Demi Moore. For awhile they even wooed Julia Roberts, who was an admitted fan of Hepburn, but who wouldn't consider taking the part out of respect for the late actress. With none of the A-list of actresses willing to tackle the role, Rudin and Pollack looked at

Hollywood's pack of up-and-comers, such as Julie Delpy and Gwyneth Paltrow, the latter of whom had worked with Pollack on *Flesh and Bone*.

But as Paltrow was quickly learning, the composition and complexion of a film ebbed and flowed like a cinematic tide. She was also learning that although you might be under consideration for a role, it didn't mean you would in fact be cast. After all the speculation about *Sabrina*, the ultimate casting of the movie came as a surprise to many, with Julia Ormond being the final choice for the Hepburn role.

As it turned out, *Sabrina* was a bust. While Ford's career is almost "turkey"-proof at this point, Ormond's certainly wasn't ignited by the experience, proving to Paltrow that when you get offered the lead role in a film, you've got to make sure there's a solid film there to back you up. Until then, Paltrow was content to hone her craft in small roles in smaller, more offbeat films, and she was prepared to wait for the role that would propel her up the Hollywood acting ladder — an ascension that seemed inevitable.

By 1994, even though Paltrow was hardly a household name, she was circling ever closer to the radar of public awareness. The cover of *Rolling Stone*'s "Hot Issue" that year featured the so-called *Melrose Place* Bod-Squad — Laura Leighton, Josie Bissett, Heather Locklear, Daphne Zuniga, and Courtney Thorne-Smith. But inside the magazine, those singled out as the next great break-out stars were designer Richard Tyler, the alternative band Green Day, the television show *My So-Called Life*, and actors Leonardo DiCaprio and Gwyneth Paltrow.

It seemed as though Paltrow's name was always popping up in the most unexpected places. In a review of the disappointing remake of *The Getaway*, in which Paltrow's *Malice* costar, Alec Baldwin, teams up with real-life love Kim Basinger to reprise the characters originally created by Steve McQueen and Ali McGraw, movie critic Harper Barnes observed: "Sometimes, as with Warren Beatty and Faye Dunaway in *Bonnie and Clyde*, Hollywood stars can redefine themselves and deepen their range by taking on grittier roles than usual. But Beatty and Dunaway had the talent to pull it off. Baldwin and Basinger, I'm afraid, are just a couple of pretty faces. Here's a suggestion. Remake *The Getaway* again, only with Michael Madsen and Gwyneth Paltrow (from *Flesh and Bone*) in the lead roles. And let Walter Hill direct it. I'd pay to see that movie."

However, not everyone was immediately smitten with Paltrow, who could occasionally come across as a tad too pretentious and precious. In *Time* magazine, Ginia Bellafante sounds exasperated when she notes: "What celebritydom possibly does not need now is another actress like

GWYNETH PALTROW, who describes her soul as pained and calls her childhood suffering existential. Wisely, though, Paltrow, who is getting raves for her performance in the thriller *Flesh and Bone*, serves up plenty of cheeriness too. How is her budding career? 'Great!' Life with actress-mom Blythe Danner? 'Great!' Romance with Robert Sean Leonard? 'Great!'"

Actually, things were not necessarily as great with Bobby as outsiders may have inferred. More comfortable than passionate, Paltrow would later put the less-than-fiery affair in perspective. "That wasn't so serious a relationship. Bobby Leonard and I are good friends," she explains to Jesse Kornbluth of *Buzz* magazine. "Sometimes you date people because they're great and you don't realize that what you're supposed to be is friends. I think I see now that all you need is to find the right person — and improvise."

While waiting for the real love of her life, Paltrow had plenty to keep her busy, as she seemed to be moving from one film to the next. In *Mrs. Parker and the Vicious Circle*, released in 1994, Paltrow got to watch the unique style of Jennifer Jason Leigh, who at the time might have been considered one of the top independent film actresses, known for her penchant for dark, edgy, over-the-top roles.

In *Mrs. Parker*, Leigh took on a role that seemed somewhat ill-suited

Paltrow and Leonardo DiCaprio looking oh-so young, 1994

ROSE HARTMAN / GLOBE PHOTOS

for her talents, portraying Dorothy Parker, who is remembered more for her acerbic wit and warp-speed comebacks than for her writing, which included some of the most funny and insightful — not to mention, inciteful — theater reviews ever written. The film faithfully re-created the 1920s atmosphere and setting of the Algonquin Round Table, as Parker's circle of friends was known. The group became famous for its daily liquid lunches, held at the Algonquin Hotel, which frequently lasted until late into the evening. Perhaps the most lasting legacy of the group was that out of their boozy binges sprang the idea for what would become the *New Yorker*, one of publishing's most revered magazines.

The members of this group of literary budding elite, which included Robert Benchley, Robert Sherwood, Edna Ferber, George S. Kaufman, and Alexander Woollcott, were known for their quick-witted verbal skills. Of them all, Parker was considered the brightest and wittiest. She was also the most tragic figure, whose failed relationships seemed to color her entire being.

Twice she married Eddie Parker, who ultimately succumbed to drugs after she left him for the last time. Her relationship with Charles MacArthur, who would later go on to marry Helen Hayes, was equally damaging. MacArthur was known as a relentless womanizer, and some believe that his infidelities while with Parker literally broke her heart. Parker would end up living out her life in bitterness and solitude.

In *Mrs. Parker and the Vicious Circle*, Paltrow was cast in the small role of Paula Hunt, but she had sufficient screen time to give the character enough "bitch bite" to measure up nicely to Leigh's Parker. Unfortunately for the film, many reviewers thought there should have been less bite and more wit. Critic Richard Schickel posed the question, "How does a Dorothy Parker biopic manage to be witless?" he wrote, "At times Alan Rudolph, the director (and co-writer) of *Mrs. Parker and the Vicious Circle*, seems to have a larger purpose, which is to challenge the supposed glamour of the bright, bibulous young writers who drew themselves up to the round table at Manhattan's Algonquin Hotel in the 1920s. Yet Rudolph remains of two minds about his subjects. He wants them to charm us, but he also wants to show how their infinite distractibility stunted their lives and careers. His ambivalence creates not an intriguing thematic tension but merely confusion."

Although Paltrow always wanted the movies in which she appeared to do well, she also understood that sometimes it was the effort that counted most. Her next few films would offer her more of an opportunity to gain as much from them professionally as she did personally. But already,

Paltrow had achieved a personal goal that she had set for herself years before when she had decided to drop out of college and pursue acting full-time. "When I started acting, I set a goal for myself," she reveals. "I said if I haven't achieved something by the time everybody else graduates — all my friends graduate — I'm going to be in big trouble and feel like I really messed up."

Paltrow recognizes, however, that "By the time everybody graduated, I had already done *Flesh and Bone* and *Mrs. Parker and the Vicious Circle*. . . . So I was already like the new whatever from *Flesh and Bone*, the new rookie, and in all the papers and stuff. So all my friends thought I was getting somewhere. So I felt validated."

Then, in 1995, Paltrow was cast in three big films. The first was *Jefferson in Paris*. *Jefferson* was intended to be the kind of seminal period piece that has made the directing-producing-writing team of James Ivory, Ismail Merchant, and Ruth Prawer Jhabvala such art-house power brokers, with hits such as *Howard's End* and *Remains of the Day* to their credit.

The premise of the film was rife with dramatic possibilities. Set between 1784 and 1789, when Thomas Jefferson was US ambassador to France, the movie spotlights Jefferson the man as opposed to Jefferson the great political leader and imaginative inventor. When the film begins, Jefferson (played by Nick Nolte) has been a widower for two years and has just been appointed ambassador to France. He brings along the eldest of his daughters, Patsy (played by Paltrow), and promptly houses her in a local Parisian convent. The film dances around Jefferson's relationship with Patsy, suggesting either that she had a slight Electra complex regarding her father or that he was just a little too interested in her.

With Patsy safely tucked away with the nuns, Jefferson begins a romance with painter Maria Cosway, although historians disagree on whether or not the two actually had a sexual affair. In any event, after one of Jefferson's other two daughters dies, he sends for his youngest, Polly, to join him in Paris. Accompanying Polly to tend to her needs is a young slave, the historically notorious Sally Hemings. Hemings was already tied to Jefferson's family in that she was Martha Jefferson's half-sister — a fact seldom discussed in high school history classes.

When she arrives in Paris, Hemings is only 15 years old. As portrayed in the film, Jefferson becomes smitten with her when his relationship with Cosway remains unconsummated. Patsy, for one, thinks her father's infatuation is "unspeakable," while Cosway comes to the conclusion that there is no future for her and Jefferson, who goes on to impregnate Hemings by the end of the film.

Although the film created a bit of a stir around the apparent creative license taken about Jefferson's possible relationship with Hemings, recent DNA testing indicates that he did indeed father several of her children. However, even that fact probably wouldn't have saved the film from the barbs tossed its way by reviewers.

"Bereft of any flesh-and-blood honesty, the last half of the movie plays like a ludicrous PBS version of Mandingo," sniped Owen Gleiberman in *Entertainment Weekly*. And *San Francisco Examiner* critic Barbara Schulgasser begged: "Nick Nolte as a hockey player. Nick Nolte as a crooked cop. Nick Nolte as a sanitation crew member. Nick Nolte as a nightclub bouncer. Fine. But Nick Nolte as Thomas Jefferson, author of the Declaration of Independence, violinist, architect, founder of a university, ambassador to France, third president of the United States? Don't get me started." Even Paltrow had to agree that the film was not cinema at its finest, calling it "bad." "But," she adds, "I did get to learn French."

Less than 48 hours after wrapping *Jefferson in Paris*, Paltrow flew to her home-away-from-home, Williamstown, Massachusetts, to begin a five-week run of *The Seagull*. With only a week's break after the play ended, she was on her way to Toronto, Canada, to begin filming her next 1995 release, *Moonlight and Valentino*, in which she starred opposite Elizabeth Perkins, Whoopi Goldberg, and Kathleen Turner.

The film was written by Ellen Simon, daughter of prodigious playwright Neil Simon, and was based on her own life. In 1987, her professor husband, Jeff Bishop, went out for a run on a rainy November morning. The date was Friday, the 13th. When Bishop was very late getting home, Simon went to go look for him and happened upon an accident scene where a policeman told her that a jogger, her husband, had been hit by a car. Driving to the hospital, Simon told herself it was probably no more serious than a sprained ankle.

But when Simon arrived at the hospital, a nurse, her shoes stained with blood, had to tell her the staggering truth. "She said, 'Your husband was hit very, very hard. He didn't make it,'" Simon recalls to Jane Wollman Rusoff in an interview for *Good Housekeeping*. "All I could say was, 'Are you sure?' I must have said it 50 times." Then she almost passed out.

What made Bishop's death even more difficult is that Simon had never really come to terms with the unexpected loss of her mother, Joan Baim Simon, who died of bone cancer in 1973 when Simon was just a teenager. "All the adults were so upset," she says. "I had to be the strong one." But when Bishop died, she couldn't keep the pain inside and finally turned to family and friends for support.

Simon says she had always assumed that she'd be able to take care of herself, "but this was too overwhelming." "So," she adds, "when my husband died and people came around and I felt safe to mourn and really cry, I realized how healing that is. So that was the catharsis, and I wanted to write about that."

What particularly interested Simon was how differently she had reacted to her mother's death than to her husband's. "With my mom I was afraid to cry one tear because I felt so alone," she says. "But when Jeff died, I let people in and could lean on them. That allowed me to feel the pain. I realized that holding it in just prolongs it: There's no place to put the grief until you feel it."

Simon found comfort, too, in her son Andrew, who was born during a previous marriage. "Every night before we went to sleep," she recalls, "we'd talk about where we imagined Jeff had gone after he died. It was a comfort seeing things through Andrew's eyes."

After Bishop's death, Simon's sister Nancy and her father's ex-wife, actress Marsha Mason, came to stay with her. Between them, her dad and his then-wife, Diane Lander, and Simon's best friend and neighbor, Claudette Melchizedek, Simon says she found the support she needed to get through her grief. "They saved my life," she says. "That's what I wanted to write about."

In the film, which was originally produced as a play, Elizabeth Perkins plays Rebecca Lott, who is sent reeling by the sudden death of her husband. Rallying around her is her sister Lucy (played by Paltrow), a chain-smoking NYU film student, her former stepmother Alberta (played by Kathleen Turner), and her best friend Sylvie (played by Whoopi Goldberg.) Rounding out the characters, in a bit of inspired casting, Jon Bon Jovi plays a painter hired to work on Rebecca's house. With him is his dog, Valentino. Whether it was the puppy appeal or something else, Rebecca has a romance with the painter, which finally results in the catharsis she needs to move on with her life.

Although many — mostly male — critics caustically dubbed *Moonlight and Valentino* a "woman's film," it did receive generally positive reviews. Kirby Tepper wrote, "Perkins has dignity, grace, and an edgy irony in her voice that make her a perfect heroine for a comedy/drama. Her humor comes from pain underneath; Perkins never allows her characters to appear superficial. She has a world-weariness and a sense of irony reminiscent of great screen comediennes such as Paulette Goddard or

Claudette Colbert. Perkins is an actress to be treasured, and even in this rather innocuous film she manages to find depth. Her final scenes are positively radiant with energy and emotion." Tepper goes on to say that the movie is, however, "stolen by Gwyneth Paltrow as gawky Lucy. Paltrow is the perfect actress for the part, eager and wide-eyed one moment, cynical and grungy the next — and all of her moments are well-timed, well-played, and just plain delightful."

Similarly, another critic noted, "To say that *Moonlight and Valentino* is a film about grieving might not give it a fair shake in the audience-enticement department. But grief is what this film does best — next to giving Gwyneth Paltrow a chance to steal every spare ounce of viewer attention from her better-known costars." While another reviewer observed that "Best of all is Paltrow, who, on the heels of *Flesh and Bone* and *Jefferson in Paris*, is fast proving she can do anything. Her Lucy is the film's most sympathetic character, a pretty student whose tarted-up exterior belies a kind heart and troubled soul."

As for herself, Paltrow was most struck by the softness of Lucy. "She's a very sweet-natured girl," she says, "and, I think, what drew me to her is the fact that she is trying to come to terms with who she is and . . . she can't hide behind cigarettes and insecurities for the rest of her life." As for Ellen Simon, the most important thing about *Moonlight and Valentino* was simply the chance to tell her story. In 1992, she was remarried, gave birth to a daughter, Nicola, and she has since written another romantic comedy, *One Fine Day*, which starred George Clooney and Michelle Pfeiffer.

Sometimes, life really does imitate the movies, and Paltrow was about to find out how a film role could literally change your life. However, she was also about to find out just how blurred the line between fantasy and reality can be.

5

Love and Consequences

EVERY NOW AND THEN a movie comes along that manages to appeal to our darkest natures without catering to the lowest common denominator. *Silence of the Lambs* is perhaps the best example of this kind of intelligent psychological thriller. More recently, *Seven* (originally entitled *Se7en*) offered moviegoers scares of an all-too-intense kind.

The movie, which was Paltrow's third big film of 1995, starred Morgan Freeman as William Somerset, a soon-to-be-retired homicide detective who teams up with his young, soon-to-be replacement, David Mills (played by Brad Pitt). A week before Somerset plans to leave the force, a serial killer presents himself with a unique MO — to punish seven people breaking the seven deadly sins within a seven-day period. His first murder involves having an obese man literally eat himself to death as penance for his sin of gluttony. The killer, who is played by Kevin Spacey, is ultimately revealed to be a cunning and intelligent religious freak. Into this mix is added Paltrow, who plays the young detective's radiant, good — and therefore doomed — wife.

Those who initially assumed *Seven* was just another cop thriller were in for a surprise, as evidenced by Roger Ebert's commentary in the *Chicago Sun-Times*: "A movie like this is all style. The material by itself could have been handled in many ways, but the director, David Fincher (*Alien 3*), goes for evocative atmosphere, and the writer, Andrew Kevin Walker, writes dialogue that for Morgan Freeman, in particular, is wise, informed and poetic. Eventually, it becomes clear that the killer's sermon is being preached directly to the two policemen, and that in order to understand it, they may have to risk their lives and souls.

"*Seven* is unique in one detail of its construction," Ebert went on to note, "it brings the killer on screen with half an hour to go, and gives him a speaking role. Instead of being simply the quarry in a chase, he is revealed as a twisted but articulate antagonist, who has devised a horrible plan for concluding his sermon."

For the first time in her career, Paltrow's character dies, winding up a decapitated head in a box. But despite the extreme darkness of the film, the set was an enjoyable place to be for a number of reasons. First and foremost, it is a pleasure to work with three-time Oscar nominee Morgan Freeman, who says he has no reason not to be easygoing. "I don't have to be angry when acting," Freeman explains. "I'm making lots of money, doing what I want. How can I be in a bad mood?" Nor does Freeman believe in making too much of movies. "I don't want the audience to get a message," he says. "I just want them to get their money's worth."

But even the perennial optimist admits that, physically, *Seven* was not the easiest of movies to make. "The set was dark, uncomfortable, and unhealthy," Freeman says. "The director, David Fincher, and others developed a chronic cough because of the water and mineral oil that was blown into the air to create the murky atmosphere."

However, at least the mood on set was kept light by the camaraderie between Freeman, Paltrow, and Pitt. "We rode Brad about being named the sexiest man in the universe," Freeman chuckles, recalling that the prop guys gave his costar a director's chair that said, *Brad Pitt*, The Sexiest Man Alive. After the chair was set out for Pitt, Freeman sulked in *faux pique*, jokingly ranting, "What am I, chopped liver? How dare they insult me by putting this here!"

Eventually, everyone let Pitt in on the joke. "I thought it was funny," Paltrow says, but she admits that Brad "didn't think it was that funny." Paltrow also claims that she happened to side with Freeman on the issue of who was the sexiest man on set: "I told Morgan someone had asked who the sexiest man alive was, and I said, 'Everyone is making all this fuss over Brad, but I'm telling you, Morgan Freeman is the sexiest man alive. You heard it here.' And he is. He's so sexy and so talented and just cool." As it turns out, the admiration was obviously mutual. "I have always been floored by her mother, Blythe Danner," Freeman comments. "And then here she comes. She's spellbinding. She has the gift," he says of Paltrow.

Paltrow also happened to have the heart of Brad Pitt. The two had actually met through mutual friends some seven months earlier, but no sparks had flown between them. However, when they hooked up again on the set of *Seven*, love was suddenly in the celluloid air. "I was so nervous the day I met him," Paltrow admits. "I was starting a movie and he was this big movie star, so I was all nervous." In fact, Paltrow tells

Reggie Nadelson of *Tattler* that when she began working on *Seven,* "I said to my best friend, 'I have such a crush on Brad Pitt.' And she said, 'Like, welcome to America.'"

Brad Pitt had been knocking around Hollywood a long time before his overnight stardom struck, but, unlike Paltrow's childhood experience, acting seemed like an almost unreachable fantasy while he was growing up in Springfield, Missouri. So it was a shocking turn of events for his family and friends when in 1987, Pitt dropped out of the University of Missouri just two weeks shy of his graduation and drove across the country to follow his dream to Hollywood.

"In my heart, and in my head, I was done with school," Pitt would later say in trying to explain his impulsiveness, which couldn't have initially sat well with his blue-collar, Southern Baptist parents. But Pitt had grown up bending the rules, so striking out on his own wasn't really out of character for the young man. That said, he still found it expedient to lie to his parents and tell them he was going to Los Angeles to enroll in design school.

Ironically, Pitt had been a journalism major in college, and although he had dabbled a bit with performing in high school, he came to Los Angeles with no formal training or experience as an actor. Needless to say, then, Pitt's arrival in Hollywood was anticlimactic, and during his first few nights in town, he actually slept in his car. Then, throughout his struggling-actor days, he scraped by with a series of odd jobs, such as driving strippers around town. Pitt also earned some notoriety as a bit of a party boy who was willing to try and promote himself through beefcake photos arranged by perhaps less-than-scrupulous Hollywood types.

But those dog days ended in 1991 with his appearance in *Thelma and Louise* in the role of J.D., the thief who steals the women's money after giving Thelma her first ever orgasm. His total screen time was a mere 15 minutes, but his boyish good looks and steel-ribbed abs made him the object of affection of female moviegoers everywhere. "I loved the guy," Pitt later said of J.D. "He just had it figured out. He knew what worked for him, and he was so damn nonchalant."

Some might have said the same thing about Pitt's offscreen lifestyle. Even before he was Brad Pitt, movie star, he managed to get noticed in 1987 by dating a young starlet named Shalane McCall, who appeared on *Dallas* for five years before disappearing into prime time obscurity. The two met when Pitt was hired for a small role on the long-running nighttime soap, and so began his pattern of dating leading ladies.

After McCall came a relationship with Robin Givens, Mike Tyson's ex-wife, whom he met while appearing on the television series *Head of the Class.* His relationship with Givens was followed by a liaison with Jill Schoelen, who had appeared with Pitt in the slasher film *Cutting Class.* In 1990, amid rumors that he and Geena Davis were having a romance, Pitt met Juliette Lewis while working on the telefilm *Too Young to Die*, and Lewis became his first real love.

Interestingly, despite his womanizing ways, Pitt's ex-girlfriends all seem to speak highly of him. "When I met him, I thought, 'Well, he'll be a silly movie star,'" Josh Mooney of *Cosmopolitan* was told by one former love of Pitt's, "but he's an exceptional person. First of all, he has no ego. I don't know how, but he doesn't, to the point where he avoids the word *I*. He'll say things convoluted, and you'll realize he's gone in this whole circle to avoid saying, I."

When Pitt and Lewis became involved, she was only 16, but for Pitt, her youth wasn't an issue. "I don' t see ages as relevant," Pitt says. "You've got to see past the surface, you know? Different people move at different speeds." Lewis was also already a respected actress in Hollywood circles, despite an eccentric personality. "She's an original," Pitt once said in defense of Juliette. "She's from another planet, but a good planet."

Pitt and Lewis were a steady couple for three years before the relationship appeared to run its course. However, even after the breakup, Pitt seemed to carry a torch for Juliette: "I still love the woman. The problem is, we grow up with this vision that love conquers all, and that's just not so, is it?" But Pitt wasn't alone for long after he and Lewis went their separate ways, and he was soon linked romantically to Julia Ormond, who, probably not-so-coincidentally, was his on-screen love interest in the film *Legends of the Fall.* After Ormond, Pitt dated an unknown actress named Jitka Pohlodek until he hooked up with Paltrow while working on *Seven*.

Of his many relationships, Brad says in self-defense, "In all fairness, we're dealing with an industry full of fascinating people, you know? I don't see anything crazy about that. They understand what you're trying to do. I hear actors say, 'I'll never date another actor.' Well, I think just the opposite."

Paltrow, by contrast, was much less experienced in the ways of the heart when she met Pitt, even though she had previously been dating musician Donovan Leitch for quite awhile. But Paltrow was only 22 when she began filming *Seven*, and she had been working more or less constantly for the previous three years. And whereas Pitt seemed to have a bevy of past romances, Paltrow's past was more eclectic, and it involved more parental supervision.

"When I was in grammar school, I had this wicked crush on a guy named Flash Mandel," Paltrow admits in *Seventeen* magazine. "Eventually I think he noticed it, too, because he asked me out on this big date — we went bowling and then to see *The Toy*, that Richard Pryor movie. It was one of those totally embarrassing things where your mom has to drive. Maybe that's why it didn't work out for me and old Flash." And, during high school, Paltrow says a sun-bleached blond California surfer broke her heart. "Oh my God, the love I felt for that boy," she recalls.

By her own admission, Paltrow's romances with Robert Sean Leonard and Donovan Leitch were not exactly passionate love affairs, so by the time she met Pitt, she was a young woman who was ready to be swept off her feet. But first she'd actually have to notice that someone else was interested in her. "It would never occur to me to flirt with somebody, even if I had a crush on them," Paltrow admits, calling herself "oblivious." "I wouldn't know if somebody was flirting with me," she adds.

Following the same line of thought, Paltrow tells *Newsday*'s John Clark, "When Brad and I met, he says, it was obvious that he liked me, and that I was an idiot. But I had no idea. I thought he was just really friendly. And then I started getting a crush on him. I'm like, 'Are you insane? You can't get a crush on Brad Pitt. Get hold of yourself.' It's funny to think back into that mind now. Now it's so different."

Paltrow also admits that she had "a few preconceptions" about Pitt. "Of course, I thought he was very handsome, from movies, you know, the way people are. But I also thought, 'Oh, he'll just be one of those young Movie Star Boys.'" But he wasn't, and the awkward stage didn't last very long between Paltrow and Pitt, because once he managed to get her attention, the attraction ignited. Later, Paltrow would say, "When we met to start work on *Seven*, playing husband and wife, it was love at second sight."

What Paltrow didn't know at the time was that it was Pitt who had suggested her for the role of his wife, Tracy, because he had remembered her impressive audition for *Legends of the Fall*. "The Tracy character was so important, because it's the only sunshine we have in the film. This is the feel-bad movie of 1995," Pitt tells Bronwen Hruska in an interview for *Newsday*. "We needed someone who could take those little seconds she gets and fill them with soul, and that's what I'd always seen in her performances — soul. She took a fantastic part and made it better."

Paltrow and Brad Pitt:
lucky in love, 1996

For their first date, Pitt took Paltrow to an intimate Italian restaurant in Los Angeles where nobody paid any attention to them. From that night on, they would become inseparable. "It was immediate," Paltrow recalls. It was also obvious to everyone working on *Seven* that Pitt and Paltrow were a couple. "The chemistry between them was real," notes costar Freeman. Indeed, Paltrow was deeply, giddily, no-doubt-about-it in love and was ready and willing to tell the world. "I am properly in love for the first time in my life," Paltrow blithely told a reporter in 1995, "and I do not care if my former boyfriends read this."

What Paltrow didn't realize was how much interest the rest of the world would have in her love affair with Pitt, but she would quickly find out and learn a painful lesson in the process. If Paltrow had wanted a private relationship, or at least a relationship that had a semblance of privacy, Brad Pitt was not the person to fall in love with. From the time that Pitt had first broken through in *Thelma and Louise*, he quickly became one of the world's most desired movie stars.

"I was with him in England for the premiere of *Legends of the Fall*," recalls the film's director, Ed Zwick. "We got out of the car in Leicester Square, and there were ten thousand girls screaming like he was the Beatles." Reflectively, Zwick adds, "Brad is one of those rare actors who carry their own lights. By that, I mean Brad is comfortable in his own skin. Few people are in front of the camera. He has self-confidence; he's comfortable in his sensuality, in his humor about himself. That's something the camera responds to." Similarly, even Pitt's costars exude a bit of awe when they speak of him. "Oh my God, the girls just love him," says Kirsten Dunst, who costarred with Pitt in *Interview with a Vampire*. "They worship him."

The irony in all this is that, by all accounts, Pitt is an extremely unassuming, private man, who has nonetheless handled the intense public and media scrutiny with amazing grace. "Brad is an extremely private person," says director Tom DiCillo, who worked with Pitt on the 1992 film *Johnny Suede*. And as Pitt himself once said, "I don't want people to know me. As soon as you have an image, you gotta break it. I don't know a thing about my favorite actors. I don't think you should. Then they become personalities."

And as Pitt observes to Joyce Persico of the *Minneapolis Star Tribune*, "People take this all so seriously. It just doesn't amount to what you think it should be. It should be more personal, but it's not that — everyone's calling you up and congratulating you, but not for the film, for the box office." He adds that "Things are buzzing around faster on the outside, so you have to stand still to see what's happening. Adjustments have to be made. I tend to sit back, see what's going on and try to avoid waves. But there was a time when there was a little more fun, when you could surprise people."

To Pitt, fame was a more compelling concept than it has been a reality. "You grow up with this belief that if you're famous, you're not going to have to worry about bills," he says. "Then they're throwing all this money at me, and I don't have much concept of that. But when you don't have to worry about bills anymore, you're really stuck with yourself. You can't say, 'If I only had money.' It's all about you, you know?" Plus, Pitt points out that, once you achieve movie-star status, "You're more liked, [but] you're also more disliked."

But for all the hassle of celebrity, there remains a fundamental joy in his work. "Every now and then, you get the individual who comes up, and you know they were moved by a movie you were involved with," Pitt tells Diane Sawyer on ABC's *Primetime Live*. "You know they were honestly moved, because that was my experience as a child," Pitt explains. "That's why I love movies. Because someone demonstrated or articulated something that I had felt, but I had never been able to put it that way, and it made sense to me, and someone showed me some clarity and it really moved me."

So, in balancing the pros and cons of fame, Pitt has developed a philosophy: "My answer to everything I don't have an answer for is, 'Lighten up, please. There are other things I want to do that have nothing to do with making movies.'" It's this genuineness that sets Pitt apart from many actors of his generation, and it's what prompted Paltrow to sum him up by saying, "He's just a good guy."

A good guy who also happens to be desired by a large number of women on the planet. If any one incident epitomized what Pitt was *not* all about, it was when, in 1995, *People* magazine decreed him "The World's Sexiest Man." "A friend of mine said they misspelled it," Pitt tells Bronwen Hruska after he was crowned. "It was supposed to be sexiest *moron*." Then, on a more serious note, he adds, "Listen, who wants to be the standard of comparison? It's some cruel and heinous joke. I think that was a cruel, cruel thing to do to me, that's what I think."

Paltrow was well aware of Pitt's discomfort with being thrust into the role of sex symbol. "He's eager to cast off this sexy image, and he does it quite effectively in *Twelve Monkeys*," she says at the movie's premiere in 1995. "Brad was so amazing in this. Look at him, he's nuts. I want to see it again." And according to Tom DiCillo, "He told me, 'You know, I woke up one day and suddenly found myself in a whirlpool.' I said, 'I feel for you, man.' I wouldn't wish what he has on anyone."

But what Pitt had — namely, the eyes of the world seemingly focused upon him — is what Paltrow stepped into when she fell in love with him. And almost instantly, Paltrow found herself caught up in a vortex of media and public scrutiny. To her credit, she didn't seem phased by the glare of attention that followed her and Pitt — at least, not in the beginning. Initially, she sounded amused by the world's fascination with Pitt. "After I got *Seven,*" she says, "I thought everyone would say, 'So, Gwyn, who do you play?' No. Everyone I know was like, 'Oh my God! Does Brad have short hair or long hair now?'"

But the global obsession with Pitt wouldn't always remain so funny to Paltrow. Just a few months into their relationship, she says with exasperation, "I'm sick of all the hoopla about Brad's hair," referring to the fact that for *Seven,* Pitt had cut off the long hair he'd been sporting since *Legends of the Fall.* "I swear, if I hear one more time, 'What happened to his hair?' I'm going to scream. Don't people have anything else to worry about?"

Nor did Paltrow appreciate those who felt free to flirt provocatively with "The World's Sexiest Man," regardless of whether she was present or not. "Grown women. Educated women. Famous women. Women with boyfriends. Women with husbands — they're all just shameless," she whines. "Women come right up to him and press their bodies against him from behind. And I'm right there."

One would think that the flirting of strangers would be preferable to the other downside of life with Pitt — the constant presence of the paparazzi. For anyone with even a modicum of fame, it's expected that you will more than likely be photographed while out and about in public. That is one of the trade-offs for the perks that accompany fame, wealth, and/or notoriety. It becomes another matter, however, when a public figure's expectation of privacy is apparently violated.

In May 1995, Pitt whisked Paltrow off for a 10-day romantic getaway to the Caribbean island of St. Barthelemy. Somehow, a determined photographer tracked them down and snapped pictures of the couple lounging nude on a veranda. The photos first appeared in a British newspaper and then popped up on America Online, to be downloaded for free by anyone with a computer.

Pitt's immediate reaction was horror, Tom DiCillo tells *Cosmopolitan.* "He can't comprehend that people would waste time doing that in the first place," DiCillo reveals. "He said, 'God damn — if I want to make money, I should just take pictures of myself and sell them on Hollywood Boulevard.'" Dryly, Pitt also noted at the time, "Meanwhile, we've got Bosnia."

Pitt's second reaction upon learning of the photographs was to sue. "You know why? Because things are printed every week, and I've got to tell you they are always wrong," he tells Diane Sawyer. "Listen to me, they are always wrong. I don't fight it. I don't say anything. I just let it go. But when this thing came out, I felt like, you know, enough is enough."

What especially irritated Pitt was that, according to him, he and Paltrow were on private property, and in order to get the photos that were taken, the photographer would have to have been trespassing. Beyond that, "If people aren't going to have any kind of common decency, which I see is dwindling, then I felt like it was time to make someone accountable for it," Pitt says. "I don't want to infringe on the press," he adds, "but the fact that Pitt has a penis and here's proof, it's not news. It's not needed. I think the laws have not kept up with technology. I don't think that our forefathers saw telephoto lenses, you know, when they were writing it out."

But the bottom line was more personal and less legal. According to Pitt, "Some things have to remain sacred. I mean, come on. They're special moments. And they're private moments. And again, you know, common decency." But obviously, not everyone sympathized with Paltrow and Pitt. "Why come out in the open, stark naked, and then get angry when pictures show up on the front page of the news? Go figure," Stella Foster asserts in *Sister 2 Sister.*

Adding to the invasion of getting caught with his pants quite literally down was the embarrassment of the timing of the photographs. Pitt says that, as the pictures were being taken, he was imitating a character from the movie *Silence of the Lambs.* "Where," Pitt explains, "he tucks his package between his legs and says how he'd like to copulate with himself." But the worst part of the entire ordeal wasn't knowing that there were nude pictures of himself about to break in the press, it was having to tell Bruce Paltrow about it. "It was my responsibility," Pitt says, "because [Gwyneth] wouldn't be going through this if she wasn't dating me."

But by that time, Pitt had already won the approval of Paltrow's protective parents. However, Danner does admit that when she and her husband first learned that their daughter was dating Pitt, their knee-jerk reaction was, "*Oh no.*" "But he's just a gem," Danner would later say, "very grounded and family-oriented and loving and real."

Ultimately, neither Paltrow nor Pitt seemed willing to bow their heads in shame over the whole ordeal. Right on the heels of the photos' publication, they attended the Broadway opening of *Hamlet*, starring Ralph Fiennes, and were seldom out of the society columns after that. If there was a premiere or opening or event, Pitt and Paltrow seemed to be there. Whether it was a performance of the play *Sylvia*, Melissa Etheridge's birthday party, the premiere of Kevin Costner's *Waterworld*, the Virgin Records party for David Bowie, dinner out at the Manhattan restaurant Villa Mosconi, or an evening at the honky-tonk bar Hogs & Heifers, Pitt and Paltrow were in the public eye a lot.

Nor were they shy about expressing their feelings for one another. "Really, all I can tell you is, I've never been happier," Pitt told reporters at the time. "She's my angel. My girl's got class." And he showed his "girl" off whenever he could. Pitt was especially anxious to have his family meet the new woman in his life, so he arranged to have Paltrow spend Christmas with him in Springfield. While there, Paltrow was once again reminded of how it was sometimes possible to become invisible when with Pitt. Once, when she was with him at a local grocery store, Pitt excused himself to go outside for a cigarette. Immediately, the checkout girl stared after him in amazement and said to Paltrow, "That was Brad Pitt," completely unaware of who Paltrow was.

In addition to introducing her to his all-important family, Pitt was busy making what appeared to be nesting noises. He bought a huge house near Beachwood Canyon, and he was also looking to buy a place in New York, where Paltrow was technically based. He also plunked down the cash for a 600-acre spread in the Ozarks, which he indicated would be the place where he would one day go to raise a family. And when he and Paltrow were shooting movies in New York and England respectively, he called the separation "A beast. A big, hairy beast."

Everything Pitt said or did reflected a man in love. However, as he well knew, juggling any relationship with two careers is tricky at best, but especially difficult when one of the partners is in the throes of a quickly advancing career and just 23 years old. But Pitt and Paltrow both seemed committed to each other and, because Pitt was older and more stable, it seemed as though the couple had a good chance to weather the storm that would no doubt blow.

6

The Turning Point

FAME BY ASSOCIATION can be thrilling to some but anathema to another, depending upon what one's ultimate goals are in life. For Paltrow, it was imperative that her peers within the industry see her as a separate entity in her own right and not just the trophy girlfriend of Hollywood's most sought-after movie star. Paltrow knew that the best way to make a name for herself was through her work, and despite her relationship with Pitt, she refused to curtail her workload, which in and of itself spoke well of her dedication and work ethic.

Even before *Seven* had wrapped, Paltrow had begun work on *Sydney* (which would be called *Hard Eight* in America), a film-noiresque movie in which she plays a prostitute. Immediately after that she would segue into *The Pallbearer* as the love interest of David Schwimmer (of *Friends* fame); then it would be back to England to star in *Emma*, her first lead role. And of *Emma*, Paltrow says, "Oh gosh, it was a very important film. It certainly defined certain things about me or what I'm capable of, at least in other people's minds. That's really nice, and it's just a sweet, sweet movie that I'm very proud of."

And Hollywood was indeed sitting up and taking notice of Paltrow. In March 1995, *Vanity Fair* unveiled what they called "The Class of 2000" — 10 young actresses that they predicted would become the top female players in the movies after the turn of the century. In addition to Paltrow, the magazine singled out Patricia Arquette, Angela Bassett, Sandra Bullock, Jennifer Jason Leigh, Uma Thurman, Nicole Kidman, Linda Fiorentino, Sarah Jessica Parker, and Julianne Moore.

"People look at her and say, 'This is someone who has a lot of class, a lot of talent. She has a name, she's Brad Pitt's girlfriend — she's bound to go far,'" says Beth Senniac, a *Vanity Fair* publicist who helped select the actresses chosen for the cover. "It puts her in a different class than a lot of other actresses."

But what many of the actresses listed had in common was the tendency to balance typical "Hollywood" fare with independent films of stature and merit. However, at the time, Paltrow claimed that she really wasn't being calculating in her choices. She also tried hard to downplay any sense of ambition she might exude: "There's no pattern. I'm not interested in that. The reason I'm doing this is me. It's not for the money, though I like the money. It's got nothing to do with fame, which is the great evil of mankind. Billing? Hype? What's the point? Who cares? Actors who are hung up on those things haven't been raised by people who love and support them. I was. So I don't have that Hollywood version of penis envy. For me, it's all about acting. I mean, I'm beyond interested in acting; I get completely lost in the moment."

Like many actors, Paltrow says it's hard to watch herself on screen. "I can't watch myself with pleasure," she says. "Not yet. I do learn about myself, but in an odd way. You don't get the acting lesson until the film is finished." That said, she admits that "Sometimes I watch myself and think, *I am my mother*."

Perhaps because she is her mother's daughter, Paltrow never seemed particularly impressed by the company she was keeping, either on screen or off. "I was never starstruck that way," she says, then admits, "But I'm totally football starstruck. But movie stars, I don't get like that anymore. It's kind of a shame, because it's kind of a fun thing as a teenager to feel, 'Oooh, Keanu Reeves.' Now it's like, 'Hey, Keanu.'"

Like *Seven*, *Sydney* (a.k.a. *Hard Eight*) was a movie with a noir flavor. The film starred Phillip Baker Hall, John C. Reilly, and Samuel L. Jackson. Notably, it was the first film by director and screenwriter Paul Thomas Anderson, who would later score big, as it were, with the porn-themed *Boogie Nights* and critically acclaimed *Magnolia*. The casting of Paltrow in the role of Clementine, Anderson relates, was a stroke of good fortune: "I got lucky because I had written the script and, through a friend, met Gwyneth Paltrow. She stood by the picture when her star rose, as did Samuel Jackson. When they became hot, I suddenly had a movie that could be financed."

Hard Eight tells the story of the relationship between John (played by Reilly) and his older mentor, Sydney (played by Hall). They first meet after John has lost all of his money in Las Vegas, where he had gone in the hopes of winning enough cash to bury his recently deceased mother. Sydney offers to teach John how to work the casino system in order to get by. Specifically, he shows him how to start with $150 and recycle it through the casino cashier cages until it appears that he's spent $2,000 and is given a free room.

Fast-forward two years. John and Sydney are now in Reno, and their relationship is moving beyond simple friendship and becoming more and more familial in nature. But two new people in their lives begin to complicate their bond — Clementine (played by Paltrow) and a low-rent security man named Jimmy (played by Jackson). Clementine is a waitress who hooks on the side, but in spite of that, John becomes drawn to her, and they begin an intimate relationship.

Instead of being a thriller like *Seven*, *Hard Eight* is mostly a character study about four people whose lives intersect at a particular moment in time and how the interaction between them ultimately changes who they are. For Paltrow, such an examination of character psyche was sheer heaven. "It's my favorite movie that I've ever done," she would say for years after. "I really jumped at the chance to play this girl. Although she's not a role model and shouldn't be a role model for young women across the land, I love that she was so specific. She had problems and she was very three-dimensional. She's very complicated. She's not intellectual whatsoever; she's not cerebral in any way. She just reacts to things. She's sweet, sad, and fucked-up."

Although the character works as a hooker, Paltrow says that to her, that was secondary, because "I didn't view her primarily as a prostitute. This was a woman who behaved in a very complicated way, which she did not understand, and her being a prostitute was incidental to me. So it wasn't like I set out and said, 'Oooh good, I'm going to be a hooker,' and have my little rite of passage into Hollywood. I just approached it like I would any other character that I've played."

She also approached working on the set the way she usually did — as an experience to be enjoyed, regardless of the subject matter of the film. As director Anderson notes, "She's always one of the actors who's fucking around and talking between takes, and then you call, *Action*, and boom, she's there." However, Paltrow's activities beyond the set didn't include a lot of real-life time at the casino tables. "I did play blackjack," she admits. "I did play a couple of hands one night, but it didn't go so well. So I just stopped; I quit while I was ahead."

For Paltrow, the most bizarre shooting experience during the making of *Hard Eight* took place when they were filming a wedding scene at a real Reno chapel. "It was so cheap and so depressing," she says. "You could not believe that anyone would really get married in a place like this." She describes the scene in greater detail in her 1997 Mr. Showbiz interview: "There were polyester red curtains, fake lattice work on the walls. The owner was this lady, and her daughter was there, and they were totally confused about what was going on. They thought it was a real wedding. The guy who was performing the ceremony didn't really know what was going on, and in the movie, when he puts the video in, you see me laughing hysterically, and that's totally real and uncontrollable. I thought I was going to completely lose control."

For all of her lightheartedness, Paltrow proved she could also dig her heels in when necessary. In fact, she came out publicly in defense of Anderson after Rysher Entertainment fired him, reedited the movie, and changed the title from *Sydney* to *Hard Eight*, which Paltrow felt made the film sound like "a porno movie — even though the movie had been positively received at various film festival screenings." Boldly, she proclaimed, "If they don't release his version, I will be on a personal crusade to murder these people for the rest of my life."

"Writing and shooting the movie was a dream," Anderson, who was only 23 when filming began, says to Paul Mungo of the *Independent on Sunday*. "I was a bit nervous before we shot the first day. I wondered if the crew might think, 'This guy's the youngest on the set and he's telling everyone what to do.' But when we started shooting it was fine." He adds that "It was only after dealing with the business side of the editing that it went wrong. I kept looking at what they wanted to do and saying, 'Are you trying to make more money?' I could never understand what they were doing, except trying to be directors with footage I had shot."

In the end, Rysher Entertainment reconsidered and announced that the dispute had been resolved, promising to release a director's cut of the film. According to Anderson, it wouldn't have happened without Paltrow's support. "She was so tough and so strong to stand up for me and to help support me," Anderson tells *Newsday*'s John Clark. "She took her job to another level by being there for me in the editing process, by constantly supporting me and giving me advice on how to deal with the situation."

Even though the film went on to receive some good reviews and was screened at both the Cannes and Sundance film festivals, it fared poorly at the American box office. "If the poor grosses of my movie helped in some way in putting [Rysher] out of business, then I'm happy," Anderson now says. "It's a really rough memory. It fucked me up. But I'll try not to sound bitter about it."

Without any real break to speak of, Paltrow went from the bowels of

Reno to the bright, cheery atmosphere of costarring in a *Friends* vehicle, playing David Schwimmer's object of desire in *The Pallbearer*, a Miramax film. Even on paper, the film didn't sound particularly scintillating, although at the time Paltrow deemed it "very funny and sweet." "I play a really nice girl," she said. "She was the least strong character in the script, but the bones were there, so I thought I could fill it in. I'm romantic for the first time."

As many critics pointed out, at times *The Pallbearer* seemed like a hybrid between an extended *Friends* episode and *The Graduate*. In the movie, Schwimmer is a mopey young man named Tom Thompson, who has no job (much less a career), no girlfriend, and no home of his own (he still lives with his mother). Out of the blue, he gets a phone call from Ruth Abernathy (played by Barbara Hershey), the mother of a high school classmate who has just died. The grieving mom is under the impression that Tom was her son's best friend and wants him to deliver the eulogy and act as a pallbearer at the funeral. Tom accepts, even though he has no memory whatsoever of the dead man.

As it turns out, Ruth is no average grieving mom and soon seduces the still-virgin Tom, making love to him in her dead son's bed. However, Tom's attention is soon stolen away when his secret high school crush, Julie (played by Paltrow), shows up for the funeral. Even though Julie initially shows no interest in Tom, naturally they end up together.

Despite some obvious plot-borrowing from *The Graduate*, not every critic was quick to pan the film. Roger Ebert, for one, noted, "Barbara Hershey's role as Mrs. Abernathy is . . . written with some freedom in it. At first she seems set up simply as a clone of Mrs. Robinson in *The Graduate*, but her character takes some unmarked turns and ends up less predictable, and much nicer, than we expect. Tom, too, is not locked into one mode of behavior, and in a way the movie is about how he grows up and learns to take charge of himself. And Gwyneth Paltrow fools us about who Julie really is, and what she really wants."

Once again, when the cameras weren't rolling, Paltrow was endearing herself to her coworkers. Meryl Poster, one of producers of *The Pallbearer*, teasingly calls Paltrow "an old Jewish lady." "She wants everybody to be in love the way she is," she explains, "she wants everybody to eat, she doesn't want anyone to worry, and God forbid you're rude to a waiter — she'll die. She's like, 'Be nice, be nice, be nice.'"

To Paltrow, however, that kind of behavior is something that should be expected, not something that one should be complimented for: "I guess I'm not the type of actress who says, 'I'm not coming out until I get my tropical-punch Gatorade.' Who needs that?" And so, it's because Paltrow was reared with such good manners that sometimes the press coverage of her private life gnawed at her. "Occasionally, I get annoyed," she says, "but it's more like a fleabite. It's not deeply upsetting. It's frustrating when people write things that aren't true, but you can't let it get to you. There's no way I'm going to let the *Star* ruin my day."

So, as much as possible, she tried to see the humor in all the false stories: "The one I liked is that Brad was giving sperm to Melissa Etheridge and her girlfriend, Julie Cypher, but I forbade it, so he called Melissa's machine and said, 'Girls, I won't be showing up with that Dixie cup anymore!'"

That said, some of the more outrageous stories had Paltrow shaking her head. "Someone reported that Brad was hobbling around at the Oscars because he was wearing my underwear to bring him luck," she recalls to Jay Carr of the *Minneapolis Star Tribune.* "What kind of moron would make that kind of thing up? It's so not true." Reflecting on the falsehoods, she adds, "I think that these people are bored. People are agitated; they're not happy in their lives, they're not peaceful, and they think we have everything. I suppose it could appear like that to the outside world. Listen, we're incredibly fortunate, and we thank God everyday for having the families that we do and the opportunities that we do. We have problems; we're not always kicking our heels and not always the Lotto couple. That's not the way life is."

Most of the speculation in the press, however, centered on the question of whether or not Paltrow was going to be the woman who would finally walk down the aisle with Pitt. Of course, few thought of it the other way around — whether Pitt was the man whom Paltrow would ultimately choose to be her husband — but such is the way of Hollywood and those who cover it.

By April 1995, there were so many rumors circulating about the alleged engagement of Pitt and Paltrow that the couple felt compelled to issue a statement. "Nobody need speculate further," announced Paltrow, who said that the stories were "totally way out of control"; so much so that "even extended family members have started calling" to ask about the couple's wedding plans.

Although Paltrow at that point denied that there was any official announcement to be made, she did comment, "It's very exciting to be with the person I know I'm going to be with, but marriage is a very serious thing." A month later, Paltrow was quoted waxing more poetically about marriage: "My father always said, 'Don't marry an actor, because actors are vain and insecure.' But Brad is the one good one — and I got him!"

What had ignited all of the speculation was the diamond Paltrow was wearing on her left ring finger during her press junket for *The Pallbearer*. When asked about the ring, she would only coyly allow, "Let's just say it was a nice gift. This is just a very sweet present. It doesn't signify anything." And if Paltrow entertained any hope that the media attention would eventually die down as she and Pitt entered their second year of togetherness, she was about to be disappointed. But this time, the focus would be more on her than on Pitt, as she was about to break out as a movie star in a very big way.

Late summer of 1995 found Paltrow back in London making yet another film, this one an adaptation of Jane Austen's romantic comedy, *Emma*, which had been the basis of the Alicia Silverstone hit, *Clueless*. What made the circumstances of this film particularly special for Paltrow was that, for the first time, she would be the undisputed star of the film. That in and of itself would be enough to cause anxiety, but in addition to carrying the movie, Paltrow had to do so with an English dialect.

An interesting sidebar to how Hollywood works is in the story of exactly how Paltrow got to star in *Emma*. Douglas McGrath, the film's screenwriter and director, had arranged a meeting with Paltrow at the suggestion of his agent, who also happened to represent Blythe Danner. McGrath, who watched *Flesh and Bone* prior to the meeting, was impressed. "The thing that actually sold me on her playing a young English girl was that she did a perfect Texas accent," McGrath says. "I know that wouldn't recommend her to most people, but I grew up in Texas, and I have never heard an actor or actress not from Texas sound remotely like a real Texan."

McGrath also tells *Time*'s Richard Corliss: "My friends and I used to just kill ourselves laughing when movie actors did Texas accents. People always sounded like the Clampetts. But Gwyneth did the most impeccable Texas accent in *Flesh and Bone*. She has an amazing ear. And, of course, everything else is perfect. Her speaking voice is a beautiful instrument, and she photographs like a dream — all the light goes to her on the set, and she seems to absorb it and then give it back. I knew she had theater training, so she could carry herself. We had many actresses, big and small, who wanted to play this part. The minute she started the read-through, the very first line, I thought, 'Everything is going to be fine; she's going to be brilliant.'"

For McGrath, though, it wasn't just the accent that sold him on Paltrow but the entire picture that she presented. "She was actually how

I pictured the part looking, too," he says, "those beautiful patrician lines, her coloring. You know, Austen doesn't give you a lot of description about how the characters look, so you pretty much put it together your own way."

But in the world of movies, casting an actor isn't merely a case of the director simply saying who they want. After the read-through, Harvey Weinstein, the independent film guru who co-owns Miramax with his brother Bob, did indeed decide to give the go-ahead to *Emma*, but there was a catch. He wanted Paltrow to do another movie for him first. According to Paltrow, "When he saw the reading, he was like, 'Okay, let's do it,' and then he was kind of up in the air, and he said, 'If you do *The Pallbearer*, we'll make *Emma*.'" She adds candidly, "He knew I really wanted to do *Emma* and that I was less keen to do *The Pallbearer*."

Meryl Poster, who at the time was a senior vice president of production at Weinstein's company, confirmed Paltrow's version of events. "Harvey really wanted her to do *The Pallbearer*," Poster says. "And so I think that in his unique way he was saying, 'Do *The Pallbearer* and I'm going to make *Emma*, and that will make you a star.'" But Poster admits that, "Because there was so much hype about her, but you hadn't really seen her carry a film before, we didn't even open up the audition process, and a lot of actresses were miffed about it."

So with her *Pallbearer* debt paid in full, Paltrow set out to start filming *Emma*. One of the most anxious moments of the filming came during the first cast read-through, during which Paltrow took on the English accent that she was planning to use throughout the film. McGrath says he suspects most of the British actors present were thinking, 'We have to help the American girl. We are the gods of the English theater.' He notes, however, that "After the read-through, not only were they excited to be in the movie with her, but I'm sure it actually made them a little insecure. You could see it as the read-through went on, because the energy kept picking up from the next person. And they were like, 'Wow, she's really good.'"

Austen's novel, published in 1816, recounts the relentless efforts of Emma Woodhouse to organize the lives of her friends. Emma can honestly be called a meddler. Her passion is poking her nose into other people's love lives, and she goes about matchmaking for them whether they want her to or not. The whole time, of course, Emma is oblivious to her own perfect match.

The film opens with the marriage of Emma's former governess Anne (Greta Scacchi) to Mr. Weston (James Cosmo), a well-to-do neighbor of theirs in Highbury, Surrey. Emma, of course, believes she is responsible for their union. Missing Anne's company, she decides to devote her energies to finding the right mate for the unworldly Harriet Smith (Toni Collette), which prevents Smith from accepting the proposal of Robert Martin (Edward Woodall), a farmer whom Emma considers unworthy of her friend. Emma encourages Harriet to have expectations for Mr. Elton (Alan Cumming), the local vicar, only to find, after a series of misunderstandings, that Elton was never entertaining hopes of winning her hand.

"It's just a great story," believes McGrath. "With Austen, not only do you get a good story, you get, for the same price, witty dialogue and very funny characters who seem like people you know. You get romance and you get beautifully written prose. When I first read the novel, just after college, I'd just read all those big, thick, heavy novels as a literature major. I found it hard to read those romantic novels of the nineteenth century particularly, because they're so humorless and turgid and they're all so upset all the time. I mean, Heathcliff — get over it!

"But this was so delightful. It was so light and effervescent and bubbly. Of the great novels it's the most amusing, for my taste. And it's not just a little social comedy. At a certain point it widens into something deeper and more romantic. And her youth allows you to forgive Emma," McGrath says, who points out that it was important to get the *right* young actress. "When you think of other actors who are 21," he reflects, "your options aren't promising. You have a grim poster staring you in the face. It's like, Shannen Doherty is Emma? I don't think so."

In fact, according to McGrath, Paltrow was the perfect Emma: "The best thing about Gwyneth is that she plays all sides of it. She doesn't soften the unpleasant things in Emma's character, nor does she inflate her good qualities. She has everything a young woman that age has, all the petulance, the vanity, the self-confidence that can only come from youth and ignorance. The tenderness, the repentance, the honest desire to help someone even though, in her case, it always seems to turn into harm. Because she doesn't always try to make herself look good, that makes her all the more endearing."

Interestingly, Paltrow's take on the character differs from McGrath's. "She's a very good heart and a very good person," Paltrow says. "She's just a little spoiled: her mother has died and she's grown up with a father who thinks she can do no wrong. What I loved about her so much is that she has faults; it's nice to see a film heroine who makes terrible mistakes and really learned from them and is very pained by them.

"And that's what was wonderful about Emma," Paltrow adds. "She's very responsible and very mature, and then in a way, she's just totally on the wrong track and sort of riding that last wave of adolescence — which I think is very real. I loved Emma immediately. I loved how spirited she was, how she had a very good heart, and I loved that she's faulty and a little misguided. I found that very human and real, and I was excited to play her. Then, of course, came all the work, which was certainly challenging — the dialect, the horses, dancing, archery, and singing and the manners. It required a lot of research beforehand. Luckily, before I went over to England, I was recovering from wisdom tooth surgery, so I had a lot of time on my hands."

In an effort not to dwell on the fact that the ultimate success of the film was contingent on her role, Paltrow played it light and loose on the set, perhaps even more so than usual. One day, says producer Steven Haft, "She would get halfway through her speech in a Dorset accent, then all of a sudden she would start sounding like Woody Allen. She had the whole crew in stitches. She does a mean Woody."

She also did a mean Emma. "The amazing thing about her," McGrath says, "is that, as a rule, she can be running around the set, singing, dancing, curled up like a cat, and then the minute action is called, she completely changes. She adopts every feature of a young woman in nineteenth-century England of that breeding and station." Producer Donna Gigliotti recalls a similar experience: "She'd be speaking in her American accent, and then the director would yell, 'Action,' and she would suddenly go into this absolutely flawless English accent. As soon as they yelled, 'Cut,' she'd say, 'Oh, Donna, I hate this bra they're making me wear.'"

"She's well in touch with her instincts, which is a great skill to have," adds Jeremy Northam, who costarred in *Emma*. "She just sails through and seems to have a blast doing it, and I think it shows on the screen, because there's a real sense of fun and mischief. I remember her ability to switch in a nanosecond from 1815 to 1995. She would snap out of her take, go straight into a thick New York accent, ask for a coffee, and do a devastating impression of Woody Allen.

"It's easy to praise Gwyneth for just getting the accent right," Northam adds. "But the language also possesses a rhetoric that we don't have anymore — the pauses, the parentheses — and she can relish those with her sense of mischief and fun. She's also technically brilliant, a great comedian, and she's wonderful to play with, full of lovely, deft touches. Emma is funny as well as romantic, and Gwyneth gives a kind of high-comedy performance you don't see very often these days. I think she's got a huge future."

Gigliotti summed it up by saying, "She's an *actress*. She can do that silly thing, the 'Let's talk about hair and makeup and clothes.' But if you dig a little deeper, you'll find a very serious person. She happens to be packaged in someone who is beautiful and talented." And Gigliotti recalls that "There were several young women who used to watch the rushes with me. They would turn to me and say, 'When did Gwyneth learn to shoot a bow and arrow?' I said, 'She knew how to do it.' In the singing scene they said, 'Whose voice did you dub for Gwyneth?' I said, 'It's her own.' They said, 'Okay, she's beautiful, she can do this accent, she's a good actress, she can sing, and she can shoot a bow and arrow. And Brad Pitt's her boyfriend. Isn't there *something* wrong with her?'" As a matter of fact, McGrath jokes that he wanted "to write in a scene where Emma jumps a motorcycle over 12 burning barrels, just to see if Gwyneth can do it."

On a more serious note, however, Gigliotti says that she remembers the first time she saw Paltrow act in the life-changing production of *Picnic* at the Williamstown Theater just a few years before: "I remember I just sat there in the audience and said, 'This is extraordinary. This girl is a major talent.' And I was proved right."

But for all of her exceptional talent and offscreen antics, being in England for an extended period of time made Paltrow homesick, not just for family and friends, but for homeland. It helped, however, that McGrath, the Texan, was there. "Yeah, Doug and I were the two Yanks on the side," Paltrow says. "It helped because we had each other to lean on; we had a similar experience, culturally."

It also helped that Pitt came to visit her whenever his own busy work schedule allowed. And even when Pitt was away, costar Alan Cumming notes mischievously that his presence was still felt: "I'd go into makeup in the morning, and she'd be drinking coffee out of a mug with a picture of Brad on it, one of those brooding, hunky ones. Very Freudian. I'd say, 'Stop that!' And she'd just laugh. If everyone went around drinking out of cups with pictures of their beloved on it, it would be a very strange world. You know, kind of getting oral gratification from something that reminds you of your boyfriend."

Once *Emma* wrapped, Paltrow was in desperate need of time off. "Emma was the role of a lifetime, a wonderful experience," she says. "It's the best-written role for a woman under 25 in the last I don't know how many years. Emma's so three-dimensional and complicated and charming and faulted — but I've never worked so hard in my life. I bit off more than I could chew doing all these movies back-to-back." Self-deprecatingly, she adds, "All I do is work. And when you work so much, you don't lose your sharpness, you lose your personality. I'm terrible; I don't have time to exercise, I smoke, I drink coffee. Something has to give."

So, for the first time in her career, Paltrow planned to take a self-imposed hiatus. After making *Hush* opposite Jessica Lange and a remake of *Great Expectations* with Ethan Hawke — both to be released in 1998 — she planned to accompany Pitt to the location of his next film, *Seven Years in Tibet.* But first she was looking forward to spending lazy days with him at his house in Los Angeles, a huge mansion once owned by Cassandra Peterson, better known as Elvira, Mistress of the Dark. Paltrow relished her moments with Pitt, and at the time, she said, "We can't go to the mall, we can't go to any of the tourist sites. But we do fine; we go to restaurants all the time and to bookstores."

After *Emma,* Paltrow also found time to catch up with her friends and went on a family trip to the Sundance Film Festival where her baby brother Jake was premiering his directorial debut. Whenever nestled in the throes of daily living, Paltrow seemed to get caught up in the domestic bliss of it all. "Hotel rooms get kind of boring and lonely after awhile," she says. "At first it's the most exciting and coolest thing in the whole world. But after awhile, it makes you really appreciate just being home to feed the dogs."

She is also a white-knuckle flier, which makes being land-bound very comforting: "You're so busy all day, stuck in your head and your own life — 'Did I feed the dog? When do we have to wake up in the morning to go to work?' — You get on a plane, and it all stops. I'm like the tiniest thing, and I'm about to go into the sky in a 50-billion-ton metal structure. I understand aerophysics and everything, but as a mammal, it terrifies me."

All of this — the reconnecting with her boyfriend and family, the relaxation, the anxiety over flying — contributed to Paltrow's feeling that "Movies are fantastic and all, but they're not what's important, you know? If I never made another movie, I would be fine. It's fun and it's exciting, but it's not what life is about." Paltrow adds, "I love what I do — don't get me wrong — but I've sort of achieved what I wanted to, and if I never worked again, it would not bother me."

Not that anyone really believed her.

7

A Star in Her Own Right

EMMA PREMIERED at Manhattan's Paris Theater in July 1996, and just as Harvey Weinstein had predicted, it did indeed make Paltrow a star in her own right. The critics seemed uniform in their effusiveness. As Richard Corliss observed, "Paltrow may not be able to — or care to — parlay the role of this adorable meddler into a multimillion-dollar picture deal, as *Clueless*'s Alicia Silverstone did. Still, *Emma* could conceivably vault Paltrow from her current status as bright ingenue to the top of the list of serious young actresses who combine Oscar éclat and box-office clout — a little Streep, a little Sandra Bullock."

Roger Ebert similarly sang Paltrow's praises, noting that she "sparkles in the title role as young Miss Woodhouse, who wants to play God in her own little patch of England." Likewise, Mike Clark's review of the film was replete with praise for Paltrow: "After standing out in *Seven* and in box-office failures from *Flesh and Bone* through *The Pallbearer*, it was only a matter of time until Paltrow exploded on screen. She does so here, and in a role that really needs her, for truth to tell, Emma's a potential pain. She's privileged, she's a gossip, she is meddlesome and in one unforgettable scene, downright rude. But we're won over by her outward charm and the warmth of her inner intentions. Never once, thanks to Paltrow, do we want to wring her neck (which, by the way, is lovely)."

At the film's premiere, it was Paltrow who took center stage, much to her weeping parents' pride. "I'm overwhelmed!" Danner proclaimed at the big event. And Paltrow's grandfather, Buster Paltrow, told reporters that, obviously, talent "runs in the family." So enthralled was the audience that scant attention was paid to the fact that Pitt was a no-show, having been unable to get away from his film location in Ireland, where he was working on *The Devil's Own*.

But even though Pitt was not present at the premiere, there was no lack of praise and support for Paltrow that night. "She reminds me so much of the young Grace Kelly," actress Arlene Dahl announced after the movie. Others took up the same chorus or offered other comparisons, from Audrey Hepburn to the queen of accents, Meryl Streep. However, when Paltrow hears people comparing her to the likes of Grace Kelly, she instantly defers: "I mean, there is only one Grace Kelly. She was a very extraordinary actress and had an extraordinary presence. Obviously, it's very flattering being compared to her, but I feel it's totally unjustified."

Regarding her ability to pull off an impeccable accent *à la* Streep, Paltrow believes it's an inherent knack: "You know, I think you're born to a certain extent with a kind of ear. When I was little I would pick out certain harmonies, and from the time I was very small I'd do accents." But when it came to actually maintaining an accent for a film, Paltrow admits, "I didn't realize it would require so much work. It's not just making the sounds but actually changing the way your jaw works. It did require a lot of work, and I did work very diligently, because I think it's very distracting when you're watching a movie and somebody's accent is here now and gone there, or it keeps changing."

What helped her immensely with her accent, Paltrow says, was the quality of the script. "Because the dialogue is so rich and is only there to accelerate the plot," she explains, "you don't have to worry about filling anything in; it's all there, so you just behave appropriately. It was a tremendous amount of fun." But Paltrow also credits her castmates for helping her muscle through: "I found it a little daunting, but the actors were so supportive and made me feel so comfortable with the work I was doing and with my accent. To think about the fact that I was carrying the movie was making me feel paralyzed, and I really felt that, on the set, we were all in this together."

"Humility, schmility," says Douglas McGrath. "There's a great sense that Gwyneth is on the verge of a major breakthrough. She *is* the next Meryl Streep. People who've seen her shine in other roles are just waiting for a part to come along that shows how many sides she has. And in *Emma*, I saw her do it all: ride a horse, dance, sing, run through every emotion. She was sparkling. Frankly, I don't think there's any kind of acting she can't do."

Indeed, McGrath became a one-man cheerleading squad for his leading lady. "She's ravishing to look at and photographs like a dream," he waxes poetic to Jay Carr of the *Minneapolis Star Tribune*. "Especially on film: she just takes the light and sends it back. Men adore her, and women love her but don't envy her. She has a beauty you can enjoy and not be threatened by because it's a kind of friendly beauty. She seems like a real person. She doesn't seem like a goddess."

McGrath also begs to differ with Paltrow about her accent. "Her English accent in *Emma* came so easily and was done so proficiently that even English people thought she was British," he says. "One of our sound supervisors wanted to know why he didn't know this lovely British actress. When I told him that she was from that little English village of New York, he almost hit the floor."

Even peers such as Julia Roberts, who herself was once recognized as being the next great "Hollywood thing," were throwing *bons mots* her way. "Gwyneth Paltrow has an incredibly interesting look, which I think trancends time," Roberts says. "She can look very today, she can look very '60s, she can look period. She can go from being incredibly, exquisitely beautiful to just plain interesting. She's got a face you want to look at for a very long time; you want to absorb it."

And if you don't believe Roberts, consider that *Vogue* chose Paltrow to be their cover girl to coincide with the release of *Emma*, and Calvin Klein pursued her to "star" in a new advertising campaign — a proposal that Paltrow wanted to accept but couldn't because of a scheduling conflict with her next movie. "To me, Gwyneth Paltrow embodies the woman of the '90s," Calvin Klein asserts. "It is not only that she is beautiful and sexy, but she also radiates a confidence and grace that is timeless."

While she might exude grace, Paltrow admits that she could never bottle it for model consumption. "Calvin asked me to do some runway stuff, but I just can't do it," she says. "For me, it's far more difficult to cultivate that silent-mystery-model thing than to go, 'Oh hi!' You have a personality when you're sashaying down the runway. I could never walk down that thing." However, Paltrow does acknowledge that Klein is one of her favorite designers, because "his clothes are classic and simple." But she is not a one-designer woman by any means. "I really like what Tom Ford is doing at Gucci," she says. "And I love Donna Karan. She's doing the costumes for *Great Expectations*, and I think they're great. I really just appreciate the whole art of fashion."

Paltrow also had admirers in other high places. In August 1996, she and McGrath were honored with a White House screening of *Emma*, which McGrath dubbed "Lincoln-plex One." President Clinton admitted that he had a fondness for all things English, in part because he had first proposed to Hillary Rodham Clinton in London, although she didn't say yes until they had returned to Arkansas. Plus, Clinton had studied at Oxford University, and he revealed to the *Emma* contingent

Paltrow and Pitt arriving at the White House for the DC premiere of *Emma*
MATT MENDELSOHN / CORBIS

that he used to "go to tea parties just to listen to the musical way the women spoke, and the film brought that back." For Paltrow, it was like no other event she'd ever experienced: "I've been to DC, but never like this." And Pitt, who accompanied her, seconded her feelings. "It was the experience of a lifetime," he said. "Obviously, I'm proud of her."

There were 50 people invited to the screening and, after cocktails, the film was finally unspoiled. McGrath describes the surreal experience of having your movie screened for the chief executive: "There's a sense of a half-second delay. [Clinton] laughs, and the people behind him laugh; he doesn't, they don't. It's like they are wired to his seat." According to Paltrow, though, the president gave the movie a big Oval Office thumbs up: "He loved it."

But as pleased as she obviously was over the kudos Clinton gave her, Paltrow was also making a concerted effort not to let all the praise go to her head. "I don't want to sound ungrateful, but if I believe people who give me overwhelming praise now, I'll have to believe them if they say something else later," she explains to Jack Garner. "It's more important to me what my family and my boyfriend think."

As for herself, Paltrow admits that *Emma* was "the first movie I've done that I've been honestly thrilled by." Of the first time she saw it in the theater, she says, "I was so pleased. It was better than I had even hoped it would be. I've never participated in a film that I felt really proud of. I was really surprised." And her surprise was probably in part because, as

Paltrow admits, "I'm not a huge Jane Austen fan. I find her a little too chatty. But I think it translates well, because it's about story-plot and circumstance and confusion and love and wit and romance. That's why her novels make such lovely films."

Even though *Emma* was a distinct period piece, one of the reasons for its success was that the human behavior depicted in the film crossed time. "Thank goodness there is not this rigorous, coded system of manners and classes that was in existence then," Paltrow says. "But the dynamics within relationships and the seductiveness of romance translate easily. And gossip is very much in place today. Gossip is a whole new industry, isn't it? Who knew it could become such a lucrative profession? It's very disturbing, especially when you're sitting where I am."

The irony was obviously not lost on Paltrow that she was starring in a film that used gossip as a plot point. "I enjoy a good tidbit about somebody as much as the next person," she admits. "But I've also seen what gossip can do and how cruel it can be."

Obviously, the level of gossip experienced by Pitt and Paltrow was directly proportional to their celebrity and fame. As Paltrow acknowledges, "His is a level of fame which is extraordinary and very frightening. It's a lot for a person to endure." And having been in the middle of that maelstrom prompted Paltrow to wish out loud, "It'd be nice if I could maintain this level I'm at right now. I have the respect of my peers and the people who make movies. I don't feel I'm being assaulted."

That said, Paltrow still maintained that all the scrutiny and all the attention really hadn't been an issue within the context of her relationship with Pitt: "I feel extremely normal and grounded with my family and the people I love." And the way in which Pitt himself chose to handle celebrity, lessons he was passing along to Paltrow, no doubt had a lot to do with her sense of security. "He's great," Paltrow said at the time. "Any kind of period that I go through, he's been through. He's very wise about it all. It's really nice; it makes me feel very safe."

But no amount of advice makes a difference unless the person receiving it has the wisdom to accept and assimilate it, and wisdom Paltrow has. "There's a part of me that's always felt kind of 40 years old," Paltrow muses. "And part of me feels that, when I'm 40, I'll really be all together, and everything will be all caught up." She goes on to say, "I'm living a full life. I'm more content than I've ever been. And I think that's partly because death has shaped the way I perceive things."

For someone still in her early twenties, Paltrow had experienced more death on a personal level than many of her peers. In high school, a hit-and-run driver killed her friend Courtney Steel at age 17. Paltrow was also stunned by the death of Harrison Kravis, one of her best friends, as a result of a car accident. "I'll never recover from Harrison's death," Paltrow tells Jesse Kornbluth of *Buzz* magazine. "Or the death of my 23-year-old cousin Keith from cancer the spring before that. At first, I missed Harrison in a tangible way. As time goes by, I miss him in a different way, and I resent the fact that I've gotten used to him not being alive."

Such loss allows Paltrow to put the rest of her life in proper perspective. So it comes as no huge shock that she was completely unaffected by not being nominated for an Oscar for her work in *Emma,* even though a huge number of critics predicted she would be. "No, I'm not disappointed," Paltrow said at the time. "I was surprised that people thought I *would* be nominated. I think it was a terrific year for women. I'm glad that people can go around and say, 'How come you weren't nominated?' Or Winona for *The Crucible,* which was fantastic."

Even though the Academy might have bypassed Paltrow, Pitt made sure she didn't emerge from the *Emma* hoopla empty-handed. In September 1996, he gave her a special present — mint-condition first editions of J. D. Salinger's *The Catcher in the Rye* and *Franny and Zooey* — which just proves that the world was dealing with two of the most beautiful, and better read, people on the planet.

Looking past *Emma,* Paltrow knew that the worst thing she could do would be to immediately accept another period-piece film. Instead, she wanted to go against type and make audiences see her in a whole new light: "I don't want to get stuck doing the same thing; that's not fun. I love playing darker parts that are more gritty." She was, in fact, carrying out the philosophy that Pitt always promoted: "As soon as you have an image, you gotta break it." However, Paltrow recognizes that "It's limiting if you say, 'Now I want to play a heroin addict.' I never expect anything. That way I don't limit myself."

At the same time, Paltrow appeared to be very comfortable at this stage of her career. "There's another level, but I don't think I want to go there," she admitted. "I'm really happy at the level that I'm at right now. I can still get away with not being recognized a lot of the time. I have a chance to do many films. It's unbelievable, opportunity-wise." And she added that "The more successful your movies are, the more exposed you are, and the more people get fixed perceptions of you. That's kind of hard for me to deal with because I like to fluctuate a lot in the kind of roles I play. If you get really successful from one movie, people keep wanting you to repeat that performance, which is something I really don't want. That's why I keep going back to independent films. I want to avoid that next surge as much as possible." Indeed, what Paltrow wanted to steer clear of was the danger of being pigeonholed into period-piece roles. Little could she have known, however, that just such a role would one day bring her the greatest fame.

8

Box Office Bombs

PALTROW'S NEXT FILM after *Emma* was the thriller *Hush* (originally called *Kilronan*), which starred Jessica Lange. In theory, *Hush* was geared to give Paltrow's career the "surge" she had talked about wanting to avoid. However, when she originally read the script, the premise sounded intriguing and, moreover, it presented an opportunity to work with Oscar-winner Lange.

The movie was primarily shot in Charlottesville and Richmond, locales that are considered the heart of Virginia's horse country. The story was, in essence, an Oedipal love triangle. Paltrow's character, Helen, has met the man of her dreams. Jackson Baring (played by Johnathon Schaech) is handsome, loving, from a well-to-do family, and has a bright future on Wall Street.

When Jackson takes Helen home for the holidays to Kilronan, his mom's sprawling horse-breeding estate in Kentucky, she meets Martha Baring (played by Lange), Jackson's mother and "the other woman" in his life. A widow, Martha is devoted in the extreme to her only son. Having grown up without parents, Helen instantly warms to Martha. That's her first mistake, and it doesn't take Helen long to see the error of her ways.

Underneath Martha's Southern charm is a steel-magnolia dementia and a plan to bring Jackson back to Kentucky, a plot now in jeopardy because of Helen. So Martha begins a psychological reign of terror on the unsuspecting Helen, who quickly catches on. "Helen understands that Martha is orchestrating their problems earlier than anyone else," Paltrow says. "That's why everyone thinks that Helen is the one with the screw loose. She catches all of the little digs in the beginning and knows what Martha is doing through most of the story."

First, Martha tampers with Helen's birth control during her initial visit, then once Helen and Jackson go back to New York, Martha arranges for Helen to be nearly mugged and raped. After Helen discovers she's pregnant and subsequently marries Jackson, the newlyweds return to the farm. This time, Martha doctors Helen's dessert with a drug used to induce premature labor. Ultimately, her idea is to kill Helen after she delivers the baby so that Mama Martha can keep the child for herself. In the end, Helen's maternal instincts take over, and Martha literally goes up in flames.

The movie was directed and written by Jonathan Darby, whose enthusiasm no doubt helped convince Paltrow to sign on. The idea for the film sprang from his fascination with the mother-son relationship, "The only love affair that always ends in departure," Darby says. "Freud probably still said it best," he observes, "that families are all imagined constructs, and each member imagines different views of family. In *Hush*, Martha wants her son never to grow up, to always be with her. Helen wants the family and the mother she never had, and Jackson wants to be free to become his own individual. And so this collision happens in this triangle between these three characters that all want their own version of family. It's a triangle that constantly changes and shifts. You see different moments in this film from different points of view.

"Ultimately, this movie is about family," Darby concludes. "In the end, each character is confronted with the truth. Jackson discovers the truth about his mother. Helen discovers the truth about herself — she can stand up to Martha and she can be a mother on her own terms. And Martha faces the truth that you can't fight nature."

One of the film's producers, Douglas Wick, says that, through consultations with psychologists, a lot of care went into fashioning Martha's disturbed behavior. "It's really hard to find a good thriller with some kind of genuine psychological base. What we came up with is 'narcissism character disorder,'" explains Darby. "It is quite a serious sickness. These are self-involved, highly dramatic people who sometimes resort to violence. They are incredibly charming, incredibly seductive, cajoling, flattering, wonderful to be around. They are the sun at the center of their universe. But if you cross them, they change very fast on you."

Alas, so can critics. The reviews of *Hush* were uniformly scathing. One reviewer noted, "If *Hush* is any indication of the future path of Jessica Lange's movie career, it won't be long before she is wielding a bloody ax and bellowing like a lunatic in the kind of psycho-killer romp associated with the cinematic twilights of Bette Davis and Tallulah Bankhead. The film is so awful it doesn't even qualify as a B-movie."

Similarly, Roger Ebert wrote, "*Hush* is the kind of movie where you walk in, watch the first 10 minutes, know exactly where it's going, and hope devoutly that you're wrong. It's one of those Devouring Woman movies where the villainess never plays a scene without a drink and a cigarette, and the hero is inattentive to the victim to the point of dementia. What's frustrating is that little of the evil-doing would be possible if Jackson behaved at any moment like a normal, intelligent person. He consistently does the wrong thing just because the film needs him to." And Barbara Schulgasser panned the film by asserting that "*Hush*, which is an absurdly bad mixture of *Rosemary's Baby* and any Bette Davis movie from the 1960s, seems to be a classic case of a grasping mother trying to possess her beloved son."

Mercifully, reviews never come out until long after the cast and crew have dispersed to other projects. When *Hush* finished with its principal photography, the wrap party was held in downtown Richmond and, as always, Paltrow managed to charm everyone there. She made a point of saying hello to and chatting with every crew member, and she was frequently seen giving high fives and hugs. "This might be normal behavior in the outside world," noted one observer at the party, "but unfortunately, among Hollywood actors it's pretty rare. Gwyneth's just a very real person."

What makes Paltrow's graciousness even more impressive is that filming *Hush* had not been a particularly enriching experience. As filming progressed, the script underwent changes, which in her mind, did not improve the final product. "I really wanted to work with Jessica. She's so brilliantly talented and such a terrific woman, and in that way it was an excellent experience. . . . [I]t was such a great lesson to just be around her and watch her work But it was just the silliest character," Paltrow says of Helen. "I mean, it was *not* a character."

As Paltrow explains in her 1997 Mr. Showbiz interview, "It was just one of those things where you go to work for the wrong reason. Unless something has been radically altered, you always know basically what you're getting into. In the situations where I feel, 'God, this really didn't turn out the way I would have liked,' I've said to myself, 'Why didn't you just listen to yourself? You knew at the beginning!' But sometimes you do a movie because you've got to pay the phone bill, you know, or whatever. You can't try and rejustify it later."

Although Paltrow's next film, *Great Expectations*, didn't light up the box office either, it was a far more fulfilling acting job. In this updated remake of Charles Dickens's classic novel, Ethan Hawke and Paltrow took center stage as opposite-ends-of-the-social-spectrum protagonists.

But those expecting a faithful adherence to the original story would have been disappointed. Other than the central relationship and bare-bones story, little else remained from the novel.

Mexican director Alfonso Cuarón, who made his Hollywood debut with *A Little Princess*, wasn't overly enthused with the idea of remaking *Great Expectations*. But he says that, after he saw the script, "I realized that I had an opportunity to do something original. I was struck by its many textures and character arcs and realized that our film would be more an elaboration than an adaptation."

Even so, Paltrow was aware that not everyone would appreciate the effort: "I'm sure that there are people who will be offended at the liberties that we've taken with the material. But I also feel that there are people who will be excited, you know, that we're sort of exploring it in a new way. . . . [A]nd it's certainly, I think, more accessible for a lot of people."

At the time, Paltrow also expressed what she saw as the value of revising an old classic: "I really don't think that there's anything wrong with taking a sort of wonderful moral story and updating it. . . . It's kind of a brave adaptation. I mean, it . . . sort of extracts the didacticism, and it extracts sort of the arc of certain characters and certain dynamics within the story. But I think that, you know, overall it's quite different. I mean, it could theoretically be called something different than *Great Expectations*. But I'm sure that there will also be . . . many high school English teachers who will be thankful that we're sort of opening the doors."

In the film, Ethan Hawke plays Finnegan Bell (Pip in the novel), who becomes obsessed with Paltrow's Estella, the beautiful niece of the eccentric millionaire, Ms. Dinsmoor (Miss Havisham in the novel). Finn and Estella first meet as children at Ms. Dinsmoor's mansion, and they are reunited there again as young adults. Finn's passion for Estella is fully ignited after they share an impulsive kiss, although she leaves him wallowing in his love by departing for New York. Years later, their paths cross again, this time in the Big Apple, where Finn is now an up-and-coming artist and Estella a socialite. Even though she is engaged, they consummate their attraction, although Estella runs relentlessly hot and cold.

One of the most talked-about scenes in the film is when Estella allows Finn to do a nude portrait of her. "That was really something else!" Paltrow enthuses. "I mean, I'm a huge art lover and I love modern painting. You know, I went in to sit there, and I was just so nervous! I was overwhelmed. Here I am being painted. I was naked, but I felt, I'll just sort of pretend. Like I'm Parisian, I'm posing. It was really extraordinary."

Paltrow and Ethan Hawke on the New York set of *Great Expectations*

However, the scenes were carefully shot so that it was more illusion than erotic zones that the audience was seeing. While Paltrow doesn't seem to have any inherent problem with nudity in film, she does have others to consider, she says, which is why she turned down the Heather Graham role in *Boogie Nights* (a film written and directed by her *Hard Eight* pal, Paul Thomas Anderson). "I've got to be careful about what I do, because I don't want to embarrass my grandfather," Paltrow says earnestly to USA *Today* writer Claudia Puig. "He would have flipped out totally. There was absolutely no way. It's not worth it to me."

As it was, even Paltrow's dad ended up choosing not to see *Great Expectations* after viewing a trailer for the film that highlighted its erotic side. When the movie was released, Paltrow explained that "Because it's a little racy and I'm sort of unrobed for a good portion of the film – I mean, you don't quite see everything, but you practically do – and it's quite sexy, Dad thought he'd take a pass. And besides, I thought, 'You know, I don't want to sit next to my father and watch this film.'"

The question of nudity is always an issue for actresses, as Paltrow had discovered. "In *Flesh and Bone* I had my shirt off, and in *Dorothy Parker* I did, too," she acknowledges to Robert Paltrow (no relation) of the *Miami Herald*. "It's one of those things they make you do starting out. I don't want to be naked in a movie. But, this character in *Great Expectations*, her sexuality and her nudity was so much a part of her manipulation. It was her power. So I didn't think the nudity was exploitive. Nudity is not something I seek out. It makes my grandparents very nervous. My mother is fine with it. My father is not fine with it. He has heart attacks."

As for filming the erotically charged sex scenes, Paltrow says the experience was made comfortable by her costar: "It wasn't too bad. I've been friends with Ethan for a long time; he's so respectful and great and sweet. He really is sort of my protector, and it wasn't that bad. It could have been much worse. But it was hard because we were very sexually aggressive, and I felt uncomfortable because of who I am. He actually made it a really wonderful experience." In the end, Paltrow found doing the nude scenes, "both empowering and liberating."

But as sweet as Paltrow considers Hawke, she sees Estella in the opposite light: a "very coldhearted, manipulative person." At the same time, however, she recognizes the character's pain: "I think that Estella is tormented, or she wouldn't have ended up in that way. I think she feels deep down really bad. She's sad and she's not behaving in a way that's true to who she is. She's a complicated person and obviously not sunny and sweet, but I tried to imbue her with as much humanity as I could."

Ultimately, Paltrow also sees Estella's transformation: "I think the good thing about her toward the end of the movie is that she starts to undue what's been done to her and assume the responsibility of what she's done. Which is all that you can ever ask of yourself. . . . When people stop and take responsibility and say, 'I'm going to behave in a way that makes me feel good and is true to who I am,' that's all you can ever really ask of yourself as a person. She makes that step, I think."

Interestingly, one of the few negative comments issued publicly about Paltrow stemmed from this role. Her costar, Josh Mostel, reportedly told the *New York Daily News* that "Gwyneth Paltrow is just the star *du jour*. I thought she was nothing but a stuck-up twit." His opinion, however, was in the vast minority. Like most directors before him, *Great Expectations*' Cuarón was thrilled with Paltrow. "It's amazing to work with Gwyneth," Cuarón raves to Claudia Puig. "You can give her the *Communist Manifesto* and tell her it's a romantic comedy, and she would read it as a romantic comedy. Anything that comes out of her mouth always comes with the right emotion."

Ah, but those pesky critics spoiled the love-in. *Hollywood Reporter* classified the film as no more than a Paltrow skin flick by begging the question, "Who needs Charles Dickens when Gwyneth Paltrow's lying around naked? The answer is right there on the screen: Everyone." And one reviewer proclaimed, "If there's any hope of enjoying *Great Expectations*, you'd best lower 'em." Another said, "If you're tempted to go out and see Hollywood's new film version of Charles Dickens's *Great Expectations*, do yourself a big favor: resist the temptation, go to your local video store and rent David Lean's exquisite 1946 British version instead." And the derision didn't end there: "There is nothing about the movie *Great Expectations* to suggest it is based on Charles Dickens's classic novel. Whatever it was about the original work that has made it endure over the decades is lost in this hollow, almost crass interpretation."

The negative response to the film was not something that Paltrow was prepared for: "When we first started, Ethan and I felt very responsible because we were calling the film *Great Expectations*. Were we doing it justice? We realized that it was an unattainable goal. You have to extract what you're interested in. That allowed us great freedom. We stopped worrying. We just accepted it for what it was." In addition, Paltrow says, "Making the picture wasn't smooth, but it was very productive. Here you had Alfonso Cuarón, who is so specific in his vision, fighting with the studio. The way he works — it's like Mozart. The entire film is completed in his head before he begins."

In defense of Cuarón's vision, Paltrow elaborates on his single-mindedness in making the film: "For example, if he wanted a shot that involved some expensive miniature camera, and the studio said it was too much money, it's like he couldn't conceive of doing it another way. It's not like he was being a brat. It's just that's how it had to be. He was fighting with the studio, and the studio was fighting with him."

And in spite of its negative reception, Paltrow defends the merits of the film: "I think the movie's beautiful and kind of cool and slick – a classic on acid. It's like candy. We took a great deal of poetic license. It's also the most sensual movie I've made. You have to surrender yourself to what the film's trying to do."

However critically savaged a film might be, Paltrow at least needed to keep true to herself, which is the main reason why she had turned down an offer to costar in *Titanic*. Her rejection of the role prompted journalist Robert Osborne to fantasize about what might have been: "Gwyneth is a true aristocrat, and she would have looked like a true aristocrat. Kate Winslet looked like a seamstress. Gwyneth would have looked like she belonged on the top deck."

Paltrow confirms that she met with director James Cameron to discuss the role but decided the film would be "just too big." This is not to say that Paltrow wouldn't have considered a major film at the time, just not *that* major film. And in response to being asked if she regrets her decision, Paltrow is emphatic: "Are you insane? *Great Expectations* had great characters and a great script. *Titanic* has a ship. I just do what I want, and I don't really care what the repercussions are, or what people say. I make the movies that I like; sometimes it's some Warner Brothers thing, but more often than not it's a little British movie that I'm going over to England to do."

And so it was that Paltrow most admired Julianne Moore at this particular point in her career: "I think she's a genius. She can do *Lost World* and then she can do *Boogie Nights*. And she's still who she is. People don't follow her. That's sort of what I want. I would like to sort of keep it there." But following Paltrow, as she would soon find out, was about to become one of Hollywood's greatest pastimes.

9

Life in the Spotlight

THE MOST IMMEDIATE DOWNSIDE of Paltrow's coming of cinematic age was that, if possible, the interest in her and Pitt increased. "For the most part, people have left me alone until recently," Paltrow tells David Hochman in *US* magazine in late 1996. "They might have said, 'Aren't you . . . ?' But now, the fact that [Brad and I are] together and are famous separately seems to be too much for people to take. People want to know everything: What are we gonna do, where we are going on vacation, what are we going to eat, are we gonna get married?"

During a Mr. Showbiz interview with Michael Szymanski, Paltrow adds, "It's been surreal; it's been a strange time. You don't expect it. You think, 'Well maybe I'll be a person that someone wants to put in movies,' but you don't realize everything else that goes along with it. You don't know going in what it's going to be like, or how invading it is, and what people will do to get information and lie about you." It's this overwhelming media attention that prompts Paltrow to tell John Clark, "It's very bizarre being part of the pop culture." But, as she reveals to Cindy Pearlman in *Ladies Home Journal*, when it all becomes too much, "I just take a deep breath and say, 'Let it go.'"

"When will Paltrow and Pitt get married?" was now the echoing refrain among the celebrity media and fans. Almost from the day they had begun dating, false stories about the two being officially engaged had surfaced, only to be dismissed and denied by Pitt and Paltrow and their families. But from all outward appearances, it was simply a matter of time. Everyone who saw the two of them felt compelled to comment on what a wonderful couple they made: "Her love affair with Brad gives her strength," opines Meryl Poster to Hochman in *US* magazine. "It's not because he's a superstar but because he's completely besotted with her. They're so crazy in love. It's like there's enough love between the both of them for everyone in the room."

Marcia Schulman, a casting agent who is a longtime friend of Pitt's, tells *People* magazine's Karen Schneider about the first time he introduced her to Paltrow: "I met her, and when she was out of earshot, Brad said, 'So, do you like her? Isn't she incredible?'" Well, according to *Seven*'s director, David Fincher, yes she is: "She's highly educated, encouraging him to read more. They make a wonderful couple." Similarly, one of *Seven*'s producers, Arnold Kopelson, notes, "They are very much in love. The chemistry between them is very obvious. Gwyneth is very confident." And he adds that "A strong woman is not threatened by the attention Brad gets. It's a reaffirmation of her selection."

Paltrow was equally demonstrative in her love for Pitt. When *Hush* wrapped, she jumped into her car at 4:00 AM and drove five hours to be with him in New York City. She also turned down the lead role in *The Avengers* remake — a part that ultimately went to Uma Thurman — so that she could spend more time with Pitt. "I almost did it, and then, just personally it was very hard," she admits in her 1997 Mr. Showbiz interview. "At that time Brad had just signed on to do a film in New York for the summer, and that would have meant a four-month separation, and I thought, 'It's a wonderful role, and I think that Uma will have a great time with it and everything. This isn't the right thing for me right now. And Uma will be so much better in it than I would, anyway. It's true!'"

In December 1996, a great gust of talk renewed the Paltrow-Pitt engagement watch when gossip columns began reporting that the two were absolutely betrothed, although no date had been set. Once again, the denials were issued en masse. A spokesperson for Pitt dismissed the conjecture as "completely fabricated." Then, on December 19, Blythe Danner told *Entertainment Tonight*, "They're not engaged. I'm the mother. I know."

Ironically, less than a day after Danner's emphatic denial, Pitt proposed to Paltrow, who had spent the better part of four months with him in Argentina, where he was filming *Seven Years in Tibet*. She accepted. According to friends, it wasn't the first time he'd asked, but Paltrow had wanted to be sure. The first thing the newly engaged couple did was call their parents, who passed the news along. "They're engaged!" Bruce Paltrow announced. Speaking on behalf of both families, he added, "We are thrilled. We think it's perfect."

To celebrate, Pitt took a break from filming and chartered a private jet to whisk him and Paltrow off to his parents' home in Springfield, where they spent the Christmas holidays with his family. From there, they went to New York and celebrated the engagement with Paltrow's parents.

But it wasn't only Pitt's and Paltrow's respective families that were pleased with the pending union. "They are like adolescents in love," Dr. Horacio Cervo Zenie, Pitt's physician on the set for *Seven Years in Tibet,* was quoted as saying. "I see them feeding each other, kissing, doing things that people who are madly in love do. As soon as Gwyneth would arrive on the set, Brad would rush off and give her a big hug. You can't help but admire that." Similarly, a woman from the town of Mendoza in West Argentina said that to see them together was like watching a movie: "But it is real life and they are not acting. They are just very much in love."

Paltrow celebrated her 24th birthday while in Argentina, and for the occasion, Pitt threw her a surprise party at a local hotel. "He blew up balloons and made a sign with sparkling letters that read, Happy Birthday, Gwyneth," recalls one hotel employee. Later, Paltrow would consider turning 24 a milestone. "I feel like that is a woman's age," she tells John Clark. "Twenty-three is still kind of on the border. To me, at 23 you can still really be a kid. I just mean in terms of a number, because obviously everybody is different. For example, if somebody said they were 24, you'd know they would have to be a woman, right?"

But as happy as Paltrow should have been at this point in her life, some cracks were already beginning to show in early 1997. Sometimes she seemed downright cranky about her profession: "The importance they place on what a movie grosses and who's hot and who's it and who's getting what out of what studio, the whole thing makes me nauseous."

Paltrow was also beginning to sound more and more miffed about the continual presence of the media in her life. "It's not that I'm defensive," she says defensively in her Mr. Showbiz interview. "Unfortunately, I'm not the one who decided to become defensive. People have become inappropriate. People have pushed too far. People have climbed one too many fences. People have scanned one too many phone calls. You know, it's very hard. I'm just tired of it. So in order to protect myself and my life and what's private and precious to me, I just talk less. I need something that is for myself. I need something that other people don't know about and shouldn't be privy to." To *US* magazine's Hochman she adds, "I can't allow the tabloids to alter any of this. I can't allow them to take the joy and freedom away. I can't let these parasites screw up my day."

But even her pique seemed to reveal not an inherent brattiness but a good upbringing. "She seems very grounded to me," says John Lyons, who produced *Hard Eight.* "Growing up in the business, she understands the vagaries of being famous." In addition, she and Pitt also seemed wise enough not to let any personal annoyance spill over into their life behind closed doors. "No, we would never let anything enter into our personal situation in any way," she tells Michael Szymanski. "I mean, I think it's flattering when someone says, 'This performance was just terrific and we're putting you on the cover of *People* magazine.' But to put someone on the cover because they're in love, or engaged — it's really trivial and it doesn't say good things about our society and what our interests are." Clearly frustrated, Paltrow adds, "There are far more interesting things to be discussing than how we got engaged or why I cut my hair. Why don't people go out if they're that bored? Go out and volunteer at a homeless shelter, you know what I mean?"

Paltrow was at the point in her life when her professional ambition was butting heads with her personal wants and desires: "At this point, everybody is expecting me to define what I am. And right now I have a lot of really wonderful options. Unfortunately, I just want to sit home and cook. That's not good for my career at all." On the same train of thought, Paltrow admits to *US*: "I'm just not that ambitious — that's what it comes down to. And I don't want to be on that manic scale. I think it's horror. I don't want to be a movie star in that sense — it's too limiting. You won't see me in *Speed III* or *Terminator IV* any time soon. I'd rather go and do some play for five weeks and learn something." Well, she had learned a lesson, of a somewhat different sort: "We'll obviously never go sunbathing again."

When they weren't working, Pitt and Paltrow tried to live their lives as normally as possible. In her mind, this was more easily achieved in Manhattan, where they would hole up in her Greenwich Village apartment, than in Los Angeles, where Pitt's house was: "We get up, walk the dog, we sit and talk a lot. We might take a bike ride. We might have brunch if it's a Sunday. We always say we're going to see a movie and never go."

And for all those who envied them as the perfect couple, think again. They did indeed have their differences. "I think we don't go out enough; he thinks we go out constantly," she once revealed. "Whenever I'm at the perfect temperature, he thinks it's too hot. When I'm too hot, he's too cold." Paltrow also admitted that he liked watching things like "ultimate fighting," which she hated, while she preferred watching the E! Channel, which *he* hated. "Other than that," she said, "we don't really fight."

Inevitably, the biggest problem in a relationship that involves two busy acting careers is the time spent apart. Early in their relationship,

Paltrow tells *US*, "The longest we've been apart was twenty-eight days, and that was hell. We make a concerted effort to be together. Not that it's torture, but if I have a day off, we're together. I've got to be with him."

Things would not change appreciably for almost two years, as both Pitt and Paltrow continued to make concerted efforts to visit each other's respective sets as much as possible. And to be sure, the work kept coming. Next up for Paltrow was an independent feature from Miramax called *Sliding Doors,* to be followed by *A Perfect Murder* and then *Duets,* a film that was doubly special because it was to be directed by her dad and would costar Pitt.

Paltrow recalls how *Sliding Doors* came about: "My agent and I are really close. He's been my agent since I was 18, and he really understands my sensibilities. It was so funny because there were about 10 movies at the same time that I was having to decide on when this was coming up. And he said, 'You know, you have to read all these movies,' and blah, blah, blah, and there were all these decisions to be made. But he said, 'The movie you're going to want to do is this movie, *Sliding Doors*, this little British movie, and I know you're going to love it, and you're going to want to do it.'" Paltrow adds, "And he was obviously right. I mean, there was just no comparison between this script and the other ones, absolutely no comparison."

Sliding Doors, which was released in 1998, took Paltrow back to England, and this time, she felt much more at home than she had during

Relaxing by the Thames while filming *Sliding Doors* in London

© METROPOLIS / GLOBE PHOTOS

the filming of *Emma*. "I was so depressed," Paltrow admits to Reggie Nadelson of *Tattler*, referring to her earlier experience. "I thought London would be a big city, like New York but with a European sensibility. It was completely different than how I expected."

Initially, Paltrow had a hard time adjusting to British society: "I thought that the British were rude and cold, but it was my fault — I didn't open myself up to the culture. I imposed feelings on it, and it was very lonely. But just under that cool layer, if you can access it, the British are very warm and very funny." Ultimately, she concludes, "I love making films in England. What happens artistically there is awesome. I love the way they do it; it's a bit clumsy, not always the well-oiled machine of Hollywood, but quirky, thoughtful. You feel it's *about* something."

Sliding Doors was not your average linear film. Written and directed by Peter Howitt, it explores two alternate realities followed by Helen (Paltrow), a publicist who is fired from her job in the opening scenes. In a rush to get home, she hurries to catch the subway. In the first reality, she just makes it past the closing subway doors. Arriving home unexpectedly early, she walks in on her boyfriend in bed with another woman. She dumps the cheat and soon finds romance with a stranger that she had met on the train that morning.

In the second reality, the subway doors slide closed just before Helen can make it on board. Because she misses the train, she ends up being mugged and never finds out about her duplicitous boyfriend's affair. What makes the movie ingenious is that the two scenarios are played out in parallel fashion until they eventually intersect at the end of the film and become a single reality.

Getting the opportunity to play not one but two versions of the same woman was exactly the kind of challenge Paltrow warmed up to. "I loved the script that Peter wrote and I obviously wanted to do everything I could to protect it and bring it to life in the best way possible," Paltrow reveals. "I fell completely in love with it, and I was just so desperate to do it." And as for Helen, Paltrow says, "The character I play is so accessible and open. That was the fun of her, just playing an Everyperson. I think half the fun of the movie is that you start to think, 'I wonder what would have happened if I hadn't turned left at that corner.'"

And the uniqueness of the project really impressed Paltrow: "It's a low-budget film and it has an independent sensibility, in that it has its own ideas, its own rhythms, its own point of view." She adds that "It has an edge. It doesn't pander to audience expectations or their intellectual shortcomings. If you trust the film, you will be rewarded. But you have

Paltrow and Brad Pitt at the premiere of *Legends of the Fall*, 1995

Paltrow appears on London TV's *Late Lunch*, 1998

Paltrow and her brother Jake at the Golden Globes, 1999

Paltrow and family at the NY premiere of *Emma*, 1996

Paltrow and Ben Affleck canoodling in Paris, 1998

On her way to a Manhattan yoga class, 1999

Celebrating her birthday while filming
The Talented Mr. Ripley, 1998

TONY ALEXANDER / GLOBE PHOTOS

TONY ALEXANDER / GLOBE PHOTOS

With Matt Damon on the set of *Ripley*
in Procida, Italy, 1998

FREDDY BAEZ / LONDON FEATURES

Paltrow and Winona Ryder partying at the Armani Rocks fashion show, 1996

GERARDO SOMOZA / OUTLINE

At the 1999 Academy Awards

At the GQ Men of the Year Awards, 1999

to keep on your toes. It's so rare when you come across a script that's that funny and that smart."

Or that complicated to act. "One of the women was more fun, the one who is in the know and in a transitional time," Paltrow admits. "There's more going on with her, but I love them both. They're the same woman at very different points. And I had to keep on top of where each one was in each story. It was like doing two movies at the same time. It was especially hard to play the one who doesn't know. I had to kind of forget what I knew to keep the behavior true to each Helen." But sometimes, it's the props that can make all the difference to an actor, such as the wig Paltrow wore as the unaware Helen: "That wig helped so much. It gave me a tangible jumping-off point from one character to the other. Those kind of things remind actors who you are and where you are."

Writer-director Howitt estimates that he spent over 10 years developing the screenplay for *Sliding Doors* and two years writing it. "I was very cautious to write stuff that was sayable, because so often you get a script as an actor, and you think, 'I can't say this,'" Howitt observes. "So I'd write something, and if I couldn't say it, I'd change it. Most scripts just say what they have to say. You have to allow characters in films and television and stories to stumble over themselves and to make mistakes happen. The premise is just like a character in the film. It's what's happening to the people in the film that's important."

What was also important to Paltrow was her perceived depth of the script and the substance of her role: "The British just sort of, I think, know how to do it for women. It's kind of exciting to be able to go back and not be scared. I'm not anxious about it; I'm not worried that they're going to, say, boot me out of the theater or run me off British soil — although maybe they will start to. I'm taking all their parts!"

She was only half joking. As had happened with *Emma,* some within the British film industry questioned the reasoning of hiring an American actress to star in a British film. "It's typical hypocrisy," accuses Howitt. "I knew I wanted her as soon as I saw *Emma.* Gwyneth simply didn't fall into any of the traps of Jane Austen — playing the costume, playing the period. A lot of British actresses are far more theatrical in that situation, but she just portrayed a young girl and the things she was going through. That's what I wanted — a completely natural Everywoman."

An Everywoman with a British accent. Unfortunately for Paltrow, she wasn't able to dredge up her *Emma* dialect for Helen. "It was a much different accent," Paltrow says. "It was hard, because I had spent so many hours with my dialect coach in *Emma,* and I had to unlearn it all completely. So while making *Sliding Doors,* any time I made a mistake, I made it as Emma, not an American. I slipped into the queen's accent."

But it wasn't her uncanny ability for accents that most enamored Paltrow to director Howitt. "She's not a trained actress and, in many ways, I think that's one of her assets," he says. "She's incredibly instinctive. There were times in the first week when I thought she couldn't care less, because she didn't seem to be doing anything. Then I looked at the rushes and thought, 'Fuck, it's brilliant. When did she do that?'"

While in London, as usual, Pitt became a familiar face on the set of Paltrow's movie and, equally as usual, the two were frequently seen out and about, including on a romantic trip to Paris. "She was incredibly close to Brad," reveals one crew member to *People*'s Tom Gliatto. "She was talking about him all the time." And when Pitt would leave to return to the United States, Paltrow's spirits would perceptively sag: "She would say, 'I need my Brad to be with me today. I am really missing him.'" Not surprisingly, then, by the time *Sliding Doors* wrapped, Paltrow was anxious to return home. "She was very, very keen to get back to Brad," the crew member adds. "She was saying that she couldn't wait."

Paltrow had said that she wanted her *Sliding Doors* character, Helen, to be an Everywoman. As it turns out, the world was about to see just how human and Everywoman Paltrow herself could be.

10

The Big Breakup

IN RETROSPECT, perhaps it was inevitable that Paltrow and Pitt's fairy-tale romance would extinguish in much the same fashion as it had ignited — unexpectedly, with heartfelt emotion and passion. And just as it was their careers that had brought them together, it was in part their work that also helped fuel the break. But in the early months of 1997, Pitt and Paltrow were still Hollywood's most romantic couple.

"My parents showed me, by example, that family is what's important in life," Paltrow said at the time. "And that's something I can share with Brad. One of the wonderful things about being with him is that, whatever I'm going through now as I become better known, he's already been through all of it. He's very grounding in that way. He is a very centered person, and he shares that."

But no matter how centered you and your mate might be, it's uncharted territory living out a relationship with the world apparently looking on — a world that never seemed to tire of whatever minutia they could glean about Pitt and Paltrow. "I don't understand what people expect," Paltrow once said in exasperation. "I'm not going to sit down with a writer and divulge intimate and private things. I'm in a very happy relationship. We're the best of friends. We go out on a date together. We go to the movies. I make dinner. We go out to dinner. We have friends over. Beyond that, I don't know what else people expect me to say."

What she would ultimately say, however, is that some of the characterizations of her that she had seen printed — basically, that she was a party-animal wild child — smacked of the green-eyed monster. "Women get crazy over Brad," she points out, as if by way of confirming her theory. "You've never seen anything like it. Women are like, 'I will marry him.' And I'm not talking about 14-year-old girls. I mean 28-year-old women. They're obsessed." But, as Paltrow notes to journalist Luaine Lee in March 1997, "There are days . . . when it seems harder because you're inundated with people doing inappropriate things. And you think, 'I really can't take this,' and [then] some days . . . you're really Zen about it. You get more and more used to it, more accustomed to the fact that it exists. You get used to it more because you're accustomed to it. But I don't think it ever gets easier."

Still, dealing with other women's inappropriate behavior wasn't as difficult as watching her intended act out erotic love scenes on camera with other female leads. "It's disgusting," Paltrow tells Lee, laughing. "It is very hard to watch. I've seen *Legends of the Fall* so many times on cable that now I'm numb to that one. And that was the hardest to get over. It's just not a comfortable thing. You're not supposed to watch that. It's a very strange thing."

It was also very strange to Paltrow the way Pitt was glamorized in the media: "I don't know who this *Brad Pitt* guy is. I know a very nice, grounded, peaceful individual. It's a very difficult position to be put in as a human being. And he handles it with such grace and such warmth." Equally strange, of course, was the surreal experience of being in the position where people think they know you simply because they know your face: "Well, they think they do, but that's kind of their prerogative. You know, I'm a public figure, and he is. There are pictures of us, and people projected all kinds of things on to us. That doesn't mean that it has any basis in reality."

On those days when Paltrow felt on the verge of simply cracking under the unrelenting pressure of it all, she would do an about-face and put things in perspective, usually by looking to her number one source of inspiration and guidance, her parents. "While I prefer not to be like my mother as an actress, I do honestly aspire to be like her in real life," Paltrow readily admits to *Cosmopolitan*'s David Ragan in May 1997. "She is absolutely unflappable, with a delightful sense of humor. The rumor once went around that I had started dating Brad only after breaking my engagement to another guy — to whom I had *never* been engaged. My mother joked, 'We were having a wedding here in the spring? I could have planted some tulips!'"

For Paltrow, the success of her and Pitt's relationship was based on their strong ties to family: "It's easier for us because we come from such good and solid families. It only helps that we're in the same business, because it gives us such a deep understanding of what the other goes through on a given day. Because there are no egos involved and it's not any of that silly Hollywood stuff — we're both not very concerned with all of that — so I think it really helps us."

The winter and spring of 1997 were, by all appearances, happy times for Paltrow, who was proudly showing off her engagement ring — an emerald-cut diamond on a silver band that Pitt had designed. In fact, Paltrow was beaming when, in January 1997, she and Pitt attended a party after the Golden Globe Awards that was being thrown by Disney. Paltrow sat talking to Madonna — one of her idols — and the conversation eventually turned to babies and motherhood. When the "Material Mom" asked Paltrow when she and Pitt were planning to have children, Paltrow told her in a year and a half. "That's our goal," she said, then joked, "We're working on it."

Pitt was equally as giddy and didn't seem to care that he spoke like a man besotted. "I knew immediately, I'll tell you that much," he tells a reporter who asks when he knew Paltrow was the one. "I got within 10 feet of her, and I got goofy. I couldn't talk. She's sunshine. She sure is. She completes my life like no other woman I've met."

As for their initial attraction to each another, although Paltrow acknowledges that it was love at second sight for her, she believes that, for Pitt, it was indeed love at first sight: "I think men know. I think when a man sees a woman across the room and says, 'That's the one!' they really know. My dad said the same thing about my mother. I know so many men who've had that experience. And we're always the ones complaining: 'I don't have a boyfriend. I want a boyfriend.' And then they go: 'You're for me!'"

So attached were Pitt and Paltrow from the very beginning that, after a month-long separation early on in their relationship, they made a pact never to go more than two weeks apart. "It's terrible being separated from each other," Brad said in May 1997. "But it makes the reunions that much sweeter."

And breakups that much more curious. On June 16, 1997, Pitt's publicist issued an official statement that surprised not only fans but many jaded industry insiders within Hollywood: Pitt and Paltrow had called off their engagement and were no longer a couple. "They have been broken up for a couple of weeks now," Cindy Guagenti said in a press statement. She also added that, "It's not because of any one specific event."

Maybe not, but it's human nature to look for reasons and, immediately, entertainment journalists set out to piece together what had led to the abrupt end of their two-and-a-half-year romance. As to be expected, Paltrow's publicist, Stephen Huvane, kept mum: "I really can't comment on what they're doing personally, because that would be infringing on their privacy."

The big breakup draws near, 1997
SONIA MOSKOWITZ / GLOBE PHOTOS

When the official representatives can't or won't answer any more questions, journalists then turn to friends and associates to fill in the blanks. While no one person ever has the full story, a lot of people often know parts of the story, and by talking to enough people, a journalist can piece together what happened. It's not too unlike a detective solving a crime. Barring a confession, they might not know exactly every detail, but they can put together enough pieces of evidence to get a conviction. In the case of legitimate journalists, if they talk to enough reliable sources, they can usually collect enough details to get a fairly trustworthy overview of what happened. Even if the celebrities involved screamingly deny it.

Consider the cases of Eddie Murphy, Robert Downey, Jr., and Ellen DeGeneres. For years, journalists had written discretely about Murphy's fascination with drag queens, Downey's drug problems, and DeGeneres's homosexual orientation. Through representatives, each of these celebrities issued strong denials, lambasting the press for making up stories — until a cop pulled Murphy over while he had a drag queen in the car, Downey was arrested and sent to jail for drug use, and DeGeneres herself came out on the cover of *Time* magazine. The point being, while entertainment journalists can and do get it wrong, they are right far more often than any celebrity would care to admit. (Whether or not journalists *should* probe into the private lives of public figures, a right legally protected under the United States Constitution, is a separate argument altogether.)

Ultimately, all a journalist needs for a major scoop are the major points of a story. What the scrutiny of Pitt and Paltrow uncovered was that, even though much had been made about their engagement and future plans, little if anything had actually been done as far as laying the groundwork for any nuptials. And then there was the incident observed in London by a celebrity photographer named Nikos just a few weeks prior to the announcement of the breakup. Nikos had seen the couple leaving a nightspot looking upset and, when they got into their limo, Paltrow was being consoled by Pitt.

In retrospect, the first concrete hint that something was amiss occurred four days prior to the official announcement of their breakup. On June 12, Pitt, who was in Manhattan filming the movie *Meet Joe Black*, was seen with a group of male friends at a party at a photographer's studio. One guest remembers that "Brad actually looked really happy, smiling and enjoying himself." The guest also recalls, "It was noticed by everyone that Gwyneth wasn't there." By contrast, even though Paltrow had accepted an invitation to attend the June 17 New York City premiere of Julia Roberts's new comedy, *My Best Friend's Wedding*, she was a no-show. A friend told a reporter that Paltrow was "stunned and devastated" by the breakup.

Not surprisingly, both Pitt and Paltrow remained mute on the subject of their now former relationship. Despite accounts to the contrary, according to Pitt's publicist, the two were still in communication with each other. "They are definitely talking," said Guagenti. "There's no animosity between them, so you never know what will happen." Guagenti also put an end to the speculation that Pitt had become involved with his latest costar from *Meet Joe Black*, British actress Claire Forlani. "There's not an iota of truth to that," she stated. "Since nobody knows the truth, everybody's making up reasons."

The accusation that Pitt had been unfaithful finally caused Paltrow to speak up. In a statement to *Newsday*, she says, "The desperation to uncover a reason why has produced information which is false, unfair, and foolish. Not only is Brad Pitt beyond reproach, but he is a man of extreme integrity and goodness." And while it was true that Pitt had earned a reputation — and rightfully so — as someone prone to fall in love with his leading ladies, others agreed with Paltrow that he had also earned the equally fair reputation as being a one-woman man. "Brad is not a womanizer," a friend of Pitt's tells Tom Gliatto of *People* magazine. "He doesn't cheat. He always has one girlfriend."

And Pitt always seems to fall hard for the woman he is with and gets caught up in the romance of it all. In late spring 1997, Pitt waxed poetic during an interview about the idea of getting married — walking down the aisle, putting the rings on, kissing the bride in front of everyone. "I can't wait, man. Oh, it's going to be great."

But the reality of marriage is something quite different. It's one thing to star in a wedding-day extravaganza, quite another to be a player in the unglamorous, day-to-day work-in-progress that being a committed partner and spouse entails. "He's commitment-shy," one of Brad's acquaintances tells Gliatto. Another friend goes into more detail: "Brad called it off. He changed his mind about a month ago. He got caught up in the frenzy of getting married, but he really didn't want to. He hasn't had a second to think about what's going on."

Complicating their personal breakup were their professional ties to one particular project. On September 15, 1997, filming was scheduled to begin on the Columbia Pictures project, *Duets* — the Bruce Paltrow film about assorted characters involved in a karaoke contest. Needless to say, when the news of the split hit the wire services, the movie's producers wanted to know whether they still had Pitt and Paltrow's commitment. And according to early reports, both were still signed on, although as one industry observer astutely commented, "I can't imagine suddenly not being engaged to someone and then going to make a movie with them."

Neither could Paltrow's dad, who was a parent first and a director second. Bruce Paltrow made the decision to recast Pitt's part and explained why, even though nobody needed him to: "Everybody loves their children. And I think that whatever each of them is going through, they need to not have this hanging over them. When we talked about doing this together, we were at a different place and a different time." Paltrow also made it clear that it was his decision to temporarily pull the plug on the movie. "Brad would never bail out on me having made a commitment," he stressed.

The Pitt-Paltrow breakup remained *the* story for most of the summer of 1997, and it didn't really lose steam until August, when magazines turned their attention to the new fall television schedule. Updates of the former couple usually found Pitt out at some function — a Malibu Beach party here, a high-profile meeting there — while Paltrow remained a shadow. "People forget that she's really young," one friend commented at the time. "The bottom line is, she's only had a few boyfriends in her lifetime."

And none had ever swept her off her feet as Pitt had done. Later, it would be revealed that after the breakup Paltrow had sought refuge with her close friend, Winona Ryder. "There are not a lot of people who can relate when you tell them that you've just broken up with your boyfriend and it's been on the cover of *People* twice," Paltrow dryly notes. Years earlier, Ryder herself had suffered through a high-profile breakup with then-fiancé Johnny Depp. "I was in pathological denial," Paltrow adds. "I've never understood or known how to handle celebrity. It looks weird to see myself on magazine covers, and I never read gossip magazines, so I was out of touch with what was being written about me."

Ironically, although the relationship was over, Pitt was still very much embroiled in his legal efforts to squelch the nude photos taken of him and Paltrow during their first romantic getaway to St. Barthelemy two years earlier — photos that were scheduled to appear in the August issue of *Playgirl* magazine. On August 7, 1997, a Los Angeles Superior Court judge decided that *Playgirl* had violated Pitt's right to privacy and ordered the magazine to recall the August issue — even though *Playgirl* representatives claimed that 300,000 issues had already been sold.

At the time, Paltrow also had some dealings with a magazine, but on a much more friendly basis. In August, Paltrow accepted an invitation to be the guest editor for the January 1998 issue of *Marie Claire*, a woman's magazine with an emphasis on style and fashion. Her duties would include choosing the cover and determining a schedule of articles. A representative for the magazine explains their reasons for wanting Paltrow: "Gwyneth embodies sophistication, beauty, intellect and also has a sense of humor." As for Paltrow, she thought it was a fun way to "be on the inside with the editors who help make the magazine happen."

From most outside appearances, the breakup between Pitt and Paltrow seemed much harder on her than on him. Later, after the initial rush of interest had died down, both would tread carefully onto the soil of their former relationship and publicly discuss, albeit in very oblique terms, what had happened. "It wasn't one thing," Pitt tells Diane Sawyer, who then asks if he still believes in happy endings. "Happy endings? No, I believe in perfect moments. And then I believe in miserable moments. And then you collect another perfect moment. But you know, listen, this is the big one. Love is a fantastic thing. It's fantastic. When you first meet and you have that first touch and there's this euphoria and it's exciting. But that's not it. I mean, that only lasts for so long. . . ."

Pitt adds that "Love is work. And so you've got to make your choice, if that's what's most important to you. What do you want? Do you want to be with someone, or do you want to play around? You make your choice. And you've got to be honest about it if you find yourself going another way, that's all. You're better off alone. Don't waste someone's time. It's very simple stuff, honesty. Yet it seems to be the toughest thing to grasp." He concludes by saying, "I have a lot of respect for love. And I think I'm speaking for the both of us here: You put yourself into a relationship and you expose yourself, and it doesn't work. Sometimes you see it's not going to be so healthy for the long run and you'd better get out. Listen, I'll go on to the next one just as open. And if it doesn't work, it doesn't work. You know, I'll keep trying."

Paltrow seemed equally as philosophical about the relationship once enough time had passed to act as an emotional buffer. "It was an insane, twisted fairy tale, a beautiful two and a half years," Paltrow says. "Just like with any wonderful relationship or romance, there's always storybook qualities to it, but then again, we're just two people. It's impossible to convey, because people don't seem to get it. But it's true, we're just two people.

"It's weird," she adds, "because people think that I had this high-profile relationship, but it wasn't high-profile. I'm talking about what was going on within the relationship. I mean, there were pictures of us all over the place, but that doesn't give anybody insight into my relationship, you know? So I feel like it was completely private, and nobody really knows anything about it. It was everybody projecting all this stuff onto the relationship. It always seemed to be in a different language from what was real between us. It was surreal more than anything else."

As for the fallout, Paltrow says, "I got some calls afterward. But I can still go out and do my own thing completely. It's great. I've kind of had a little life do-over, and it's great. At 25 years old, to understand as much as I have, I feel pretty fortunate." And as always, the protective presence of her parents was never far off: "I'm secure in who I am and what I owe to my parents. They worry sometimes that I might need to slow down, but they're incredibly proud. And the way they raised me always was with such love and support. Because of that, I don't place too much stock in Hollywood or what people think of me. It's all fleeting, and you never know when everybody is going to turn on you. But people can say whatever they want. They can't hurt me. And that's a really good thing to possess.

"If I just stay the way they raised me," Paltrow adds, "then I'll be able to sail through it without any real heartbreak." Indeed, Paltrow was about to show the world that she is a woman who was brought up with both refinement and reserve — a true, if reluctant, princess.

11

Flying Solo

FOR HER FIRST POST-PITT FILM, Paltrow left behind the world of independents and dipped her thespian toes into the murky waters of a Hollywood big-budget picture. A *Perfect Murder* was an updated remake of Alfred Hitchcock's 1954 film, *Dial M for Murder,* which starred Ray Milland as a husband who plots to have his wife (played by Grace Kelly) murdered. The remake, which was released in 1998, starred Michael Douglas, a longtime friend of Blythe Danner and Bruce Paltrow who specifically requested that Gwyneth be hired for the role of his wife — despite the 29-year age difference between them. She agreed in part because of Douglas's ties to her family and in part because, occasionally, agents like to see their clients in high-profile, commercial studio films.

At the time, Paltrow acknowledged, "It's my first big Hollywood movie. It's a smart, fun thriller, and Michael is so scary." But she also admitted, "It sounds like I'm selling out. But I'm not really. It won't be about aliens. It's not stupid, entirely." Besides, she added, "I was always a big Hitchcock fan. But to be completely honest, *Dial M for Murder* isn't my favorite of his films. I think artistically what he was trying to do was keep it a stage play — it's one of his least cinematic films. So I felt like we could really do something different."

Looked at in one way, it might be construed as curious that Michael Douglas would request the much younger daughter of two old friends to play his love interest in a movie. Some might also construe it as macho posturing of the worst kind for Douglas to have needled Bruce Paltrow about the love scenes he and Gwyneth were slated to do, with Papa Paltrow reportedly not amused by the idea. According to Gwyneth, however, "We never shot a sex scene between Michael and I, and one was never planned. That was just a joke, whereby Michael was teasing my father about the fact that he was playing my husband, and about physical contact that he had with me in the movie." She adds, "But it wasn't

Paltrow and her *Perfect Murder* costar, Michael Douglas, 1998
ALBERT FERREIRA / GLOBE PHOTOS

serious trepidation, it was just old friends ribbing each other a little bit. It was all a joke that Michael started to tease my dad with. Michael and my father have been friends all their lives."

However, to others, Douglas joked, "Gwyneth sat on my knee as a little girl. Now she's a big girl sitting on my knee." After the film wrapped, he would say, "Was it odd being romantic with someone when I'm a friend of her parents? Ha! I sort of take pride in the fact that most of the actresses I work with are pretty comfortable during the whole process, no matter what their age."

But the proliferation of young women being cast in parts that might be better suited to their more "senior" peers is a touchy subject these days among most Hollywood actresses past 30. As Meryl Streep once said at a Women in Film Crystal Awards luncheon in Los Angeles, "The lack of good female parts for elderly women like me has two good things about it; first, I get to spend a lot more time at home with my children . . . and I've forgotten what the second good thing is." Streep, then 49, expressed the hope that movies would stop depicting the "myth that it's a good fantasy for a girl to want to grow up, stop eating, and at 25 marry a 60-year-old and have a fabulous 10 years escorting him into his dotage. That's a time-honored fantasy for him. What's hers?"

However, in August 1998, producer Bonnie Bruckheimer tells *People* magazine that she doesn't necessarily blame older male actors for the increased presence of young female costars in film, claiming they are "probably not the ones saying, 'I demand that I have a 22-year-old costar!' It's suggested to them, and, sure, their egos will say, 'Um, yeah, sure, I'll take Gwyneth Paltrow!'"

Well, actually Bonnie, in the case of *A Perfect Murder*, it *was* Douglas's suggestion. Paltrow, aware of the ongoing controversy over Hollywood's tendency to cast 20-something leading ladies opposite 50- and 60-something-year-old leading men, defends the casting choices in the movie: "I think this whole Hollywood phenomenon is pretty creepy, but the age difference really works for this film. There's supposed to be an uncomfortable difference in age between our characters. In the context of the film it makes sense, and there are a lot of those situations when people marry much older. Obviously, though, if I was married to Michael Douglas in real life, that *would* be creepy."

For the record, it seems clear that Douglas doesn't share Paltrow's views: "Older men date young ladies all the time." But as Paltrow tells Hal Rubenstein of *In Style*: "Hollywood's masters-of-the-universe mentality is distasteful to me. In *Murder* there *was* something intrinsically wrong with my being with Michael that serviced the plot. But pairing Jack Nicholson with Helen Hunt? I don't want to see hot women like Susan Sarandon or Sigourney Weaver portraying grandmothers while 70-year-old guys play opposite Liv Tyler."

Despite the strangeness of the situation, Paltrow says it was comfortable working with Douglas: "The pluses were that I've known him since I was a little girl, so in that regard I think he was my champion and wanted me to succeed, and he was very supportive of me." She admits, however, "If there were any negatives, it would just be that I could never regard him as a peer. He was always very much my dad's friend. I had to resist the temptation to call him *Mr. Douglas*."

To Bruce Paltrow's relief, the movie's most erotically charged love scenes were between Gwyneth and Viggo Mortensen, who played her lover. As for the love scenes, Mortensen says, "I wanted to make sure Gwyneth was comfortable. So I sang to her in Spanish. I sang her a bunch of Argentine tango songs." But while music might soothe the savage beast, it doesn't completely make up for the fact that movie love scenes are filmed in a room full of gawking crew members. "It's always strange when you're lying in bed naked with someone you don't know well," Mortensen admits. "It's weird, but it's also sort of fun."

It can also cause speculation, and for awhile, rumors were swirling that Mortensen and Paltrow were a romantic item, which her costar flatly denies. "There is absolutely nothing to the rumors that we were a couple. I don't know where it came from," Mortensen says, pointing out, "I mean, I had a real nice sex scene with Christopher Walken in *The Prophecy*, and no one linked us together."

Directed by Andrew Davis, who had scored a huge commercial hit with *The Fugitive*, the filming of *A Perfect Murder* began October 13, 1997. (In a kind of nostalgic twist, a lot of the movie was shot on 92nd Street, the same street where Paltrow grew up.) In the updated story line, Paltrow plays Emily Bradford Taylor, the heiress trophy-wife of financially troubled industrialist Steven Taylor (Douglas), who devises a plot to have his wife murdered so that he can collect her $100 million trust fund.

From the outset, it's fairly obvious that Emily and Steven's marriage is a loveless one, more business relationship than love match. Emily, who works as a multilingual translator for the United Nations, is having a passionate affair with David (Mortensen), a struggling artist who lives and works in his Brooklyn loft and who apparently longs for him and Emily to be together on a more permanent basis. Eventually, Steven finds out about Emily and David, which sets in motion his murderous scheme — he hires David to "off" his wife. Obviously, David wasn't quite as head over heels as he appeared. As in the original, the murder attempt fails, and soon Steven is dancing as fast as he can to cover his tracks. But in this particular version of Hitchcock's thriller, Emily's husband gets his comeuppance in the end.

In addition to the surreal experience of playing the wife of her dad's best friend, Paltrow also had to adjust to making a movie where dialogue and plot seemed to be of secondary importance to the action. It was the first time she ever had to work with a stunt double: "I'd never done anything like that before, and it was a challenge. But it's hard, because when you're doing a close-up that involves so much emotion, it's a tricky thing to do: all of a sudden you're inserted in the scene for just one bit, and it's supposed to be very charged and emotional. You have to work yourself up into this frenzy." She adds, however, "Thank god for the stunt double. She did the heaviest parts. I just did the close-up stuff, 'cause I'm a big wimp."

Whether or not the film was ultimately an educational experience for Paltrow, she did learn that while making a blockbuster can be rewarding in a way, it also made her long for the smaller, more character-driven films that she preferred. "When I got the script, I thought it was really fun," Paltrow recalls. "With a movie like *A Perfect Murder*, my thinking was, this could be one of those movies you watch on Spectravision when you drive up to Santa Barbara for the weekend and get in a hotel and cuddle in bed. That sounded like fun. And it was a really good experience, but halfway through I thought, 'I've got to stick to my little movies.'"

Clearly, in taking the role, Paltrow was very influenced by the film's high-profile status. As she tells David Hochman in *Entertainment Weekly*, "Looking back, there really wasn't anything to sink my teeth into. My role wasn't particularly interesting, but I wanted to work with Michael Douglas, and I had never done a big studio movie like that. I've done lots of these little movies, and, maybe people are seeing me as too precious. I just couldn't believe they wanted me in a big movie like that." She doesn't, however, regret taking the part: "Do I point to that one and I say, 'I'm really proud of my acting in that?' No. But I don't think it discredits me. There's nothing intrinsically wrong with doing a fun, Hollywood movie. Everyone throws in their commercial movies once in a while, then you go back and do the movies that mean something to you and in which you can do different kinds of work."

If Paltrow has a professional mantra, it is to avoid the perils of "mega-movie stardom." She claims that "It ruins your life. You can't go anywhere. People get so possessive. They think they know you. They can only see you in one way. They pay you all these millions. If the movie doesn't have a huge opening weekend, it's your fault. What kind of pressure is that? Terrible. Hollywood's values are so screwed up. Entertainment is America's main export, but it's so corrupt."

One of Paltrow's biggest worries is to be typecast via the Hollywood machinery, and she cites Julia Roberts, who spoke at a industry convention that she attended, as an example. "I remember Julia Roberts getting up and talking about *My Best Friend's Wedding*," Paltrow recalls. "She's so charming. She's so accessible and funny. She was like, 'I'm funny in this movie and have my long, red, curly hair like you guys like.' Everybody laughed. But it *is* what they want. They want her as *Pretty Woman*. Everyone couldn't wait to say *Mary Reilly* was so terrible. If you had no idea who she was and you saw that movie, you'd say she's really talented. It's suffocating. I would never want that."

That said, Paltrow admits that there will no doubt be more big-budget, mainstream features in her future: "Of course I want to do some Hollywood films. I want to earn some money, after all." And, as it turns out, a fatter bank account is about all she got for *A Perfect Murder*. Tampering with a well-known film is always risky business at best, especially any movie directed by Alfred Hitchcock, one of the great stylists of all time. Even those films of his that are average fare (such as, according to film historians, *Dial M for Murder*) still exude an aura of skill and cinematic know-how that can be hard to match, particularly in this day and age of music-videoesque quick cuts and dialogue written for the attention-span impaired.

A Perfect Murder was perfectly skewered by most critics. One reviewer wrote, "Gwyneth Paltrow, an uneven but promising actress, has nothing to do in Andrew Davis's snoozy, slack thriller *A Perfect Murder* — but, oh, her clothes! Or, specifically, the way Paltrow wears them. . . ." But Paltrow was aware that her wardrobe had been chosen with great care, as well as her diamond-laden look. "I can think of worse accessories," she says, then admits, "It *was* kind of hilarious. The night that we were doing the scene at the Metropolitan Museum of Art I actually had an armed guard, because Cartier had lent us some really beautiful things. I think the necklace cost $180,000 — some ridiculous price."

But the hoards of negative reviews went well beyond ridiculing Paltrow's wardrobe. Stephanie Zacharek of *Salon* magazine stated, "*A Perfect Murder* needs Paltrow, not because her performance is so riveting — as the part is written, there's hardly anything she could have done with it — but because otherwise, Davis's picture would have no warmth, but no crisp coolness, either. Extremes in temperature are useful things in a thriller — think of the iciness of *Basic Instinct* or the sizzle of *Dressed to Kill* — but *A Perfect Murder* is more like a handful of anemic ice cubes floating in a lukewarm puddle." Similarly, Roger Ebert complained, "Director Andrew Davis (*The Fugitive*), along with novice writer Patrick Smith Kelly, doesn't deserve much sympathy for mucking with what was once a tautly tidy thriller and turning it into a humorless *Dial M for Mediocrity* — updated, of course, with cell phones."

But, as dismissed as *A Perfect Murder* was by critics, *Sliding Doors* seemed to have a never-ending life of its own. The film was a hit at Robert Redford's Sundance Film Festival and added to Paltrow's reputation as one of the independent film world's up-and-coming queens. And for Paltrow, arriving at Sundance as the star of not one but two entries — *Great Expectations* was also featured — was thrilling. "This is pretty crazy. I thought Sundance was a peaceful respite in the mountains. I'd go see my movie. I'd hang out. It didn't quite work that way," she says.

Sliding Doors' director, Peter Howitt, however, wasn't afraid to poke at the reverence often bestowed to Sundance's founder: "You come to the Sundance Film Festival's opening night just so you could meet Robert Redford, and he doesn't even bother to show up. I always thought Paul Newman was better in that movie [*Butch Cassidy and the Sundance Kid*], anyway."

At Sundance, Paltrow seemed more than just philosophical when discussing *Sliding Doors*. At times, there was a sense that she was speaking personally. "If you've ever had your heart broken, you remember and connect with these two films so palpably," she says of *Great Expectations* and *Sliding Doors*. "But out of heartbreak always comes the most interesting evolutions, the most interesting changes, when you wake up and say, 'I will never make those mistakes again. I will never make the same choices.'"

Paltrow also admits that she had been worried that attending the film festival would leave her vulnerable to a barrage of questions about her breakup with Pitt, but she was pleasantly surprised to find the press keeping a respectful emotional distance: "I really had a lot of trepidation — I thought it was going to be a bloodbath. But people only want to talk about my work and about the subject of my films, and the two are quite different. *Sliding Doors* is really a labor of love. I'm very proud of the film. I put a lot of my heart into it. I think it's really sweet, resonant, and smart. It's rare that I feel this way about a film. I learned so much."

But *Sliding Doors* wasn't only a great experience for Paltrow professionally, it was also significant for her on a personal level: "It's one of those times when there was this great opening. I started seeing things in a different way. I started understanding things I didn't understand. Suddenly, I was incredibly thirsty to figure out who I really was. I worry that the more successful I get, the less people will think of me as an actor."

Ultimately, from the film, Paltrow gained profound personal insight: "I'd spent all this time working and never taking time to understand who I am as a woman and what I really want, what kind of choices I want to make. Things started to become clear, not only in work, but in getting my priorities in order. I'm 25 years old, and I'm going to move into the second chapter of my life. What am I going to accomplish? Who am I and what am I going to do? This film resonated for me in that way because it's about choices and destiny."

Finally, Paltrow concludes, "It's so well written and funny and heartbreaking — and so good. I think the moral is that you always make the right choice. Even though it sometimes feels like, 'Wow, I've really made the wrong choice here,' there are very specific and clear reasons why you go through the things you do. Then, in the end, it's all the way it's supposed to be. We constantly second-guess the choices we make, but then it's all part of God's plan. Which I believe."

More than anything, Paltrow tells Sherryl Connelly of the *New York Daily News*, she had learned that "you can't change who you are to make someone feel better. And you have to express who you are, so there is no confusion. And that's true no matter who you're dealing with — your parents, your best friends or anybody." Upon further reflection, she adds, "It's an interesting concept, that of regret and what would I do differently given the option. But I think that regret is a total waste of time, a complete anti-lesson. So I would never regret anything, I would just try and avoid re-creating those situations."

When *Marie Claire* had recruited Paltrow to be their guest editor, they also asked her to embark on an adventure. For a planned feature that would be entitled "Castaway," Paltrow spent three days alone on a deserted Caribbean island near Belize, where she was asked to keep a journal of her experiences. And this was definitely *not* a spa outing. Among the few supplies that Paltrow took were a pound of rice, a Swiss Army knife, fishhooks, matches, and a hammock.

One of Paltrow's journal entries reveals the extent to which she completely got in touch with her emotions: "My mind takes me in a new direction every few minutes. Yesterday, after spending the day setting up and resting, swimming and snorkeling, I knelt down to light my fire and was overcome with emotion. Out of nowhere I started crying large, hot tears. Lots of things were going through my mind. Life things, love things. For a moment, sitting by my fire, I felt lonelier than I ever had in my life. It was the sharpest, most deeply resonating pang of loneliness. I just sat there crying, embracing the feeling instead of trying to talk myself out of it. I think that's something we all do and shouldn't. I think when we experience emotion we should delve into it and live through it. We are always trying to shut off pain or control our happiness. Why? To live is to feel. So I sat there and let go. And when I stopped, I felt really strong and centered and quiet. I was able to look at things with a better perspective."

Paltrow also writes that, while on the island, she often went nude during the day. "I'm positive there are no paparazzi out there," she jokes, "not that I'd put it past them." More than anything, though, the actress looked at the adventure as an exercise in survival, and she discovered "that I am stronger than I thought. I am braver than I thought." Which, Paltrow later points out, doesn't mean, "I think I can do everything and I refuse to regard myself as this very accomplished person. As soon as you're comfortable with what you can do, what you expect of yourself, then that's all you're going to give. But if you're scared or don't know what you're capable of, then you can't do anything."

What Paltrow needed to learn was how to utilize that strength to confront and resolve issues that frequently reared their heads, such as believing she had finally made a name and reputation for herself on her own merits. "It's hard when you take your work very seriously, and you want the focus to be on your work," she says. And as she told Philip Wuntch of the *Dallas Morning News*, "Because acting and producing and directing were the professions I was familiar with as a child, people think acting must come very easily to me. From a technical viewpoint, I *did* have the advantage of watching my parents rehearse and create. But acting is truly so personal. It's a strange, absolutely wonderful and quirky job. You dress up. You recite lines. And you go deep into character, without being sure what the outcome will be. Hopefully, you feel this terrific sensation when you and the character become one."

Although she had gone very far, very fast, Paltrow saw time from a different perspective. "I think it's taken me a lot longer than it would have taken anybody else to achieve respect, because first there was my mother, and people thought I was getting roles because of my parents," Paltrow says. "Then they said, 'Oh, she gets parts because of her boyfriend.' You start to think, 'Well there must be a reason this is happening this way, and I'll just ride through it, and keep doing my work.' At the end of the day, hopefully that will speak for itself."

Thanks to a little hindsight, Paltrow was able to appreciate, more than ever, her parents' lifelong concern for her. "When I was little, I'd want to audition for a commercial, and they'd say, 'Absolutely not!'" Paltrow recalls to Steve Murray of the *Atlanta Journal Constitution*. "Then, in dinner conversation with my mother, I'd say, 'I want to be an actress.' And she'd say, 'No, you want to be an anthropologist or an art historian, don't you?' And I understand why — because it's painful; there's so much rejection in this business. It's awful."

But what made up for all of its inherent awfulness, and all the doubt and second-guessing, was the sheer joy that Paltrow garnered from acting. "I love stepping into somebody else's skin and understanding their psychological makeup and the way they go about things. It's just a magical experience. It's very difficult to describe when you hit a moment and everything's just perfect and you've tapped into something," she says, then tries anyway. "It feels like flying."

And the time was about to come for Paltrow to positively soar.

12

Back in the Game

AFTER NEWS of Paltrow and Pitt's breakup went out over the wire services and into seemingly every magazine and newspaper in North America and around the world, Paltrow took refuge with her close friend Winona Ryder. She spent a lot of her time coming to terms with the unexpected turn her life's road had taken, writing her thoughts and feelings down in journals.

"I guess I still don't understand the public ramification of being one half of such a well-known couple," she said at the time. "I didn't think it affected me while we were together, and it will probably be some time before I understand the dynamics of that. Right now it's too close. Maybe when I'm 80, and I sit down to write my memoirs, I'll have a better understanding."

Like anyone adjusting to suddenly living without the daily presence of someone you thought would always be there, Paltrow's emotions seemed to fluctuate. Sometimes, she sounded almost flippant. "We were just two blond, blue-eyed people who kind of looked good together and did movies," she was once quoted as saying. "Everybody always wanted to know why we broke up. We broke up because we were just two blond actors who had gone as far as we could go. We had it, and it was finished."

Other times, however, she seemed concerned about what people might think of Pitt: "There was no cheating on any one's part in our relationship. Brad never did anything wrong. There is no sweeter, kinder, nicer man in the world. He doesn't deserve the speculation that bombarded him after our breakup." But in retrospect, Paltrow isn't sure that she should have responded to the accusations, because "responding to any of it gives import to what people have written. But I just felt it was very unfair to paint him badly, to say he was a bad guy, to say he didn't want to settle down — things that would be very hurtful to him, and things that weren't true." She sums it up to Claudia Puig by saying,

"He's a really wonderful guy, and that was a beautiful and complicated chapter of my life that's now closed."

Paltrow also had moments of pique against her media nemeses. "They literally make things up," she fumes about the tabloids. "Like, 'A pal says that Gwyneth said, I'm just not yet ready for marriage. I want to pursue my own career. Look at all the couples in young Hollywood that don't survive this madness.' Unbelievable! They just lie. 'Gwyneth says yes to marriage after saying no to three proposals.' It's just garbage."

Then, there was the thoughtful side of Paltrow: "It's been a really interesting and horrible and wonderful time. I've learned so much. Instead of questioning how did I get here, I'm asking myself, *Where do I go? What is my path?* Which is a good thing to learn when you're 25." She adds that "Before 25, it's sort of kid territory. It's like you can totally get away with kids' stuff before then, but at 25 you better get it together. It's comforting to sort of turn yourself into a kid and act like a kid and want people to treat you like a kid. You just feel all silly and comfortable. Now, at 25, it's like you've got to step up and be a grown-up."

Paltrow emerged from her summer of introspection perceptibly matured. "I think she's dealt with the breakup amazingly well," says Paltrow's best friend Mary Wigmore. "She's worked really hard to understand how to deal with it — not just the relationship, but the press. She's done a lot of work with herself." And considering the intensity of her relationship with Pitt, it wasn't surprising to hear Paltrow say, "I've never been without a boyfriend for even a month. I've always had a boyfriend, and it was always serious. I'd always go from one serious relationship to another, and I thought it was time I got to know myself. . . . I needed to spend time with myself."

What was surprising, then, was that by the end of the summer, Paltrow suddenly found herself in another high-profile relationship, this time with rising star Ben Affleck: "Yep, I'm dating again. It's great to be by yourself, but it's also great to be with someone." Affleck, along with childhood friend Matt Damon, was generating a deafening buzz for having cowritten and costarred in *Good Will Hunting*. In the movie, Damon plays the lead role of the Boston townie who happens to be a math genius, and Affleck plays his best friend who encourages him to leave town and follow his opportunities and the woman he loves.

The making of the film was the culmination of a lifelong dream that Affleck and Damon had shared since childhood. While most kids have a best friend from whom they are inseparable for a period of time, Affleck and Damon never grew apart; they simply grew closer the older they

DAVE PARKER / GLOBE PHOTOS

Paltrow and Ben Affleck spotted leaving Heathrow Airport for New York, 1998

got. Their relationship was, and still is, as close as one between two brothers, but without the familial rivalry. They were soul mates before they even knew what the term meant. And they might have never been friends if it weren't for the insistence of their mothers, who were both teachers.

Damon was ten and Affleck was eight when they were first introduced, and it wasn't exactly like at first sight. "I was pretty much forced into hanging out with Ben," Damon laughs. "I remember exactly what Ben was like as a kid: gregarious and outgoing. Except when he used to ring my bell then cower on the other side of the street because he was afraid of the little kids at the school next door to my house. But believe me, it's no surprise that he grew into the totally obnoxious guy he is now."

While working but still-struggling actors sharing a small apartment in Los Angeles, Affleck and Damon decided to write the script for *Good Will Hunting* as an acting vehicle for themselves, weary of waiting for Hollywood to make them stars. Against all probability, the gambit worked.

Much of *Good Will Hunting*, at least the periphery, is autobiographical in nature. Affleck grew up in a blue-collar neighborhood of Cambridge, Massachusetts. When he was 12, his dad, who once worked as a janitor at Harvard, moved out, leaving Affleck's mom Chris to raise him and his younger brother Casey. Affleck readily admits that he wasn't always a model child, dabbling in "underage drinking, pot smoking, and all the attendant shenanigans. I'm not a paragon of virtue."

After graduating from high school in 1990, Affleck spent a semester at the University of Vermont, then transferred to Occidental College in California, only to drop out to pursue acting full time. Like Damon, Affleck worked fairly steadily but never broke out of his crowded pack of peers, which at the time included Brendan Fraser and Chris O'Donnell. That's when the two began their unlikely venture with *Good Will Hunting*. Ironically, by the time their film began production, both Affleck and Damon had managed to break through in *Chasing Amy* and John Grisham's *The Rainmaker* respectively.

Through the summer of 1997, Affleck had been involved with his high school sweetheart, Cheyenne Rothman. But not long after her breakup with Pitt, Paltrow ran into Affleck in New York, and they began quietly dating, making Rothman Affleck's ex-girlfriend. Years later, Affleck would try to explain his breakup with Rothman: "Basically, I was in love with someone for years and years, and ultimately, I felt she just didn't love me in the same way, which was extremely painful."

Although they tried to remain inconspicuous, Paltrow and Affleck were spotted on various outings, including a dinner engagement with Paltrow's mom at Aubergine restaurant. Naturally, as rumors of their relationship became verified fact, the entertainment media was agog over the new couple, but this time, Paltrow seemed determined not to repeat her perceived mistakes of the past. "I've just been through a very public relationship, and it isn't a pleasant experience," Paltrow said with a measure of understatement. However, she allowed that Affleck was "really nice; we're very good friends."

It seemed clear that, this time, Paltrow wasn't about to allow her relationship to enter the public consciousness: "[I]f there's one thing I've learned, it's that I'm not going to talk about relationships anymore. I don't talk about my personal life. I did it in the past, because I didn't think about it. But it's just not a good idea. I think it's private. You dilute it, and you really mess with it when you start to let other people in, let alone the whole world in."

Paltrow says she has now developed "an organized philosophy" about the media. She admits that "I brought it on myself. I contributed a lot to the media attention. I used to talk about everything. I'm not guarded at all. I've had to really learn to be. I used to tell everybody everything. It didn't occur to me not to. I said things about being in a relationship that felt wrong to me even as I was saying them. It wasn't about whether I wanted to say more. I was more concerned about hurting the reporter's feelings or coming off as being overly self-protective." But, she adds, "You always learn, unless you're an idiot. You always learn from the previous experiences. I've just gotten burned far too many times, so I'm not going to talk about Ben. This one is for me."

While she might have tried to keep mum about her relationship with Affleck, she wasn't necessarily shy about showing it off in public. During the Sundance Film Festival, arriving to give an interview at the Riverhorse restaurant, Paltrow and Affleck gave the assembled journalists and patrons a bit of a show when he bent her over his arm and kissed her with dramatic flair. Then, in December 1997, Affleck and Paltrow spent a couple of weekends together enjoying Manhattan during the holidays.

In January 1998, Affleck and Damon won a Golden Globe Award for their *Good Will Hunting* screenplay, and the two immediately became strong Oscar-winning candidates, as well. Certainly, that was Paltrow's belief. "They're going to get that Oscar," she announced. "I told them they'd win the Globe, and I'm telling everyone they're getting the Oscar. They absolutely deserve it."

Paltrow and Ben Affleck enjoy a leisurely lunch
BAUER / GRIFFIN / SHOOTING STAR

Paltrow also took time to visit Affleck on the set of his big-budget Hollywood blockbuster, *Armageddon,* in which he starred opposite Bruce Willis and Liv Tyler. The production budget for *Armageddon* made *A Perfect Murder* look like a student film. "I could make a movie on what they're spending on the props for Ben's film," Paltrow marveled.

The Affleck and Damon saga took a wee twist when Paltrow took it upon herself to act as matchmaker, introducing Ben's best friend, Matt, to her best friend, Winona. Whether or not this was the impetus for Damon to break up with Minnie Driver on national television is still debated by those involved. Damon's *Good Will Hunting* costar Driver, with whom he became romantically involved, claimed she was stunned to hear him tell Oprah Winfrey that they were no longer seeing each other. According to Driver, that was news to her.

In any event, Damon and Ryder began dating, Affleck and Paltrow seemed cozier than ever, and the cuteness of it all was just too much. "It was so gay," Affleck would later tell Evgenia Peretz in *Vanity Fair,* referring to the foursome. "If I had gone by the tabloid stories of it, I would have been like, 'Look at these fucking chumps. I just want to smack these people.' And I kind of wanted to smack myself. But it was one of those things you kind of can't help. What are you going to say? 'Look, dude, don't go out with her because it'll look really weak.'"

In February 1998, Affleck and Damon were indeed nominated for a Best Original Screenplay Academy Award, and for the next month, the two basked in the thrill of being Oscar-nominated writers. But it was Damon who garnered most of the attention from the movie, mostly because he was the one who had starred as the title character, Will Hunting, while Affleck had taken the less flashy supporting best-friend role. However, within Hollywood circles, Affleck, with his movie-idol bearing and cleft-chin good looks, was considered *mucho* hot property. He was also appreciated for being fun to work with. "Big Ben is one of the funniest guys I've ever been around," says Chris Rock, who worked with Affleck in the comedy *Dogma* and who is himself no slouch in the yuks department. "He does incredible impressions. He does a mean Adam Sandler. He's really, really confident — which borders on obnoxious — but he's so funny, you don't care."

However, Affleck was also gaining an equal name for being just a straight-ahead guy — a reputation furthered by his decision to bring his mom to the Oscars as his date. In a year when Leonardo DiCaprio exhibited some puckish behavior by skipping the Oscars after not being nominated for *Titanic*, Affleck and Damon seemed like the "golden boys next door made good," and the fans showered them with cheers and applause, especially after they realized the boys were escorting their mothers.

"When Moms is asking for the ticket, you have to give it to her," Affleck joked. Showing their good natures, Paltrow and Ryder happily eschewed the award show and, instead, met up with their beaux after the ceremony was over. In so doing, they missed watching their honeys win the Oscar and give an amusing tag-team acceptance speech. Afterward, Affleck remarked, "I thought I was remarkably composed, considering I nearly wet my pants."

For as high as Affleck was on the night of the Oscars, he also experienced his share of lows. Like Paltrow, he was learning the less pleasant side of fame. "I've been tempted to slug a few photographers," he admits. "They'll say the most vulgar things. Two years ago, if somebody said to me, 'Hey, I saw your mother at the Academy Awards and she looks like a real slut' — I love my mother; she's like a saint — I'd punch them in the nose." But now, he says, "The rules have changed. It's not worth it. You're gonna get sued."

But for the most part, Affleck finds life to be pretty much the same, because, he says, his friends are still the same guys he hung out with before the million-dollar salaries started being thrown at him and because he refuses to let celebrity and fame sway him. "My ambition was never to be famous," he says in an interview with *People* magazine in July

1998. "I always thought of that as a somewhat undesirable quality." Others attest to that sentiment. "I was out with him in LA," says friend, Chris Moore, "and a waitress was going crazy on him. He handles it really well, and he tries to be polite. He still says *Thank you*."

That kind of easygoing personality, not too dissimilar to Pitt when you think about it, was a nice compliment to Paltrow's more edgy feelings about celebrity, of which she once tellingly observed was "such an empty pursuit. It's like you get famous and everyone around you starts changing just when you need them the most. You need them to react to you as *you*, the person you are, but they believe you've become someone else." At the same time, Paltrow praised her friends for continuing to accept her despite the change in her public life. Like Affleck, she maintains close contact with the people who knew her before she was Gwyneth Paltrow, movie star — the people who knew her when she was just plain Gwynny.

"It hasn't changed the way I live all that much," says Paltrow of stardom. "My best friends literally are from kindergarten, then from seventh grade when I moved to New York City. I'm friends with people that I've known my whole life, and my celebrity is not a factor in our friendship." She adds that "When it first started happening, when I first started being successful, my friends in New York would say, 'This is too weird,' and then forget about it. They think it's hilarious. They all make fun of me. They have been my friends forever. They're real with me. They're not afraid to contradict me, and that's how I want it."

That said, Paltrow sometimes worries that her success might be difficult for her best friend Mary, also an actress, with whom she lived for awhile: "She's been my best friend since kindergarten. She's auditioning now, and she's doing really well. But I think it's hard. When we're in a room together, just us or with our friends, it's just Mary and Gwynny. But when we go out somewhere, it's *Gwyneth Paltrow's* friend, and I think that's kind of unpleasant, you know what I mean?" But, Paltrow adds, "She's really open with me about it, and we talk about it. And I do what I can. She's so smart, and she's so above all of the bull. She sees right through everybody. I'm really lucky to have her."

It was also friends like Mary who occasionally had to remind Paltrow that she wasn't anonymous anymore. For instance, she remembers the time she had left to go visit Mary after she'd been "waiting for two messengers all day." Paltrow taped a note on the front door of her building, directing the messengers to drop the packages in her slot, and jotted down her apartment number. Paltrow admits, "I didn't think about it

Paltrow helps Liv Tyler and Ben Affleck celebrate the release of *Armageddon*, 1998

until Mary said, 'You're crazy, you can't do that! Anybody walking down the street could read which apartment you live in.' But I think it would be a shame if it were something that I thought about. [Celebrity]'s not going to change my behavior. I don't think I will."

It was important for Paltrow to remain a part of the nonacting world: "You know, I go to the market, I do all my own stuff. But sometimes, you're like eating, and you go, 'I wish everybody would stop staring at me. And I wish people would stop eavesdropping on my conversation.' Sometimes it gets sort of heavy. But I think the minute that you say, 'Well I'm not going to do this anymore,' well then you become a freak. Then you remove yourself from society, and you have no foundation in the normal world." She insists that "You just can't do that. I refuse to do that. I mean, I refuse to kind of say, 'Yes, I'm larger than life. You know, I'm this actress and this celebrity, and so therefore I remove myself from the world.' That's just death. I couldn't live that way."

But the upsides of celebrity show themselves in unexpected ways. "There are a lot of bad things about being famous, and amazing things, too," Paltrow muses to Merle Ginsberg in a W magazine interview. "But one of the best things is when you're in the street and you see a kid coming toward you, a girl going through her teenage angst, and she'll see you and her whole mood changes. It's a pretty amazing power — to be able to make somebody feel good. It's sweet."

For as lucky as Paltrow felt to have the friends that she did, Affleck felt just as fortunate to have her. He rhapsodizes to *USA Today* that she is "the woman that I love." However, Affleck was also content to take things slowly, noting, self-deprecatingly, that, "Almost every relationship I've ever been in has basically been a train wreck."

If anyone was making out like a bandit from the Affleck and Paltrow love match, it was jeweler Harry Winston. For Affleck's 26th birthday in August 1998, Paltrow surprised him with the $21,000 platinum wristwatch that Winston had lent him to wear to the Oscars (a purchase she made after Damon had told her how much his friend had admired the timepiece). Ironically, Paltrow had recently told a reporter that she was staving off buying herself a Cartier watch that she had wanted: "I'm spending an awful lot at the moment because I'm decorating my new apartment. That means I have to forgo something, so I guess that." Not only was she talented and brainy, but practical, too.

However, Paltrow wouldn't do without trinkets for long. A month later, for her 26th birthday, Affleck surprised her with a pair of Winston diamond stud earrings. What made the gift particularly special was that he delivered the earrings to Paltrow in person in Italy, where she was filming *The Talented Mr. Ripley* with Affleck's best bud, Damon.

As she passed another year of life, Paltrow seemed to be relaxing into the role of "actress cum celebrity" more and more, although she frequently peered into the future and wondered where it was all going to lead. But the only way to find out was to live her life and follow where the movie roles took her, such as back to London to star in a little film called *Shakespeare in Love*.

13

Shakespearean Pursuits

SHAKESPEARE IN LOVE was exactly the kind of film that Paltrow loved — a classy, well-written, modestly budgeted movie populated by characters that actors could really take a bit out of. Directed by John Madden, the script was written by the extremely literate Tom Stoppard and Marc Norman, who fashioned an ingenious screenplay.

"This is the best screenplay I've ever read. Stoppard has a kind of genius that's unparalleled," Paltrow says. "He's able to take this terrific premise and make it work in a way that's accessible. It's a great concept, but he makes it funny, sexy, and romantic. It's the kind of writing you hope every script you do will have, but that's sadly not the case." Still, Paltrow is quick to defend her previous films: "I don't think there's anything wrong with movies like *A Perfect Murder*. I love being in a hotel and watching a Hollywood thriller. But for the artist in me, Shakespeare felt like food after being starved. It had been a long time since I'd read anything that rich. I mean, it just felt like a dream come true, in terms of how rich the language was."

The movie had originally been developed for Julia Roberts and Daniel Day-Lewis to play Viola de Lesseps and William Shakespeare respectively. After they collectively dropped out, the script sat gathering dust. Then, Harvey Weinstein bought the rights specifically for Paltrow. "I don't usually get movies that Julia passes on, so this was a wonderful surprise," Paltrow admits. "I'm usually the girl studios think of when Winona Ryder or Claire Danes have turned them down. When Julia passes on a project, it goes through people like Sandra Bullock and Nicole Kidman long before someone thinks of me." Weinstein, however, saw the script as tailor-made for Miramax's unofficial queen.

Shakespeare in Love follows the travails of a struggling, still-unknown William Shakespeare, who is suffering a debilitating bout of writer's block, which is preventing him from finishing his new comedy, *Romeo and Ethel, the Pirate's Daughter*. What young Will needs is a muse.

A lot is riding on Shakespeare finishing the play. The owner of the theater, Henslowe, has given a loan shark a piece of the expected production, so if the production doesn't happen, the owner stands to lose some body parts. Furthermore, Henslowe's best performers are out on the road, making his predicament even more dire. Miraculously, however, Shakespeare gets the muse he yearned for in the person of Viola de Lesseps, a wealthy young woman whose passion is the theater.

At that time in history, 1593, women were hardly allowed to attend plays, much less appear on stage. "I can't imagine being in that situation," Paltrow admits. "That's why I admired my character so much. She went in there and did her own thing. I would not be that brave, I can tell you that. Nor am I quite as innocent as she is. She's like this open flower. She's never been hurt, so that gives you an unlimited capacity for romance."

So zealous is Viola that she disguises herself as a boy so that she can audition to participate in Shakespeare's new play before being married off to Lord Wessex, as commanded by Queen Elizabeth. After their nuptials, Wessex intends to whisk Viola off to Virginia in the wild New World. Viola's goal is simply to be cast in a small role, but instead she is chosen to play Romeo.

"Viola is probably the strongest character I've played," Paltrow reveals. "Underneath all that Elizabethan finery, she's a real pioneer woman. You can actually visualize her going to America and making a home for herself and her family in Virginia." But, she adds, "It's just rare that you come across a role like that. Viola's so strong and proactive. You know, she's really in touch with not only what she's feeling and who she is, but what she becomes and what she ends up feeling. . . . [S]he's very in touch with her growth, and I just admired her. It was really fun to play."

Even though, a few years earlier, Paltrow had been quoted as saying, "If I could live back then, with no press helicopters, without *Hard Copy*, without the *National Enquirer*, I would have been a very happy girl," she rethought that position and joked that, realistically, she couldn't see herself "in any age before there were some modern conveniences. I need plumbing."

At first, Viola is able to pull off the charade, until Will sees her at an Elizabethan dance, falls immediately in love, and, eventually, figures out that she is the "young man" cast as Romeo. Therein starts Will's great love affair, and through this passion, he shrugs off his writer's block and is inspired to create his first great play, now a love story called *Romeo and Juliet* — a testament to true love that will become a classic for the ages, even if his affair with Viola is fated to be but a magical moment in time. Interestingly, the movie is set at a time when Shakespeare is already married, but his wife and kids are back home at Stratford-upon-Avon. Without the convenience of modern transportation, there is no threat of his family popping in on him, leaving Will without much worry that his wife will find out about Viola.

Starring opposite Paltrow's Viola is Joseph Fiennes as the young Bard, and also appearing in the movie are Dame Judi Dench as Queen Elizabeth, Geoffrey Rush, Tom Wilkinson, Colin Firth, Simon Callow, Rupert Everett as Christopher Marlowe, Antony Sher, and Ben Affleck as a famous actor. "Pretty awesome," Paltrow says of the cast. But beyond the brilliant casting, what makes *Shakespeare in Love* particularly clever is that, despite its period setting and the rich, iambic pentameter-laced dialogue, the movie has a very modern feel. Specifically, it clearly satirizes Hollywood moviemaking while, at the same time, humanizing the man considered by many to be the greatest playwright the English language has ever produced.

"I mean, I think this is just a really charming way to look at him," Paltrow comments. "Whoever he was, he was just a guy, you know? Tom Stoppard's script just operates on so many levels. He's using history — what Shakespeare has written, has theoretically written and would write — and it's woven together so well. It's just infinitely playable." And, as Paltrow points out, "There's great mythology about Shakespeare, but there are few facts. He was married and had children, but we don't know much about him. From many of the myths, it seems his marriage was not an enduring success, and there have been many theories about a mystery woman in his life. From his writings, you can tell he was capable of enormous passion; he knew about the joy and pain of a deeply caring relationship."

Once again, Paltrow had been cast in a film that required a British accent and, once again, she had to forget everything she had learned about previously and start from scratch: "I have an accent coach — whom I always have, the same lady from *Sliding Doors* — who really cracks the whip, and I did a series of exercises every morning." As Paltrow recalls to the Toronto *Sun*'s Jim Slotek, "There were just tons of exercises. And this fabulous guy from the Royal Shakespeare Company helped us working on text and voice and articulation. It was beautiful 'cause I never went to drama school and I felt, 'Jesus, if I would have really gone to school, just think what I would've gotten with it.'"

Fortunately, though, Paltrow acknowledges that she was blessed "to have been born with an ear for [accents], but I mess up all the time. I'll make mistakes when I work with her, but by the time I commit to film, she's worked out the kinks. But I listen to myself and hear mistakes, so I'm sure other people can, too, but my English friends are supportive."

There were times, however, when Paltrow worried that her quest for perfection might have been a bit wearying for her costars: "There was one monologue from *Measure for Measure* that I always did the whole time. It drove everyone crazy!" But it also impressed them. "Her ability to hit the accent is extraordinary," costar Fiennes says. "I haven't done much film, so it was remarkable to watch someone just nail it, someone who understands the discipline of Shakespeare, and has the poise and brilliance to get it right, and doesn't need 15 takes."

In addition to providing her with an opportunity to flaunt her expertise with dialects, *Shakespeare in Love* offered Paltrow a new acting experience — gender reversal. "I was playing a woman who was playing a boy and who also played Juliet. It was a lot to keep straight," Paltrow understates. In an interview with Prairie Miller, she says, "It was a new experience for me. I learned how to talk lower, and how to walk. The costume department made me this heavy, triangular-shaped beanbag to place in my tights to force me to walk differently. It was great to have that weight, that shift in gravity helped a great deal."

Uppermost in Paltrow's mind was trying to be realistic enough so that her male costars would be able to suspend their disbelief: "I was really worried and preoccupied. I just thought, 'How am I going to be able to do this, and is it realistic enough so that the other guys in the theater would believe I was a boy?' The good thing is I didn't have to worry about the audience believing I'm a boy. What I had to my advantage is the fact you know that it's me. You're all complicit. So that took a lot of the pressure off."

Most fascinating to Paltrow was how differently her castmates reacted to her when she was dressed as a boy. "Cross-dressing is so much fun, but it was a strange experience when I would go to work as the boy," she says. "Suddenly, I was this boy with a mustache, and it was interesting to see the change in all the other boys on the set. I became this kind of bizarre object, and everyone was sort of staring at me. They were like, 'Oh God.' It's strangely exciting, you know? And all these British men were looking, and it was so strange. I was this new species coming toward them, then they finally got used to me and treated me as a boy, and their energy was very masculine."

Paltrow elaborates on the cross-dressing experience: "It's amazing the different energy you get from men when you're wearing facial hair, a boy's wig, and men's clothing. It didn't take long for them to forget I was a girl. The days I was in full male makeup, it was a very different energy from when I came in as this frail, pale blonde girl. The guys would end up treating me like one of the boys; I was treated more like an equal. When I was dressed as a boy, I was one of them. It's like they had forgotten I was a girl. They would knock me around and talk about girls. Then I came on for the scenes as a woman, all corseted, and they'd be like, 'Wow, oh yeah, you're a girl!'" Paltrow, however, saw herself in a somewhat different vein. "I'm not very manly, so when I cross-dressed I tended to think of myself as this gay Elizabethan guy who wanted to be an actor," she tells Louis Hobson in the Edmonton *Sun*.

But the novelty of gender-bending wore off before long, leaving Paltrow looking forward to being able to don an Elizabethan gown or two: "Period pieces are the ultimate dress-up roles. When you are wearing period costumes, you don't see yourself in the mirror." However, she admits, "The clothes were slightly uncomfortable. Physically, it was challenging, because there were so many hours getting ready, and the costumes were incredibly heavy, especially the Juliet dress I wear through the last quarter of the film. I had bruises on my shoulders from it. My back would be thrown out from that dress. I had to go to a chiropractor."

Then there were the scenes in which Paltrow didn't need to worry about any clothes at all. Literally. Unlike her experience in *Great Expectations*, where she enlisted the use of a body double, in *Shakespeare in Love*, Paltrow bared more than just her thespian soul. "The film is so beautifully romantic, I felt the nude scenes worked for the movie, so I agreed to do them," Paltrow explains. "Especially because it was film where I was playing a boy, and the contrast of that. I just felt that it was really important to the story. Some people will probably be taken off guard, but I think that's a good thing."

Besides, as Paltrow points out wryly, "You can already download pictures of me on the Internet, you know what I mean? And to start letting that kind of thing affect my artistic choices, I might as well quit. It's just totally antithetical to why I do what I do." She elaborates, "My grandpa's not going to be that psyched. But it's the way I choose to express myself. And I don't think it in any way demeans me or makes me like, 'Oh, I'm just another woman who took my shirt off.' It's not like I have a boob job and I'm doing it to titillate men. I'm doing it because I'm trying to express something and reveal something in a film, and I'm glad that I did it.

"At the center, the spine of this film, was a love relationship that was filled with unparalleled love and passion," Paltrow continues. "You have to watch it and be swept away by how much they love each other. If you didn't see these people so painfully in love with each other, then the film wouldn't work. And more importantly, the message of the film wouldn't work." She concludes that "The purpose of the story is to show that you can have passionate love, and it doesn't necessarily have to turn into the person who you spend your life with. It can be an incredible experience that propels you forward to do other things and live other lives. I felt it was important to show a good romance in all its aspects. I felt that to try and convey that and be a puritan at the same time, you know, making sure the sheets are up and that kind of thing, is stupid. So we had to do the scene like it would really happen, so the passion would seem real."

Plus, what made the experience safe, says Paltrow, were costar Fiennes and director Madden: "I was dealing with really sensitive men. Joe is very sweet and angelic and very, very shy. I was naughty. I'm naturally outgoing and loud, and I prodded him into fooling around on the set." Clearly, Paltrow is effusive when talking about Fiennes, who did an incredible job with his role as Shakespeare. "He had a tougher job than any of us," she says. "He was playing Shakespeare. That's slightly daunting. He really humanized him and made him so earthy and real."

Shakespeare in Love was Fiennes's second high-profile role in 1998. His other big part that year was in the film *Elizabeth*, in which he starred opposite Cate Blanchett in the role of the Virgin Queen's first great love, Robert Dudley, Earl of Leicester. While to most North Americans Fiennes was initially best known for being movie star Ralph's younger brother, in Britain, he had already begun establishing his own identity. After spending several relatively uneventful seasons at the Royal Shakespeare Company (RSC), he earned notice in theater performances such as Dennis Potter's *Son of Man* and Ivan Turgenev's *A Month in the Country*. His successes on stage were followed by film roles in Bernardo Bertolucci's *Stealing Beauty* and *Martha, Meet Frank, Daniel and Laurence*.

While some may have suspected that Fiennes, the youngest of six children, was simply following in his big brother's footsteps, in truth, all the Fiennes offspring were reared to be intimate with the arts. Their father, Mark, was a onetime tenant farmer turned freelance photographer, and their mother, Jini, who died in 1993 at the age of 53, was a writer and painter.

While growing up, Fiennes and his siblings led a nomadic existence, moving to and fro between London, the West Country, and Ireland. "I wish I could paint a picture for you of a kind of bohemian idyll, but it wasn't," Fiennes admits to Maggie O'Farrell of the *Independent on Sunday,* referring to his childhood. "It was a normal, messy, smelly, noisy environment; a mad, chaotic adventure. Although being one of six children meant always having enough of you to play games."

According to some of the Fiennes brood, Jini was a volatile, difficult personality, and her last novel, *Blood Ties,* is viewed by some as being a searingly bleak vision of family life. But Fiennes doesn't necessarily agree, and in any event, he adopts the philosophy that "As a kid you adapt to anything. And I see my family as close friends as much as siblings. But I was a bit of a tearaway."

Indeed, Fiennes left school when he was just 16 — ostensibly to study art — and took off for Tuscany where he helped restore a twelfth-century villa. "I was quite isolated for about six months," he says. "It was important to get away and clear my head, with my passion intact and focused. And becoming an actor was like a strange thing that happens when you're picked up by the scruff of the neck and plonked in the right place."

A year after leaving school, Fiennes moved to London and found backstage work at the National Theatre. "Working backstage as a teenager made me realize there's not much glamour in this profession — just lots of hard work," Fiennes notes. "That's a good thing to learn early on." By this time, Ralph, the eldest of the Fiennes children, was already established as one of Britain's up-and-coming young actors. Undaunted, Fiennes secured an agent and was accepted at the Guildhall School of Music and Drama before moving on to the RSC, where he discovered that being the romantic lead isn't always the best part to play.

"There are fewer facets in a romantic lead," Fiennes believes. "When I was with the RSC I did three mooning lovers on the trot, and I found I couldn't get the creative energy to leap between those extremes. Roll on the beer gut and bald head, I say. The character parts." However, with his brooding good looks, Fiennes was inevitably destined to be of heartthrob material. And just as inevitably, as his star rose, so did comparisons with his older brother. Fiennes usually took the brother-relationship questions in stride, although occasionally exasperation crept in. "That is one of the few journalistic angles which is the obvious one," he once responded, before adding resignedly, "I can't blame them. I mean, if I was a journalist, I'd do the same."

But as far as feeling as though he is in his brother's shadow, Fiennes says that's a media supposition with no basis in reality. "Not at all. Everyone follows their individual path," he says of his siblings, most of whom are involved in movies in one fashion or another. Martha is a director, Sophie is a producer and designer, and Magnus is a musician. Joseph's twin brother Jacob, however, chose to be a gamekeeper. "We don't go to each others' houses and swap notes," he insists. "Ralph and I don't sit about discussing acting, you know. And when we do, it's less talking shop and more the joy of domesticity."

Not that Fiennes is averse to talking shop when it comes to discussing his films, although he admits, "It's a bit of a shock, the amount one has to give of oneself to promote a project. I'm aware of the intrusion, and I find it overwhelming at times, I guess." But not as difficult as playing the title character in *Shakespeare in Love*. "I found the acute concentration one has to achieve over a span of 30 seconds for 15 weeks grueling. But part of Shakespeare's robust physicality was a metaphor for the mercurial brilliance of his brain," he tells *Newsday*'s Jan Stuart.

One aspect of acting that Fiennes says he enjoys most is researching his characters, especially one as historically mysterious and nationally revered as William Shakespeare. "Reading some plays was a real chance for me to catch up on the horrendous schooling I had," Fiennes admits. However, his research only goes so far, because he believes "There's a fine marriage between the information you collect and the world of the script. Often you can do too much. You have to be prepared to give yourself and your ideas up to the writer's imagination."

But what Fiennes learned about Shakespeare is that "There is next to nothing known about him. You can collect an idea, a profile of the man from his sonnets and his work, and you're astounded because his knowledge was so extensive. But then it's a can of worms because, if you look at any of his plays, you don't quite know where his bias lies: his religion — is he a Protestant or a Catholic? — his politics, his sexuality. For every fact about him there is another that contradicts it. William Shakespeare is an impossible man to nail down."

Which is exactly why Fiennes thinks academics "are infuriating." "For every expert on Shakespeare," he says, "there is another one to cancel his theory out. It drives you up the wall. I think the greatest form of finding out the truth is through fantasy. You can profile him from the sonnets and the plays, but his take on life is a mystery. From my sense, that's great. No one can say I did it wrong."

However, Fiennes acknowledges, "Shakespeare's sacred ground, isn't he, for theatergoers, academics, poets, and playwrights? Yes, there was a feeling of trepidation in taking him on, so I just learned the lines and hit the mark." And as he points out: "The script isn't an in-depth look at Shakespeare and whether he really was the genius behind the pen. It's Stoppard's play on wit, and at the end of the day, I felt it was less about him and more about the deeply unsettled and competitive world a young writer lives in. The sex appeal and mystique of the theater have always had a fascination for those outside it. And there are great parallels between Cheapside and Los Angeles. The frailties and vanities haven't changed much."

What Fiennes does believe the film accomplishes is to make Shakespeare familiar: "If you want to make idols accessible — which I think Shakespeare should be — then you have to bring a human touch, make it self-effacing and warm. And that's what Tom does. What he's saying is that 400 years ago isn't that long, and the parallels between the Elizabethan age — and its competitive nature in terms of the different theaters — is probably very similar to London or LA."

Paltrow agrees that the liberty Stoppard took in imagining what life was like for Shakespeare when he was a struggling writer gives the movie a definite sense of place. "The movie can't help but being fanciful, since we know so little about Shakespeare," she says. "But John Madden tried to make it look as realistic as possible. He and Lisa Westcott, the makeup designer, made sure that Joseph's fingers were stained with ink from writing with a feather, so he really would look like an ink-stained wretch. And none of the teeth, particularly Geoffrey Rush's, look perfect. And I had to be stuck into a corset, which really transported me into another world."

Like Paltrow, Fiennes considers lovemaking scenes in films a necessary discomfort of the job. "Give me a sword fight any day. Love scenes are never glamorous. It's so technical, and there are so many people around. If anything, they're intimidating," he says, adding that it was especially stressful working on such scenes with Paltrow, because her then-boyfriend, Affleck, had a supporting role in the film. Affleck, however, stayed away from the set on the days the scenes were shot. "You don't want to get on the wrong side of Ben. He's a really big guy,"

Onscreen lovers: Paltrow and Joseph Fiennes at the London premiere of *Shakespeare in Love*

DAVE BENETT / GLOBE PHOTOS

Fiennes says jokingly to Louis Hobson. "Fortunately Paltrow, Affleck and director Madden all have a great sense of humor. We spent most of the camera set-up time laughing and joking. I was most grateful."

In the film, Affleck appears in what is essentially a cameo, as Ned Alleyn, a successful and self-important actor. "As soon as Ben read the script, he wanted to be part of the project," Paltrow tells Hobson. "He contacted John Madden on his own, auditioned and got the role. I always love it when a movie star can lose himself completely in a role, and that's what Ben does in this movie." Big Ben aside, as for his leading lady, Fiennes says affectionately, "all the crew, myself included, managed to fall in love with her. She is genuinely stunning."

Paltrow returns the compliment, telling Robert Denerstein of the *Denver Rocky Mountain News* that Fiennes made the love scenes feel "comfortable and sweet." She adds that "It was very easy. They can be at times odd, but we were just so silly. We turn into like young children together. We'd giggle the whole time. It was not at all uncomfortable. And he's such a respectful person that he didn't make me feel strange, or anything like that. He's so kind and so sweet, and really supportive." Furthermore, Paltrow recognizes that "Everyone sees the movie and says the chemistry is incredible. I guess we just liked each other and our chemistries and our styles just meshed. It was wonderful — we became friends really quickly."

Despite the film's highly charged love scenes, director Madden muses that there's a distinct possibility that Shakespeare was gay. "Or at the very least, he was bisexual," he says, noting that "The first group of his sonnets were dedicated to a man with the initials W.H." However, he asserts, "I wouldn't make claims in any direction, except to say that Shakespeare is probably more than anything we imagine him to be. I should guess he was pansexual."

While filming *Shakespeare in Love*, Paltrow furthered her reputation as being both a consummate professional and the set cutup. "It was uncanny, really," says Madden. "The take would start, and she would transform herself into another culture and place. Then it would be over, and the first word out of her mouth would be, 'Awesome,' like the California-born girl she was."

Most surprising to Madden and others was her grasp of Shakespeare while doing the actual scenes from *Romeo and Juliet* at the film's end, as even Paltrow is the first to admit that she was Shakespeare-challenged prior to the film: "I've never been a Shakespearean actress. I mean, I had done like a lion in a high school Shakespeare play, but I don't count that. But I read everything I could before we started the movie, because I was going to England and I didn't want to really embarrass myself."

Which is not to say that she was unfamiliar with the Bard. "I grew up with my mother always doing Shakespeare, or her friends always doing Shakespeare," Paltrow says. "I saw Shakespeare in the Berkshires all the time. I mean, every summer we were in Williamstown, and every summer [Mom] did *Much Ado About Nothing* in the park with Kevin Kline when I was in high school. She dragged us to every experimental, bizarre Shakespeare production, with, you know, dance interpretations in like burned-out East Village churches. It's just something that I was always very exposed to. . . ."

Even though she may not be a classically trained Shakespearean actor, Paltrow believes you can't be "an actor and not be a fan of Shakespeare; if you value text and language, you just can't not be. I mean, I suppose you can be like Bruce Willis or something. And I don't know that he's not a fan of Shakespeare, but just in terms that you can be an action star and not necessarily be a Shakespeare fan.

"I mean, that's a very big generalization," she continues, "but I challenge someone to explain that Shakespeare's not the father of poetry and language, especially in theater. It's impossible. And the language is just unparalleled, really. There were some days when we were shooting the *Romeo and Juliet* things, and you just thought about what was happening. It was so moving and beautiful." Reflecting further, she adds, "The fact that I don't do more theater is strange, just because it's my way of doing my own thing. I really want to do it now, and [this film] illuminated that for me."

But as rewarding as Viola was to play, the role took a toll on Paltrow. "I've never worked so hard on anything in my life," she claims. "Normally, I feel I have something left of myself at home, but I was bleeding to death. I had to give everything I had intellectually, looking at the structure, doing the research. Emotionally, too, it was very demanding. Not only because I was dealing with research of the period, but also I had to keep everything straight about whether I was a boy or a girl. And to do Romeo *and* Juliet — there was a lot going on, it really kept me busy. I was using everything that I had and was so spent to the bone every day."

The thrill, however, of speaking the film's rich dialogue energized her: "It's rare to do a movie with that kind of language. There are lots of successful movies that are horribly written." And her surrounding castmates, all the way to the extras, gave her encouragement. "When they filmed the scenes from *Romeo and Juliet*, Paltrow says, "we pretty much did it straight through. The audience was filled with people who really were watching. Those extras were fantastic. They really sold the scene. They would clap when a cut was called. It was very nice."

As usual, though, Paltrow has nice things to say about everyone who worked on the film: "I mean the whole cast is just extraordinary. It's a very gifted group of people. They are people with a lot of talent and a lot of technique, and they just are extraordinary. I watch them and I wish I'd been at the RSC. But you feel really supported. It's a nice way to work." Which was one of the reasons Paltrow considered England her filmatic home away from home: "I'm really happy here, and the work is great. I'm afraid they're going to take away my work permit; they're going to be like, 'There are enough British actresses here who can do this! You're not allowed back.'"

Not bloody likely, if directors like Madden have anything to say about it. Madden says he first encountered Paltrow when he was working on a different project. "I met her for another movie about five or six years ago, and she was just a complete knockout," he says. "When this project came around, she was just the natural choice for me."

Ironically, when Paltrow first learned of the script, she initially passed on it, because she "was really burned out." But a few months later, a producer at Miramax finally convinced her to read it. "He said to me, 'You're crazy. You gotta do this,'" Paltrow recalls. "So I read it, and I thought it was incredibly well written, and I'd never read anything like it." And it would prove, ultimately, to be the film that would bring Paltrow to the cinematic masses.

14

The Talented Miss Paltrow

FOR MOST OF her career, Gwyneth has gone directly from one film to the next. And so, after completing *Shakespeare in Love*, she headed straight to Italy where she was set to costar with Matt Damon in the psychological thriller, *The Talented Mr. Ripley*. The movie, which was released in 1999, is centered around a character first created in a series of works by novelist Patricia Highsmith. In the book, Tom Ripley is sent to Italy to coax the son of a wealthy executive back home, and winds up committing murder:

> He felt alone, yet not at all lonely. It was very much like the feeling on Christmas Eve in Paris, a feeling that everyone was watching him, as if he had an audience made up of the entire world, a feeling that kept him on his mettle, because to make a mistake would be catastrophic. Yet he felt absolutely confident he would not make a mistake. It gave his existence a peculiar, delicious atmosphere of purity, like that, Tom thought, which a fine actor probably feels when he plays an important role on a stage with the conviction that the role he is playing could not be played better by anyone else. He was himself and yet not himself. He felt blameless and free, despite the fact that he consciously controlled every move he made.

The seeds of the Ripley character were first planted when Highsmith saw a man walking on a beach in Positano, Italy. "I wondered why he was there alone at 6:00 AM," she explains. "Later I thought about a man sent to Positano on a mission, and maybe he failed."

Over the course of five novels, readers watched Ripley go from a man of modest means to a prosperous gentleman who also happens to be a murderer. "I rather like criminals and find them extremely interesting," Highsmith once said. "I find the public passion for justice quite boring and artificial, for neither life nor nature cares if justice is ever done or not."

Although she chose to make Europe her home as an adult, Highsmith was born in Fort Worth, Texas, in 1921. An only child, her parents separated before she was born. Highsmith's mother later told her that, while carrying her, she'd tried to induce an abortion by drinking turpentine. Her mother eventually married artist Stanley Highsmith, and when Patricia was six, the family moved to New York City, where she was raised by her grandmother.

A seminal moment in Highsmith's childhood came when, at eight, she read *The Human Mind* by psychiatrist Karl Menninger. "It was a book of case histories — kleptomaniacs, pyromaniacs, serial murderers — practically anything that could go wrong mentally," she recalls. "The very fact that it was real made it more interesting and more important than fairy tales. I saw that the people looked outwardly normal, and I realized there could be such people around me."

Highsmith attended Barnard College in New York City. After she graduated in 1942, she worked briefly for a comic book publisher before concentrating on novels. On the recommendation of Truman Capote, Patricia attended the Yaddo writers' colony in Saratoga Springs, New York, in the summer of 1948. It was there that she completed *Strangers on a Train*, her first notable success, which was published in 1950 and which Alfred Hitchcock later made into a film. The storyline of that book is vintage Highsmith: A psychopath named Bruno meets an unhappily married man. After he murders the man's wife, Bruno demands that the stranger kill Bruno's father in return for the favor.

Highsmith, who died in 1996, spent her final years a virtual recluse, living in a small mountain village near Locarno, Switzerland, with her cats. "If I saw a kitten and a little human baby sitting on the curb starving," she says in a 1992 interview, "I would feed the kitten first."

Damon, looking to shed himself of the good guy roles he had played in *Good Will Hunting* and *Saving Private Ryan*, took on the title role of *The Talented Mr. Ripley*, which had formerly been made into the René Clément film, *Plein Soleil* (*Purple Noon*), starring Alain Delon. The director of *Ripley* was Anthony Minghella, who had enjoyed enormous success with *The English Patient*.

Originally, Minghella was not slated to direct the film; he had only been hired to write the script. But, he says, "The minute I started working on the script, I thought there was no way I wanted to give it up to someone else." So began his four-year association with Highsmith's killer.

For Minghella, adaptations offer a unique challenge. "I love literature and it is my mission to intensify my own reading experience and translate that into film," he says. "In the retelling of any story, especially between different mediums, you are bound to play around with the narrative and change certain emphases. I can understand why people feel proprietorial about their favorite books, but all I try to do is animate my own reading experience. In a way, that is what all of us do when we read a book — we create a filmstrip of the novel on our own internal screens.

"I think one of the reasons film has become such a pungent medium is because it taps into this imaginative process, it manages to bring some of those internal screens into reality. But when the movie image does not match what you *see* on your own internal screen, this is when the two worlds collide and people can feel fed up with you."

That said, Minghella believes it is creative suicide to regard adaptation as tampering with a classic. "I don't think you can be over-reverential," he asserts to the *Daily Telegraph*'s David Critten. "The novel will remain the same after I've made the film, so you don't have to genuflect. And what's an authentic adaptation of a book, anyway? A book on tape is the closest you can get to it. Other than that, you have to do something different.

"Part of adaptation is that you're trying to write your way back to the book, to those things that arrested you in the first place. You have to find your way through the thicket of writing to what's essential about the story. It's just like when you retell a joke — you emphasize those elements that move or excite or amuse you."

As for *Ripley*, Minghella later admits, "It's true that I've made a great deal of changes to the book. In fact I've made so many changes and it's so long since I've read the book that I would be hard-pressed to tell you all of them. People who love Patricia Highsmith, who want to be literal, will feel the violation of my adaptation. But I'm not going to try to apologize for that." Finally, he cautions that "people should not think they've read the novel just by seeing the film — the two works are distinct and separate. I don't want to provide a service for people who are too lazy to read novels."

The central plot of the movie is about what happens after Tom Ripley kills his friend, Dickie Greenleaf, and takes over his identity. "It's this bizarre lust triangle between me and Matt and Jude," is how Paltrow explains it. "Although Matt falls in love with Jude, no sex is involved. It's very interesting but very weird."

The movie begins with Tom Ripley playing piano at an afternoon soiree. Surrounded by social glitterati, it's easy to believe he's the Yale graduate his crested jacket suggests he is. Before leaving the party, Tom meets a man who asks him if he knew his son, Dickie Greenleaf, at college. Ripley's split-second decision to lie and say, "Of course," will forever change his life. Mr. Greenleaf then asks Tom if he would consider traveling to Italy to retrieve his wayward son, an aspiring jazz musician who has become an expatriate. The father will pay Tom's way, plus expenses. After only the briefest of hesitations, Tom says yes. It's not until Tom leaves the party and meets up with a friend that the audience realizes the Yale jacket is borrowed. Tom's only association with the university is that he worked there.

On the cruise to Europe, Ripley quickly adapts to his new surroundings and begins to imagine leaving his past self behind. He takes the first real steps toward reinventing himself while disembarking the ship. On his way to retrieve his luggage, he meets fellow American Meredith Logue, played beautifully by Cate Blanchett; Tom introduces himself as Dickie Greenleaf. Meredith, the daughter of wealthy parents, has come to Italy with her family and is obviously smitten with this handsome young man.

Tom wastes no time finding Dickie, played by a blond and golden-skinned Jude Law, whom he first sees sunbathing with his beauty-queen girlfriend, Marge Sherwood. In the book, Highsmith makes a point of noting Marge's plainness, but the casting of Paltrow obviously changes that aspect of the character dramatically. Gwyneth's Marge is beautiful but understated and initially very welcoming of Ripley, who had introduced himself to Dickie as an old college classmate. Marge invites Ripley to join them, which he readily does.

Somewhat surprisingly, yet calculatingly, Ripley ends part of his charade almost immediately, letting Dickie know that he had been sent to Italy by Dickie's anxious father. In an attempt to be accepted, Tom agrees to string the father along so he'll continue to send money, which the threesome then happily spend. Even so, it is still obvious that Tom is not really one of Dickie's group; he's just a temporary visitor — a diversion and an amusement.

This becomes painfully clear when Dickie's uncouth, blue-blood friend, Freddie Miles, shows up. Freddie, played by Philip Seymour Hoffman, instinctively senses that something's amiss with Tom and lets him know through piercing looks and pointed questions, all delivered with a patronizing smugness. But Ripley allows himself the fantasy of believing he's found a place of belonging. He and Dickie go to jazz clubs and sing together, sharing a microphone. It's obvious that Ripley's attraction to Dickie goes deeper than just a friend's. He gently tests the waters, as it were, one night when he asks Dickie if he can share a bath with him. Dickie makes it clear he's not interested.

Soon enough, Dickie begins to tire of Ripley, and when the father cuts off the cash flow, Dickie tells Tom it's time for him to go. They agree to go on one last excursion. While out in a boat, Dickie turns on Ripley, cruelly calling him a leach and spurning Tom's affections. In a moment of blind, passion-fueled fury, Tom kills Dickie, pulverizing his head with an oar. He gets rid of the body and then swims to shore.

From this point on, the movie becomes a game of cat and mouse, with Ripley gradually taking over Dickie's life. With his gift of mimicking voices and his talent for forgery, Ripley is able to create the impression that Dickie is still very much alive. He sends Marge a break-up letter and writes his trust for more money. He moves into a Rome apartment and seems fairly secure until Freddie Miles turns up and finds out from the landlady that Tom is calling himself Dickie. When Freddie confronts Tom, Ripley bashes in *his* skull. He then goes to great pains to leave a trail of eyewitnesses who will later testify that they saw Dickie Greenleaf putting Freddie Miles into his sports car. Dickie now goes from simply being missing to being a missing murder suspect.

Dickie's father comes to Italy with a private investigator, hoping to discover his son's whereabouts. Marge, who by this point is coming unglued, comes to Rome accompanied by her friend Peter, with the hope of talking to Dickie. She is the one person who sees through Tom and refuses to believe Dickie would either leave her or kill Freddie.

Dickie's troubled past, however, seems to corroborate Ripley's account; because Dickie has a history of violent attacks against people, his father and the private investigator believe that Dickie snapped, killed Freddie, and then ended his own life. When Marge physically goes after Ripley, she is dismissed as being upset and hysterical. To make matters worse, her friend Peter has become infatuated with Tom.

Before heading home to America, Dickie's father shows his appreciation by transferring Dickie's trust over to Ripley. Tom has become the person he always dreamed of being. He now has money, a sensitive, caring lover in Peter, and the respect of those deferential to his new-found wealth.

But Tom's cushy new situation is suddenly jeopardized. While en route to Greece with Peter, Ripley runs into Meredith, who only knows him as Dickie Greenleaf. Realizing that his machinations will be revealed when Meredith meets Peter, Tom can see only one way out. In their cabin, Ripley tells a bemused Peter that he'd rather be "a fake somebody than a real nobody." While sobbing, he strangles Peter and then throws his body overboard. The film ends with Tom huddled on his cabin floor, grappling with the realization that in killing the one he loved, he had murdered something in himself as well.

"I was trying to honor the book, which is about a man who commits murder and isn't caught," Minghella told *Time*'s Richard Corliss. "But I also wanted to investigate what that actually means. At the end of the film, Ripley is imprisoned by the consequences of his own action. There's a difference between public accountability and private justice. He appears to have gotten away; he seems to get away with everything. In a way he's sentenced to freedom. It's painful to have this talent for escape, for being able to improvise one's way out of any situation. To Ripley, it's a curse."

For Minghella, Ripley is a perfectly fascinating character. "Probably like most of us," he says, "I could identify with his sense of self-loathing, his low self-esteem, combined with his rather superior attitude and his fine aesthetic judgments. Growing up as part of an Italian working-class family on the Isle of Wight, I always felt that I never quite belonged anywhere. Yet at the same time I had this high appreciation for culture and the arts. It's an anomaly which I think I share with Ripley." Finally, Minghella says, "The crux of the story is Ripley's obsession with Dickie and so, just as Dickie has his Marge, played by Gwyneth Paltrow, Ripley feels he has to find himself someone similar."

The biggest difference between Highsmith's vision of Ripley and Minghella's is that the director has inserted a strain of conscience into the character. "This is where, I suppose, there is a collision between Highsmith's view of the character and my own," Minghella admits. "I'm not saying mine is right — Ripley is, after all, her creation — but I feel for a film version to make sense to me, there has to be a kind of moral framework. So in the film, Ripley's punishment comes about as a result of trying to take on the identity of Dickie Greenleaf. In doing so, he has annihilated the possibility of being himself."

For however weird the content of the movie was, filming in Italy was as enjoyable as one would expect. As Paltrow muses, "We shot it in Rome, which was incredible to walk around in. You walk by buildings 2,000 years old and realize you're looking at the birth of civilization. You feel very small."

Ironically, Gwyneth says that she and Matt were cast in the film prior to really knowing each other. "At the time, I knew who Matt and Ben were from *Good Will Hunting*, which was one of my favorite films, but I didn't know either of them personally."

The "double couple" took advantage of the Italian locations, after both Affleck and Winona Ryder flew over to join Paltrow and Damon. When they weren't a foursome, Paltrow and Ryder would go off on shopping outings while Affleck and Damon stayed behind to hash out some ideas for a new screenplay to follow up their Oscar-winning effort.

But even tucked away in Italy, Damon still managed to become the focus of global media attention when the Italian press reported the rumor that he was anorexic. Paltrow explains how the story started. "The plot calls for Matt to look as close as possible to Jude Law who plays my boyfriend," she says. "Jude is really slight so Matt had to lose all this weight. He did it properly with a dietitian. Matt wanted to look particularly slim for a beach shot so he fasted for four days before the day we filmed and that day they added all this gray makeup to make him look thinner still." She admits that "It was scary. He looked emaciated. He had to wear this little Speedo suit and the Italian paparazzi got shots of him." As she adds wryly, "So much for Matt's hunk image."

But Damon has never seemed particularly concerned with image. For him it's all about the work, and taking on the character of Ripley offered challenges that would make many other actors shy away. While in the book, Ripley's sexual preference is more suggested than detailed, in the movie, it is the force that eventually spurs the climactic moment in the film. It says a lot about contemporary American society that the two studios marketing the film were more concerned with the fact that Thomas Ripley is gay, than with the fact he is a serial killer.

Costar Hoffman says he remembers thinking when reading the novel, "Wow, she says so much through the back door. But Anthony, because of the time we live in, can say things in a more overt way. And it's really not anything Matt can worry about. He's an actor and he's playing a character. And if he's going to do that, he's got to do it fully. And if he does it fully, then hopefully he'll convince people. And if he convinces people, then that's just good work."

Cate Blanchett, who plays the Ripley-enamored Meredith, adds, "Whenever you make a film it's a risk, but I think Ripley's a part to swing a cat in, there are so many hidden pockets in the character. If I were Matt I would have relished it."

But actors don't control the bankbook, and it was widely reported during production that Paramount wanted Minghella to downplay the script's homoeroticism. The director admits to David Critten of the

Daily Telegraph that the reports were not inaccurate. "Maybe the stories you heard had some accuracy," he says discretely, "But no one tried to invade the process. I had the final cut and there's not a frame of the film that isn't as I wanted it to be.

"It's not surprising the studio would be nervous," Minghella explains. "It was a lot of money for them to lose. And I'm astonished by what's happened to this film."

To Damon, Ripley's sexuality wasn't his primary motivating factor. Rather, he saw Ripley as someone who had spent his entire life on the outside looking in, someone who was so unhappy in his own skin and so desperate to be loved and included that he falls prey to his dark side. That said, he knew that a certain segment of the movie-going population would focus only on Ripley's homosexual tendencies.

"From the moment the decision was made to make this movie we knew this was going to come," he tells Chris Nashawaty of *Entertainment Weekly*. "If it's phrased in a really reductive way, *a fag serial killer*, then Ripley can't be the audience." But the truth, says Damon, is that Ripley *is* one of them: "Everyone's felt like an outsider before. I have hundreds of episodes from high school I'd love to replay, but a lot cooler. I was short until my junior year, so my sophomore year was terrifying."

In a *Time* magazine interview with Belinda Luscombe, Damon says, "I really relate to Ripley. I always did. I think most people will."

Damon also admits to Luscombe that working with Paltrow was an acting exercise in itself. "Gwyneth can walk into a scene and be talking about something else, and they say 'Action!' and she turns into the person she's playing," Matt says of his costar. "My life would be a lot easier if I could do that."

As in any film, a movie's success or failure in large part rests on whether or not the audience accepts a particular actor in a particular role. In Paltrow's case, the role of Marge seemed well suited to her, although interestingly, Gwyneth needed a little convincing. "In the original draft of the screenplay, I think Gwyneth felt maybe the part wasn't as big for her and as substantial as it could be," Harvey Weinstein says, whose Miramax studio coproduced the film with Paramount. "But Anthony so wanted to work with her, he addressed some of those issues and enlarged her part."

As Dickie, Jude Law was all bronzed skin and affluent ennui; he embodied Dickie so fully that his portrayal would later earn him an Oscar nomination for Best Supporting Actor. The recognition vindicated Minghella, who had to vigorously campaign with Paramount to cast Law in the first place.

"It may be easier for British actors to essay issues of class," Minghella says tactfully. "But I also wanted something specific. Jude has such effervescence. I feel he lives life with the volume controls turned up. I wanted someone who could be a satyr, the absolute opposite to the tonalities Matt would bring. Jude was in a category of one. And when I get obsessed with actors, I don't surrender them easily."

While American audiences may think of Law as a newcomer, he's considered one of the most dashing of Britain's new generation of actors, which includes his close friend, Ewan McGregor, better known as Obi-Wan in the latest *Star Wars* installment, *The Phantom Menace*.

Law and McGregor met at an audition over a decade ago when they were both still teenagers. "We were in our late teens and both auditioned for this cheeky little movie about a 1960s rock band," Jude tells the Calgary *Sun*'s Louis Hobson. "The director chose Ewan and I to be partners and sent us away with $50 to spend the afternoon creating an improv scene. We went to the nearest pub and got drunk. We didn't get cast, but we've been the best of mates ever since."

Although that pub excursion may not reflect it, Law says he has enjoyed a lifelong love affair with acting. "Acting was all I wanted, and I never saw any reason why I wouldn't be on stage, or in a film, or on TV," says Jude, who joined the National Youth Music Theatre company when still just a child. "I went to school as sort of a part-time job, and the theater company was what was going to happen."

Law, who was named after the title character of Thomas Hardy's *Jude the Obscure*, left school for good when he was sixteen so he could appear on the British soap opera, *Families*. After a year, he left and returned to the theater. His work eventually led to Britain's National Theatre and the Royal Shakespeare Company, where he earned an Olivier Award in 1994 for his performance in Cocteau's *Les Parents Terribles*. That same year he married actress Sadie Frost, who costarred with him as car thieves in the critically panned British film, *Shopping*.

Flush from its success in London's West End, *Les Parents Terribles* was renamed *Indiscretions* and went on to Broadway where Law reprised his role as Michael. Again, the critics swooned; Jude was nominated for a Tony and won a Theater World Award. Although his acting charmed critics, it was his nude scene in the play that many audience members will recall.

In fact, Law has appeared nude so often on stage and in film, including numerous times in *The Talented Mr. Ripley*, that he likes to joke about it, saying he and buddy McGregor "are starkers in most of our movies."

On a more serious note, Law says, "I don't have any problems with nudity if it is essential to the plot of a film. I feel that nudity can add dramatic tension to a scene. The thing is, once you've done a nude scene, directors and producers are all over you to do one for their film."

After the sting of the drubbing he took from critics of *Shopping*, his stage success gave Law the courage to try more film work. His first American movie was the futuristic, sci-fi *Gattaca*, which envisions a world in which genetic engineering is the norm and old-time procreation is considered subhuman.

His next role was in the critically acclaimed film, *Wilde*. Law played Oscar Wilde's lover, Lord Alfred "Bosie" Douglas, opposite Stephen Fry as Wilde. Because of Bosie, Wilde would ultimately be convicted of *gross indecency* — in other words, of homosexual conduct — and sent to jail. Unlike so many American actors who shy away from homosexual roles, the biggest problem for Law was that, historically, Bosie was almost universally loathed.

"I couldn't find a single nice thing about Bosie anywhere," Law tells Juan Morales in *Details*. "But I refused to play him as a villain, because he's not. There's a lovely element in the film, which is that Oscar wrote that he despised conformity, and hated pomposity, and yet he constantly wanted to avoid Bosie's father, and never really wanted anything to come out, but Bosie's attitude was, 'Look we're in love, who cares? Let's tell the world.' He was very out for a gay man at that time."

More than anything, his choices of roles reflect Law's philosophy about acting. "I just like characters that have fullness," he tells Anna Murphy of the *Sunday Telegraph*. "Like with Bosie, here was someone who everybody said was a complete shit. But I thought, 'He was the apple of Oscar's eye, there must have been *something* about him.'

"I think sometimes you have to work hard to find the nice things in people . . . sometimes you have to work hard to find the darker things. It's the same in life. Often that is the process of a relationship with someone."

Because of his need to find depth in his characters, Law wasn't particularly enthused by the role of Dickie Greenleaf, and, in fact, was ready to turn it down. "I couldn't see beyond this rich, charismatic dude," he explains to Murphy. "I didn't want to short-shrift myself with a role that didn't leave me anywhere to go."

But he changed his mind after meeting with director Minghella. "I hadn't seen all the colors that Dickie had to resonate through the film, that I had to make people like him. That was the real challenge, because if you show a British audience a person who has everything, they are immediately going to dislike him."

Also pivotal was the part of Freddie Miles, Ripley's nemesis, one of three high-profile roles for Philip Seymour Hoffman in 1999. Hoffman plays a nurse in *Magnolia* and a drag queen in *Flawless*, opposite Robert De Niro. Says *Flawless* director Joel Schumacher, "[Hoffman's] just one of these great born character actors."

"I've tried to do roles of all stripes that keep the work coming and me interested," shrugs the actor.

But working on *Ripley* was a particular test of endurance because he was simultaneously shooting *Flawless*, about a drag queen who gives speech lessons to a homophobic stroke victim, played by De Niro. However, Hoffman learned to use the Italian location as a kind of vacation, particularly since his shooting schedule was so light. "Matt, Jude, and Gwyneth did all the work," Hoffman tells Daniel Fierman of *Entertainment Weekly*. "Cate and I only worked like once a week. So we just tooled around and ate at a different restaurant every night. The other guys wanted to kill us."

For Gwyneth, the fairy-tale location wasn't as much of a romp as she had thought it would be. Back home, both her beloved grandfather and father were sick, and the separation wore on Paltrow. "I was having a very difficult time," Paltrow admits to Tamara Conniff of *Newsday*. "It was actually among the saddest I've ever been in my life. It was sort of this cruel irony that I was in the most beautiful country with all this incredible food and great friends, and I just felt that I was in the wrong place. I wanted to be with the people who I felt needed me."

Coincidentally, her character goes through her own inner turmoil. "Gwyneth goes somewhere in this film she's never been before," Minghella says. "There are very few actors that can make sense of that journey with the skill that she did." Paltrow is self-effacing when speaking about her acting ability. She would much rather talk about practicing yoga or her new apartment in Manhattan.

Of Marge, Paltrow told *Newsday*'s Conniff, "I approached her like two different people — the person she is in the beginning and the person she is in the end."

For Minghella, working with his youthful cast was a departure. "It's the first time I've worked with actors who aren't my peer group," Minghella says. "I was dad. When I cast them, they were all promising.

Gwyneth was just about to do *Shakespeare in Love*, Matt hadn't opened in *Good Will Hunting*, Cate hadn't quite finished *Elizabeth*.

"The shadow of their celebrity started to cross the film before it even started, and the expectation level for the film grew. But all of them are actors before they are movie stars."

For all the apprehension about the subject matter of *The Talented Mr. Ripley*, the homosexual elements failed to raise any significant protests or attention. Although over two hours long and definitely not holiday-season light, the film opened in December 1999 to generally good reviews. *Salon*'s Charles Taylor's unimpressed snipe was the exception:

> *The Talented Mr. Ripley* is, in a way, a predictable failure. Having earned the kind of praise he did with *The English Patient*, Minghella isn't going back to the modest style and the organic emotion of *Truly, Madly, Deeply*, his first and still his best film. It's even more depressing to see these glamorous young stars sealed up in the kind of glossy prestige picture whose boring refinement works against the very idea of star power. In a weird way, Minghella has remained true to Tom Ripley's fantasies: He's made a movie that is killingly tasteful. . . .

Most praised Minghella's efforts to bring a difficult novel to life on screen. *Time* movie critic Richard Corliss writes:

> Set mostly in southern Italy, Minghella's tantalizing movie captures the pulse, temperature and texture of the idle rich at play and the yearning of Ripley, who wants that good life so much he'd kill for it. Inhabiting this very dolce vita is a quintet of smart-looking young performers — Jude Law, Gwyneth Paltrow, Cate Blanchett, Philip Seymour Hoffman and Jack Davenport — giving vigorous life and fine shading to roles of wealth or breeding. They parade their star quality (or supporting-actor quality) not by screaming and cussing Method style but by radiating an unforced glamour that recalls Hollywood in its Golden Age.

Philip Wuntch from the *Dallas Morning News* adds:

> *The Talented Mr. Ripley* seduces but never abandons its audience. Based on Patricia Highsmith's classic tale of seduction, deception and murder, the luxurious film arrives with great expectations, courtesy of its Oscar-decorated cast and director. Virtually all those expectations are met, and some are even surpassed. Just don't expect

> a fun-in-the-sun romance; *The Talented Mr. Ripley* is dark, insinuating and compelling.

Filmed for a modest 40 million dollars, the film had passed the $80 million mark for domestic release, ensuring financial success for Miramax and Paramount. Also, the movie won Anthony Minghella and Philip Seymour Hoffman awards from the National Board of Review for their work. Additionally, Minghella was nominated for an Oscar for his adapted screenplay. All in all, a successful outcome for a project many had believed would never make it to the screen.

Although Highsmith left behind more books featuring Thomas Ripley, Anthony Minghella won't be making a movie out of any of them. "It's just a cruel story to live with for such a long time," he says. "I don't think I want to go back there anytime too soon."

15

Accolades and Awards

NOT LONG AFTER *Ripley* wrapped and Paltrow came back to America, she hit the promotion trail. When magazines and newspapers began previewing the movies not to miss in 1999, leading the pack were two highly anticipated World War II epics: Steven Spielberg's *Saving Private Ryan* and Terrence Malick's *The Thin Red Line*. Nowhere on the radar was *Shakespeare in Love*, despite it's A-list pedigree. Even after audiences discovered *Shakespeare*, it was still considered to be a dark horse as the award season approached. But that's when the Miramax publicity machine cranked into high gear, and suddenly, it seemed as if Paltrow was everywhere promoting the film.

Although she faced the same questions over and over, she made an effort to give thoughtful answers, instead of just spewing out mentally prerecorded responses. And when she talked about *Shakespeare in Love*, her professed affection for the movie rang genuine: "I think Shakespeare would have loved this, because he was a master of that kind of chaotic comedy with lots of things going on." Indeed, the film did have "lots of things going on," including a heroine that the Bard, possibly the original feminist, would have appreciated.

"She wasn't the traditional objectified muse," Paltrow says of Viola. "She brought out the best in him, and was his partner. Who she was and what she represented to him brought out a whole creativity." She adds that "It was a really interesting character for me because she was so strong, and so proactive in dressing as a boy to audition, and all of that. Even though the story is about him, she's an important element in the story. It's not your basic love-interest part." Well, no, considering her cross-dressing tendencies: "It's funny because in England, they are very into that kind of thing."

The more Paltrow discussed *Shakespeare in Love*, the more she seemed to appreciate that the experience had caused her to raise her own personal

Paltrow with Hillary Clinton at the New York premiere of *Shakespeare in Love*, 1998

bar. "Every film doesn't have to be as brilliant as this," she tells Robert Denerstein. "But I want to be careful about what I do. I want the work to feed me." And as with most actors, for Paltrow, the word is the thing: "If it's not a brilliant script, and the whole project isn't just wonderful, then I wouldn't do a leading part 'cause it's too much in your life and a lot of pressure, and all of a sudden you're carrying this thing. If its going to work it should work 'cause the piece should work, not just because you're bringing something more to it."

And a brilliant script and compelling role is exactly what she saw in *Shakespeare in Love*: "It's like anyone could do this part, it's such a great, well written and the script is so good, I felt really, really comfortable doing it. It's also really fun to do smaller roles where you get the kind of play things that you wouldn't ordinarily get to play, and do whatever you want."

Paltrow acknowledges that she had been extremely fortunate up to this point in her career, because, "The films I've been able to do are kind of smart and interesting with nothing exploding or sinking or whatever. . . . The kind of film that I like to perform in has its own kind of audiences. They're not for everybody."

She also recognizes the kind of movie that she doesn't want to do anymore. "Doing a movie like *A Perfect Murder* was strange because it's not really the kind of movie I do, but I wanted to experience the slick, big-budget Hollywood machine kind of movie," Paltrow admits. "It's fun, but it's not difficult, and it's not really engaging work. But when you do a movie like *Shakespeare in Love*, you feel like an artist. It doesn't go as smoothly, it's all quirky and backwards, but it's artful. You feel like you're learning and discovering things, and you feel like you know why you do this job."

When asked by a teasing journalist, "How about *Scream 3*?" Paltrow answers dryly, "How about not?" Nor should anyone expect to see Paltrow being the scenery in any *Rambo* or *Die Hard* film any time soon. "I know, never say never, but honestly, that doesn't appeal to me. I would never say I'd never do an action movie, but I can't see myself packing a weapon right now. My idea of selling out was *A Perfect Murder*, but I enjoyed it and it was entertaining." According to Paltrow, "Movies are so arduous you have to love what you're doing. As long as there's an audience, I'll seek out another *Sliding Doors*." And yet, she allows, "Maybe it would be interesting to play a cartoony thing. I'd like to do a Cat Woman kind of role. That would be fun."

Most rewarding for Paltrow is that she has yet to be typecast, although she *has* been sent an awful lot of period film scripts: "It's nice that I've been offered different kinds of roles a lot of times. People recognize that I can do character parts. I just hope that people don't get possessive of me that way. Like how they get over the sweetheart type of girl. It's hard when you see an actor or actress you respect, like Julia Roberts, continuously being asked to play the same role because that's what the American people demand. Anytime anyone gets too comfortable with the way they perceive me, what I should do, or how I should behave in a movie, then it's time for me to reverse it in some way."

Paltrow is also partial to working with less-established directors. "To me, it's just so much more exhilarating to work with somebody who's fresh out of the gate. There's this great enthusiasm when you work with first-time directors that you just get when you work with more seasoned, older guys." To back up her point, she says, "I was in Douglas McGrath's first movie, Peter Howitt's first movie, and I was in Paul Thomas Anderson's first movie. I think I've made good choices. These are smart guys. These are guys who are going to go on and do great things. They've written it, so they have a very clear perspective. They have a real vision about the material because it's been born out of them."

Her preferences, in large part, are directly related to her desire to be an actress, not a movie star — the latter phenomenon being "uncharted territory." Later in 1998, she admits, "It's just a different step and not necessarily one that I encourage or want to have arrived at, but there's really nothing I can do. I don't know how to handle it. I feel sort of like an impostor. I just hope that people aren't mad at me if I don't deliver. I hope they don't come to resent me. I can just be me, and if I fulfill something for you, that's great. And if I don't, don't think that I was supposed to and then hate me for it."

But Paltrow had to admit that, up to this point, she had been relatively untouched by negative reactions of any kind. "I've been lucky," she says. "No matter what they've said about my family, my boyfriend, I've always been fortunate in that people who criticize movies, well, I've always come out pretty well." And, as she tells Prairie Miller, one of the greatest misconceptions she thinks people have about her is that, because of her appearance, "they think I'm this very cool, stuck-up blond; that I'm either classy or bitchy. In this culture, if you're smart and blond, you're a bitch and you're cold and you're stuck-up. But I am so goofy, and I am so not what they think."

Paltrow's point was exemplified by *Movieline* magazine, which deemed her Most Stuck-Up, a designation that only amuses her: "I heard all about it. But it is so wrong, so untrue. I've never been stuck-up about things that some people are snobbish about. I just know that I like some people instantly, and there are others I don't like. But I don't care about anyone's social standing or bank account. But I am articulate, and sometimes it's easy to pin that label on a woman who's tall, blond and articulate." Upon reflection, she adds, "Actually, though, the more I thought about being named Most Stuck-Up, the more I kind of got to like it. Because I know it's not an accurate label, it proves that I'm kind of unknowable. And I like that. I like the fact that people perceive me differently, because I can keep the best parts of myself private for my friends and my family. I want to keep it like that."

Who Paltrow is can be gleaned indirectly, like when she reveals, "I read things that make my mind feel clearer, that make me feel less complicated, that get the junk out of my mind so I can really see where I am." She admits that "For a long time I didn't know who I was. I didn't know what was important to me." So Paltrow started reading poetry, and she developed an affinity for Walt Whitman, whom she believes "understands what it is to be tiny and unimportant." She also started taking yoga classes with Madonna's instructor.

Paltrow also admits to being bothered by the breadth and scope of suffering in the world: "I get so insane when I watch the news and read the paper, and I get so upset about things in the world, especially children who do not have enough money to eat and don't have homes. I really have to stop watching the news because I just can't stand it anymore." And as she asserts in her 1997 Mr. Showbiz interview, "Even when you watch TV now, it's all about sensationalizing violence or hunger or awful things. I've just been reading a lot now and I'm trying to tune out the world a little bit."

But it's hard to be a hermit while promoting a movie. Especially when that movie is a Miramax film and you are suddenly the subject of an ever-deafening Hollywood buzz. John Madden, for one, thought it was about time for that buzz. "She deserves it. I don't think anybody has begun to see her range yet. And I believe that certain roles belong to certain actors. That one absolutely belongs to her," Madden says of Viola. "And it explodes her talent and her abilities."

As critics published their picks for the leading contenders to snag acting awards, Paltrow's name was on every list that mattered. The first major Hollywood award recognition Paltrow received was a Golden Globe nomination for Best Actress for her performance in *Shakespeare in Love*. For years, the Golden Globes, put on by the Hollywood Foreign

Looking like a winner at the 1999 Golden Globe Awards

Press Association (HFPA), have tried to present themselves as *the* precursor to the Academy Awards (even though within the Hollywood community there are decidedly mixed feelings about the organization behind them).

For years, the HFPA was considered a bit of a joke, and most of the Hollywood film community either ignored the Golden Globes or attended the ceremony mostly to drink and party. The attitude, in large part, stemmed from the Globes' reputation of being "buyable." Those filmmakers and actors who spent the most money taking the fewer than 100 members of the Foreign Press out to lunches and dinners, or sent out the coolest *chatchkas*, seemed to have the best shot at winning. The most notorious example was when Pia Zadora, then married to multi-millionaire T.K. Riklis, won the Golden Globe for Best Newcomer for her performance in the critically panned film *Butterfly*.

But what gave the Golden Globes their current high-profile clout was the HFPA network's decision to go into partnership, as it were, with network television, which turned the Golden Globes into "must-see" award TV. Despite the apparent increase in its respectability quotient, however, the HFPA can still be the target of scathing criticism. "We are not talking about respected critics here, or even the carefully selected representatives of major newspapers and media organizations from around the world," offers one editorial. "No, the HFPA is little more than a pampered clique, an 82-member body largely made up of freelancers and part-timers which jealously guards its privileges and makes it supremely difficult for outsiders — even bona fide reporters from major publications such as *Le Monde* — to penetrate its world of special advance screenings, celebrity lunches and all-expenses-paid trips to film festivals."

Nevertheless, because many see the Golden Globes as a kind of predictor of the Oscars, and because the telecast garners huge ratings, most of the Hollywood community turns a blind eye to the disproportionate power of the 80-odd members of the HFPA and shows up at the ceremonies in all their glittery finest.

Each year the Golden Globes are held at the end of January, shortly before the Oscar nominations are announced. In 1999, in the Best Actress categories, British actress Cate Blanchett won for her dramatic work in *Elizabeth*, and to nobody's surprise, Paltrow was honored as Best Actress in a comedy. As she stood in front of her peers, Paltrow emotionally singled out "my Grandpa Buster who's had an even tougher year. Hang in there, Grandpa. Thank you so much. Thank you."

Besides the fact that Paltrow genuinely excelled as Viola and deserved

Paltrow's adoring grandparents

kudos for her work, she also had the Miramax publicity brain trust behind her and all the support Harvey Weinstein could muster for the woman he calls "one of the finest actresses in America and somebody I think about for every single movie."

Weinstein is the closest thing to a good old-fashioned movie mogul that Hollywood has to offer these days. And just like his precursors, Weinstein can be tough and difficult — yet prescient when it comes to movies. Among the movies he has shepherded to the screen have been *The Piano*, *Pulp Fiction*, *Il Postino*, and *The English Patient*. And as is often the case with such a creative dictator, he is both loved and hated, depending upon who's talking. Even those who like Harvey have their run-ins with him. "He's been good to me, but we definitely fight," Paltrow admits, with money being high on the list of sore subjects. "One day, he'll be saying, 'We have to cut your price to do this kind of film,' that it's an artistic movie; the next day, he'll be announcing that it's a $40 million coproduction with Universal for which I've made about 10 cents to the dollar."

They have also had their creative differences. "Sometimes he'll want to change something that would make the movie conceivably more commercial," Paltrow says. "Sometimes he's absolutely right, and sometimes he's absolutely wrong." But one thing she freely acknowledges is the important role that Weinstein played in her career when he hired her for *Emma*. "He's a real movie-maker and he can be brilliant. I definitely have a lot of respect for him." However, she pointedly adds, "If I want to pay rent, eventually I have to do another movie somewhere else."

Even after taking home her Golden Globe, Paltrow seemed reluctant to entertain the notion of even being nominated for an Academy Award, much less winning one. "How does Oscar sound to me?" she says during one interview. "It sounds like a boy's name. And Oscar is the Grouch on *Sesame Street*." Then, on a more serious note, she adds, "It's not really something I think about. Sure, as a kid, you're like, 'Wow, I wonder what that would be like to be nominated or to win.' But I never did the 'thank you' thing in front of the mirror, and it's certainly not a goal. If it was, I would be in need of some serious psychotherapy. It shouldn't be the focus. It shouldn't be the goal. I work my ass off, and just having my parents come to the screening, like they did the other night, and seeing them both cry at the end; to me, that was all I needed.

"I think it's wonderful to be acknowledged," Paltrow concludes, "and it's a very old tradition, which is really nice, but they shouldn't mean so much to you. You hear people get so upset, saying, 'I wasn't nominated,' or 'I didn't win.' Well, it's not about that. You should be happy with the work that you've done, and making the people you love proud. The other part is gravy if it happens."

It happened. In February 1999, Paltrow was nominated in the Best Actress category along with Cate Blanchett (*Elizabeth*), Fernanda Montenegro (*Central Station*), Meryl Streep (*One True Thing*), and Emily Watson (*Hilary and Jackie*).

The next two months would be a blur of publicity, and once again, a time of personal transition. The first clue came when a reporter asked Paltrow — regarding her relationship with Ben Affleck — if she was now the happiest she had ever been. Paltrow looked at the journalist directly and said, "Let's not go overboard."

Although it wasn't quite the shocker her breakup with Brad Pitt had been, Paltrow's split from Affleck was nevertheless unexpected, even surprising many of their acquaintances. In December 1998, the then-couple appeared together at the Manhattan premiere of *Shakespeare in Love*. But on New Year's Eve, Affleck was spotted celebrating without Paltrow. A week later, however, they had taken a romantic getaway to a bed-and-breakfast in Savannah, Georgia. "If they were mad at each other, it sure didn't show," assistant manager of the B & B, Denise Harrison, says in a January 1999 issue of *People* magazine.

Shakespeare in Love's director, John Madden, found himself denying rumors that there had been tension on the set between Ben and costar Joseph Fiennes, the implication being that perhaps Gwyneth had been stepping out with Joe. "Complete rubbish," Madden snorts, saying that regardless of what happened later, during filming, Affleck and Paltrow "were very much together and incredibly happy." However, by late January, it seemed clear that the bloom had apparently fallen off the love rose. But unlike the painful break from Pitt, Paltrow and Affleck seemed more capable of remaining, if not exactly best friends, then at least in communication with one another.

In some ways, Affleck still seemed gun-shy from the emotional fallout he had suffered in his relationship with longtime girlfriend, Cheyenne Rothman. In an interview during the summer of 1998, he muses, "Women want to take a guy and make him different. I can bend real far, but then it snaps back."

While the assumption that Paltrow hadn't necessarily wanted to end her engagement to Pitt was still out there, she seemed to be the one controlling things with Affleck, at least in the early days following their breakup. During her acceptance speech at the Golden Globes, she thanked her "good *friend*" Ben, who was later shown talking "thisclose" to Paltrow, although her body language screamed, "invasion of personal space."

After they stopped dating, the usual assortment of explanations drifted forth, including the recurring rumor that their relationship had been a ruse from the beginning because it was really Affleck and Damon who were lovers. It's almost a right of passage for any young, handsome actor to face rumors that he's gay. And in some cases, it's absolutely true. In most others, it's merely wishful thinking on the part of the wishers. Some of the speculation about Affleck and Damon may have started after *Interview* magazine published pictures of the two looking as if they were about to passionately embrace — that, and Damon's role in *The Talented Mr. Ripley*, fed fuel to the embers.

"Not only is every actor gay, but somebody has a friend who slept with them," Affleck tells Evgenia Peretz with a tinge of sarcasm. "Maybe there are gay people who are in the closet in Hollywood — I'm sure there probably are — but I'm sure they didn't sleep with *Henry's friend*." Overall, though, both Affleck and Damon maintained good humor about the speculation. "I like to think that if I were gay I would be out, Rupert Everett-style," Ben says.

Although Affleck and Paltrow would keep people guessing about the true status of their friendship — were they or weren't they a *couple*? — in the end it would become clear that, at least for now, there was no commitment between the two of them. But it was obvious that Affleck most definitely still cared about Paltrow, noting that she "has a lot of things that haven't come across in her public image. She's extremely funny, she's extraordinarily smart — not because she's a 'sixteen hundred on the SAT' girl, but smart in the way she kind of gets it. She's actually the funny, down-to-earth fat girl in the beautiful girl's body."

As for what ultimately sent them in different directions, Affleck is careful not to reveal too much. "People's stories always seem more interesting and more full of intrigue from the office-gossip perspective," he notes. "But when you're on the inside of your own relationship, you know the answers to those kinds of questions are much more mundane than when it's all shrouded in mystery and infused with conjecture."

In other words, sometimes people just don't fit in the way that meets both people's needs and wants. Which is why the best of friends don't always make the best of lovers. While it might be too maudlin to suggest that Affleck still carries a torch for Paltrow, it seems clear that he's got some soul-searching left to do: "The reason I'm single is because I wouldn't want to be with anybody right now who would be willing to be with me."

On the other hand, Paltrow seemingly emerged from her yearlong romance with Affleck with increased confidence. "There's honor in being single," she said at the time. "There's hope in holding out. I'm only twenty-five. That's young. I know people who got married when they were young and now they're getting divorced. Right now, I feel fortunate, happy, and centered. I don't see any reason to change any part of my life for awhile. Everything's good. I feel good."

As she matured, Paltrow seemed to better appreciate how far she had come as an evolving person, and at times, seemed to view herself from a distance. "My dad told me the other morning that he loves being with me now," she commented "But then, I'm becoming my parents. I'm very calm now — I don't go running out late any more."

And after two serious, adult relationships that came complete with career issues, Paltrow could also better appreciate just what her parents had accomplished by keeping their marriage intact and healthy for all their years together. "At a certain point after a relationship ends, I try and figure out what went wrong," she admits, although adds, "I think I'm ridiculously optimistic. And sometimes the worst of times brings that out in me even more strongly. I always see the upside. Or understand the human aspect. And it's not as if you can shut off the pain of life and what it brings you. But I think if you face it head-on, with an open heart and open mind, you can surmount anything. I really believe that."

She chose to look at the sum of her life experiences as necessary lessons learned. "I'm in a good place," she says. "When you turn twenty-five and you reach a milestone, a quarter of a century — and hopefully you'll at least have another one — you ask yourself, 'Am I going to change my life in the best possible way?' I think you just need to focus on making good choices."

One choice that was a no-brainer was working with her father Bruce. Although their film, *Duets*, appeared to be derailed after her breakup with Pitt, the elder Paltrow managed to keep the project together and eventually replaced Pitt with newcomer Scott Speedman, whose only credit of note was starring on the WB series, *Felicity*. On the popular young-adult soap, Speedman plays Ben, the object of Felicity's desire whom she follows to college in New York.

Duets began filming in January 1999, and even though Paltrow had again been complaining of being overworked, she viewed this project in a different light. "Yeah, this isn't work to me," she said. "I don't count this! It's just going to be really fun. I've never worked with my dad before. I always begged him to be in *St. Elsewhere*, but he never would. So this is great." And Bruce felt the same way: "It's been my dream. She got to work with her mother [in the miniseries *Cruel Doubt*] and now it's my turn."

The film, which Gwyneth describes as "a six-character movie about karaoke singers," was a low-budget effort of love for all concerned. One of the film's costars, Maria Bello, said that to prepare for their roles as karaoke singers, the cast made an excursion to a karaoke bar where, not surprisingly, it turned out that Paltrow sang great. "I have a small part," she said when work on the film began. "Then I'm going to take a hiatus — maybe six or nine months. I've been working too much. Part of the great lesson about doing *Shakespeare in Love* is that I don't want to work for the sake of working."

On March 7, 1999, the next big awards event took place, the Screen Actors Guild (SAG) Awards. Although the SAG Awards are only five years old, they are considered a special honor, because they are determined by one's acting peers. And because of that fact, the SAG Awards might ultimately be a much better predictor of the Academy Awards than the Golden Globes, since many of the people who vote for the SAG Awards, also vote for the Oscars.

To most observers, the SAG Award for Best Actress was a two-woman race between Cate Blanchett, who had received glowing reviews for her performance in *Elizabeth*, and Paltrow. The room held its collective breath as the winner was announced — Gwyneth Paltrow. As she addressed the audience, Paltrow singled out her mother as "the most brilliant, beautiful, profound actress I know." She also said, "This is just such an honor to be recognized by my peers. You'll never know quite what this means to me." In an apparent oversight that would be pointed out repeatedly, Paltrow neglected to thank or even mention her costar, Joseph Fiennes.

If there had been any doubt before, it was now clear that Paltrow was the undisputed front-runner for the Oscar. However, backstage at the SAG Awards, she studiously avoided answering questions regarding her chances. "Not going there mentally," she smiled, adding politely. "Thanks for the question."

Again, few were surprised that *Shakespeare in Love* also won the ensemble-acting prize for a film. Even so, while many assumed that

At the Screen Actors Guild
Awards, 1999

Shakespeare in Love was sure to be recognized for its acting and writing, they still predicted that *Saving Private Ryan*'s searing portrayal of war would walk off with the Oscar for Best Picture. Of course, Harvey Weinstein had other ideas. But his determined promotional campaign finally took Gwyneth to the brink, and she asked for her participation to be scaled back. "I'm so sick of myself!" she complains when confronted with her latest cover photo on *Entertainment Weekly*. "I am sick of it. This is the last cover of a magazine that I'm doing until I'm 30. I can't stand myself anymore. I'm so sick of my face, and my boring sound bites, my stupid interviews."

However, one perk she did call in was the opportunity to meet Kathy Bates, who was nominated in the Best Supporting Actress category for her work in *Primary Colors*. But to Paltrow, such bonuses, whether it was getting to meet a respected peer or getting a seat in a popular restaurant, were just a measure of payback. "It's not fair," she readily admits, "but I have to figure, there's got to be some payback for having people watch how much you eat and how you chew and if your napkin is on your lap, and asking you for autographs throughout your dinner.

"But you only feel as exposed as you let yourself. I've felt far more exposed in my life than I do now. I sort of learned how to keep what I need to keep to myself, and I learned how to feel like my own person, since it's possible that my every thought can be documented somewhere."

The attention on Paltrow and the other nominees peaked in the week leading up to the Oscar telecast, which was itself undergoing an overhaul. For the first time ever, the Academy of Motion Picture Arts and Sciences (AMPAS) would present the Oscars on a Sunday night, and, in another departure, would open the telecast with a live half hour preshow, to be hosted by Academy Award-winning actress, Geena Davis.

Oscar director Gil Cates and AMPAS President Robert Rehme readily admitted that the idea for the preshow stemmed from the proliferation of pre-Awards shows being produced by non-Academy affiliated companies. "It seemed foolish that we shouldn't do it," says Rehme, who also adds that the Academy was not attempting to curb the other shows, despite the new restriction that nobody else could broadcast live during the half-hour during which the Academy's preshow would air. "It wasn't motivated about knocking the other people off the air. I assume they're still going to be on the air in a somewhat adjusted format, that's all. They can run the footage they take during that half hour later, they just can't broadcast live during that half-hour."

While the addition of a pre-Awards show seemed like a natural evolution, the move to Sunday was made despite some resistance from opponents both inside and outside the Academy. But both Cates and Rehme were emphatic about their reasons for the change. In addition to practical concerns, such as less traffic, they also suggested that there were other advantages to having the ceremony on Sunday. The first being that they could start the show earlier, at 5:30 PM Eastern Time, in an attempt to finish the broadcast as close to midnight as possible. "And, moving to Sunday could also be an improvement in the ratings," Rehme says. "All the major events, like the Super Bowl, are on Sunday, and the Oscars should be on Sunday, so we have Sunday at the Oscars. It's something that I've wanted to do for a long time." Cates adds that he sees a Sunday telecast as being a boom in terms of star power, making it easier to get celebrities to participate in the big event, because "they're not working on Sundays."

Those potentially most affected by the switch to Sunday were the movie exhibitors, because traditionally, Sunday is one of their biggest box office days, while Monday is one of the slowest. Rehme admits that he discussed the issue with some exhibitors, but in the end, he decided that keeping "the Oscar show healthy, keep[ing] those ratings high and hav[ing] as many people as possible watch it, outweighed their concerns," once again demonstrating that the ties between award shows and television superseded other matters.

Of course, all the nominees cared about was getting through the ceremony and pre-Awards festivities. For the Miramax crowd, that included the now traditional Oscar-eve party, during which the actors are "urged" to participate in lampooning performances from films not their own. This particular year had Roberto Benigni, the exuberant-to-the-point-of-annoying star of *Life Is Beautiful*, doing a takeoff on Joseph Fiennes by telling Paltrow, "I want to kiss your *Golden* Globes!" In return, Gwyneth did her impersonation of Benigni with the aid of a plastic nose and glasses.

Finally, Sunday, March 21, arrived, and as expected, Paltrow proved to be the belle of the ball — literally and figuratively.

16

The Big Prize

THE ACADEMY AWARDS CEREMONY has become an event not only to honor creative excellence but also to showcase Hollywood's most glamorous dressers. There are probably just as many, if not more, features about who wore what to the Oscars than there are about the actual awards. As such, it is tailor-made for a woman like Paltrow.

Her parents and ex-boyfriends can attest to her shopaholic tendencies, and long before she earned recognition for her work, Paltrow had been the darling of fashion designers and magazine editors for her eclectic style and her ability to wear clothes better than most. "I was in a Diesel shop and saw these pants," Paltrow recalls. "I asked my friend, 'Are Diesels kind of tacky?' She said, 'Not if *you* wear them.' I liked hearing that."

In addition to her slim, 5' 10" physique, which is perfect for most designers' fashions, Paltrow's patrician, blond, New York looks also heighten her aura of style. And her professed love of clothes only makes her that much more adored by designers. "I'm fascinated by all forms of expression, whether it's Cubist painting or dresses," she says to Hal Rubenstein. "I think fashion's a totally noble art form, the most immediate interpretation of where our culture is at the moment. Plus, c'mon, I'm a girl."

In addition to old favorite Calvin Klein, Paltrow is also partial to Dolce & Gabbana and Prada, although she sometimes isn't sure she likes being on the Seventh Avenue fashion hit list. "It's very flattering when people say they would love to dress you," she admits. "But I remember reading an article once while I was getting a manicure and a New York designer was quoted saying, 'Oh, we'd love to dress Gwyneth Paltrow. What a mannequin!' And I thought, 'I don't really know how to take that.'"

In the end, she decided not to take it negatively, and continued her love affair with haute couture, showing up at the Manhattan zoo known as "Collection Week" — an event at which the top designers present their new clothing lines — in 1998. "I'm going to Mr. Armani's presentation tomorrow, and since it's only my second fashion show ever, I wanted to look right," she tells a reporter. Not that anyone has ever accused her of being fashion challenged.

Part of Paltrow's style is simple confidence. "I may not be the most confident woman in the world, but I'm sure of my aesthetic choices. I don't need advice about whether to buy an Ellsworth Kelly drawing, or a Calvin Klein coat. I know what I like. When I look back at pictures of me in high school, I was sort of a minimalist," she notes. And Paltrow says she never went through "the big-hair-and-makeup phase." She always leaned toward a more spare look — a response, she assumes, to the fashion tyranny of having to wear a uniform, which she admits, she "hiked up to here." It wasn't until she was out of school that she developed her current style, which includes everything from motorcycle jackets and jeans to cashmere, often in combination. "Mixing the elements is what personal style is all about."

Although she is a favorite cover girl — even appearing on the cover of *Vogue* — Paltrow says she never really gave much thought to the fact that she might be a style role model. But with the Oscars, she would suddenly be on fashion display for hundreds of millions of people the world over, causing her to quip, "I may wake up paralyzed tomorrow and never leave the house again." For her big night, Paltrow wore a bubble-gum pink Ralph Lauren ball gown with her hair primly done up. She arrived at the ceremony positively glowing on the arm of her father, who was proud to the point of melancholy. She later said her object was "to look sweet."

Hosted by Whoopie Goldberg, the 1999 Academy Awards reflected everything wonderful and not-so-wonderful about the movie business. Yes, it was emotional and star-studded and had moments of terrific creativity, but it was also inflated, overblown, and filled with lulls. But it was still impossible not to watch.

When, early in the telecast, Dame Judy Dench won Best Supporting Actress for her work in *Shakespeare in Love*, some thought it was the beginning of the Night of the Bard, but in the end, the awards spread themselves out. Among the films nominated for Best Picture — *Shakespeare in Love*, *Saving Private Ryan*, *Life Is Beautiful*, *Gods and Monsters*, and *The Thin Red Line* — only *The Thin Red Line* was shut out of a major award.

However, when it came time for the Best Actress Award, it almost

Mutual admiration society:
Paltrow and Giorgio Armani

KEVIN MAZUR / LONDON FEATURES

seemed a forgone conclusion to perhaps everyone but Paltrow herself. When her name was announced, her hands flew to her face and then she fiercely embraced her father. Up on stage, her self-control broke down quickly during her acceptance speech. Choking back tears, she began by acknowledging her fellow nominees: "I don't feel very deserving of this in your presence." Then, she got more personal, dedicating the award to Harrison Kravis and Keith Paltrow, and adding, "I would not have been able to play this role had I not understood love of a tremendous magnitude, and for that I thank my family and my mother, Blythe Danner, who I love more than anything, and especially my father, Bruce Paltrow, who has surmounted insurmountable obstacles this year." By the time Paltrow turned to leave the stage, she was almost weeping.

Backstage, once she had regained some of her composure, Paltrow admitted, "It's hard when you have adrenaline going and your friends and your parents are here with you. It's impossible not to be overly emotional or to keep them under control — as is evidenced by my teary acceptance speech. You can't help but be swept away by the whole fairytale aspect of these awards and what they mean. It is just — shock. I'm completely overwhelmed."

Paltrow also elaborated, to a degree, upon her comments regarding her father. She explained that her father had been ill but that he asked her not to disclose details, although she indicated he was going to be all right. "It looked like he wouldn't be able to direct the movie that he's been trying to direct," she said, "but he did, and it's a beautiful job." When one journalist asked what she was going to do now, Paltrow's thoughts were completely in the present. "What am I going to do now? Maybe go have a cocktail."

While Paltrow was making the rounds backstage, the show went on, and when Steven Spielberg won the Best Director Oscar, it seemed to assure *Saving Private Ryan* of the big prize, because historically, the Best Picture Award goes to the movie that wins for best director. There have been only 18 instances when the two awards didn't go in tandem. For example, in 1981, Warren Beatty won the Best Director Oscar for *Reds*, while the year's Best Picture Award went to *Chariots of Fire*. Then, in 1989, *Driving Miss Daisy* won Best Picture, but Oliver Stone was named Best Director for *Born on the Fourth of July*. That year, *Driving Miss Daisy*'s director, Bruce Beresford, wasn't even nominated for his directing.

And tradition was about to be broken again. To the delighted surprise of those in attendance, *Shakespeare in Love* was named Best Picture of 1998. The *Saving Private Ryan* contingent sat in stunned shock, while

WILLIAM NORTON / CORBIS

members of *Shakespeare*'s cast and production team leapt and whooped in joy.

Some of the more cynical members of the film community would later claim that Miramax has effectively "bought" the Oscar via its determined, multimillion-dollar advertising campaign — estimated to be in the $15 million range — which included not just *Shakespeare in Love* but *Life Is Beautiful*, as well. Others complained that Miramax executives bad-mouthed *Saving Private Ryan* throughout the voting period.

Looked at objectively, however, much of the griping comes across as little more than sour grapes, such as the complaints of Bill Mechanic, chairman of Fox Film Entertainment, whose movie, *The Thin Red Line*, came up empty at the Oscars. "The entire Academy process is overbloated," Mechanic says. "It's like the process of trying to win an election. It's no longer about the material or the merit. It's about how much money you spend. It's not what the Academy founders set out to do."

He also accused the Weinstein brothers of being obsessed with winning Oscars above all else. "More than any other company, Miramax was set up for specialized movies and tend to be movies that the Academy recognizes," he says. "They've focused on one thing: the Academy Awards process. The rest of us are in the business of making different types of films, some of them meriting Academy attention, some not." In other words, these companies also do films like *Verne and Ernest Go to Hollywood*, while Miramax concentrates on films considered to be of a higher quality — which is exactly what they set out to do as a niche independent production company.

While less hostile, other competing executives also seemed to be feeling sorry for themselves. "What makes [Weinstein] unusual is the results," says Mark Urman, copresident of Lion's Gate Films, which had distributed *Gods and Monsters* and *Affliction*. "Look at what happened at the Oscars. The machinery Harvey puts in place is like a juggernaut. All predictions, all sense of logic and, in some instances, a sense of fairness are thrown out the window."

Weinstein's response was to shrug off the criticism and admire his Oscars, while others tried to analyze what had happened. Even executives at Walt Disney Studios, whose parent company owns Miramax, were pleasantly surprised. "I was stunned that *Shakespeare in Love* won after the Spielberg award," admits Joe Roth, chairman of Disney Studios. "It seemed like *Private Ryan* had all the criteria to take Best Picture. Why didn't it? Perhaps *Shakespeare* was able to convince a lot of women voters to vote for it." And one producer notes that "*Saving Private Ryan* suffers on cassettes. If you see it at home, you are by no means as impressed with it as you were in a movie theater. And *Shakespeare in Love* is a more intimate picture; it plays well on cassette. It may actually be enhanced by watching it at home."

The issue of Academy members being allowed to view films on video instead of in a theater is a prickly subject being debated within the industry. "You're a member of the Motion Picture Academy, not the television video academy," asserts Terry Press, the marketing chief at DreamWorks. "These movies are meant to be seen in movie theaters, all of them. They're not meant to be stopped and started and paused when the phone rings or to feed the dog."

Others suggested that *Shakespeare* might have triumphed because actors make up such a large voting block of the Academy and *Shakespeare in Love* is an actor's film, in both dialogue and subject matter. Whatever the reason, while *Saving Private Ryan* may have been the favorite to win, nobody could complain that *Shakespeare in Love* wasn't worthy of the award. Both films exemplified the best movies have to offer, and while the opposing executives took pot shots, it's interesting to note that Spielberg himself chose not to join the fray.

But while the weeks following the Academy Awards ceremony would be replete with analyses of the results, Oscar night was a scene of camaraderie and mutual admiration. Miramax, never a company to pass up the chance for a party, held its post-Oscar bash at the Beverly Hills Hotel's Polo Lounge, where Paltrow partied with her family and, to the surprise of many in the room, her *Duets* costar, Scott Speedman. Making the party especially interesting was the fact that Ben Affleck was also there, although he was clearly not with Paltrow. Instead, he spent his time chatting with singer Mariah Carey, with whom he would later be romantically linked.

Whether or not she fully appreciated it, Paltrow's life had turned a corner, in ways both obvious and subtle. This fact seemed to dawn on her when a journalist asked her how it now felt to be more famous than her famous parents: "God, you know, it's strange — I've never thought about it! I'm still trying to figure out what the advantages are to my situation. It's funny when your cousins call you and say, 'I've stopped having to spell my last name in restaurants. Thank you!' It's just such a strange thing to bring to your family. I think my parents get a kick out of it." But Paltrow also recognizes that there is a flipside to fame. "Then there's people who are going to sort of pick on you," she says, "and the more successful you are, the worse it gets, you know. These are just mean-spirited people who don't know me, and I laugh it off, but if I looked too closely at it all, it might hurt my feelings. Sometimes, ignoring it is better."

After the Oscars, some of the pot shots hurled at Paltrow seemed to truly come out of nowhere. Former teen star has-been, Corey Feldman, who frittered away his career thanks to a nasty flirtation with heroin and jail, lashed out inexplicably. "Look at Gwyneth Paltrow," Feldman fumes to David Spitz in *Time* magazine. "She did twenty movies in four years because her parents are in the business! She's not a great actress! How can you not be bitter when . . . it should be you up there winning the Academy Award?" (Hey, Corey — can you spell *delusional*?) And a more prominent member of the Hollywood community also took Paltrow to patronizing task. Sharon Stone meowed that Gwyneth was "very young and lives in a rarefied air that's very thin. It's like she's not getting enough oxygen."

However, not everyone emitted rancor. Julia Roberts, for one, showed grace when quizzed over whether or not she had any misgivings or second thoughts for having dropped out of what had turned out to be an Oscar-winning role in *Shakespeare in Love*. Roberts recalls having gone to London eight years earlier to participate in the casting search for the actor to play Shakespeare opposite her then-planned Viola. "This was the first time I met Hugh Grant," Julia says. "He was one of several British actors who read opposite me," Roberts says, although ultimately it was Daniel Day-Lewis who won the role. But, according to Roberts, the movie "just never came to pass. And the script was very different from what Gwyneth Paltrow eventually starred in." As for any lingering thoughts of 'It could have been me,' Roberts demurs. "I did not do any stomping about," she assures. "I've been attached to other projects that have never been made or have gone on to be made by other people. It's all part of the business."

In the end, Paltrow learned that, like any life endeavor, being a successful actor has its upside as well as its underbelly, and what she ultimately gains or loses from it depends in great part on the approach she takes to dealing with both the good and the bad. True maturity has less to do with aging than with understanding ourselves and our place in life. By this criterion, Gwyneth Paltrow seems on her way to being not just a successful actress but a successful person.

After the hoopla of the Oscars had died down, Paltrow made good on her promise to take time off. She was determined to lay low, even though her agents were as busy as ever lining up her next films. The first of these films was to be *Bounce*. What made her inclusion in the cast particularly notable was that the film would costar Ben Affleck.

In the movie, Affleck's character gives his seat on a flight to a man desperate to get back home to his wife, while he stays behind to have a one-night stand. After the plane crashes and kills everyone aboard, he is consumed by guilt and starts drinking heavily. Eventually, he goes to rehab and straightens out, but hoping to find closure, he searches out the dead man's wife, played by Paltrow, and of course, they start to fall in love. However, Paltrow's character has no idea the part that her new man played in her husband's death.

Because they were formerly lovers, Affleck and Paltrow's decision to work together generated all kinds of speculation. Since it is uncommon for ex-paramours to remain on truly good terms, it was immediately assumed that they were once again a romantic item. The rumor mill was further fed by a report from Hollywood columnist Marilyn Beck that Paltrow had spent a lot of time visiting Affleck on the Vancouver set of his movie *Reindeer Games*. Add to that the revelation that Affleck had finally settled down enough to buy himself a house in Los Angeles, and the gossip columns had them nearly married with children. While Paltrow and Affleck may indeed have entertained an on-again, off-again relationship for a while, in the end they just remained good friends, with Affleck later being linked to everyone from Mariah Carey to Jerry Seinfeld's ex, Shoshanna Lonstein.

So the question for entertainment journalist types became, just who *is* Paltrow dating? At one point, she was linked to Lee Eastman, the cousin of Stella McCartney, Paul and Linda's designer daughter. Most recently, there have been rumors about both Scott Speedman, her *Duets* costar and David Schwimmer, her costar on *The Pallbearer*. Then again, Paltrow was seen canoodling with her old flame Affleck at the 2000 Academy Awards after parties.

Either way, Paltrow has been steering clear of any serious involvement, perhaps wanting time to get some perspective. "I think you can always learn from your mistakes and you can always learn from what you have done wrong and what you've done right," Paltrow says, insisting that it is possible to live in such a way that "you can learn and grow from your past relationships." But then she wryly notes, "I think all that I know about men . . . is already too much. Just leave it as it is now. I'm such close friends with so many men."

However, she did have one notable love affair in the summer of 1999 — with Williamstown, Massachusetts, where she appeared as Rosalind in the Theater Festival's production of *As You Like It*. For the residents, it was like the hometown girl made good was returning to her roots. "The whole town's abuzz," crowed one proud local.

Indeed, in many ways Paltrow found herself in familiar territory, especially because the role of Rosalind required her to once again dress up as a man. However, the reason for the deception is quite different from Viola's motivation in *Shakespeare in Love*: Rosalind is the daughter of an exiled duke and, as a result, has been banished from the protected world of the royal court, forcing her to fend for herself in the big, often cruel world.

Appearing opposite Paltrow as her beloved Orlando was Alessandro Nivola, whose film credits include small roles in *Face/Off* and *Inventing the Abbotts*. Nivola wasn't coy about the importance of being cast opposite Paltrow: "It was a madhouse. Every night, the audience had some celebrities. One day, I think Kevin Kline, Paul Newman, Joanne Woodward and Mia Farrow all came to the show. Every day there was such pressure on, but I don't think anyone had as much pressure as [Paltrow] did. There were people like Steven Spielberg, agents, producers, and directors all coming to see Gwyneth and talk to her afterwards," recalls Nivola. "I'm not naive enough to pretend it couldn't be helpful to my career, as I was playing her lover."

Of course, to Paltrow, doing the play was all about her love of theater rather than career advancement. As Michael Richard, the festival's producer, notes, "We pay nothing, compared to anybody. Everyone gets the same pay, same campus housing, same shared restrooms. It's to Gwyneth's great credit that she's got the world in the palm of her hand, she can do anything she wants, and she's actually doing what she wants, which is this."

For Paltrow, there is nothing like acting in a play written by Shakespeare, whom she considers "a brilliant man, [whose] writing has never been paralleled." Although, as she says, most professions — especially technological ones — advance and improve over time, the same cannot be said for the theater. Because of Shakespeare, Paltrow believes, "The best came first in a lot of ways." But when asked what she would do if she had the chance to meet the Bard, her girlishness rears its head. "I'd probably ask him to bathe," she laughs. "'Cause you know how they were back then."

Overall, Paltrow's stage turn charmed the critics as much as the audiences. *Newsday* prints:

With its famously brief rehearsal period, Williamstown is not the place you'd expect to see actors, however talented, forged into a brilliant Shakespearean company. But under the direction of Barry Edelstein, they pull off a small miracle, speaking Shakespeare's intricate language as if it were their daily form of address and conveying the narrative clearly and comprehensibly.

Paltrow, whether flitting around girlishly in Rosalind's blazingly red strapless ballgown, or striding boyishly through the woods in Ganymede's tweedy knickers, is a striking physical presence on the stage. Although her voice doesn't project quite as well as it ought, she dominates every scene in which she appears, bantering with Celia, teasing Orlando, and, in drag, promising to make everything end happily by magically producing Rosalind.

Because she has become known for what many call her "ethereal" beauty, people often wonder if Paltrow would ever be willing to sacrifice on-screen beauty for a role, the way Sally Field did in *Norma Ray* and Meryl Streep has done countless times. "I would, I guess," Paltrow says, but admits, "I wouldn't like it. I'm just as vain as the next boring actress. But I don't mind looking grubby, I don't mind looking ugly, I wouldn't mind gaining weight if it was right for the thing. I know that certain people think that I have a certain amount of pulchritude. I guess it helps in a way — and in a lot of times I think it hurts. I've tried out for millions of movies and didn't get them. I have a strange look. When I was nineteen, I was stranger looking than I am now! I was still kind of baking until I was twenty-two or so.

"There *are* roles that people wouldn't think of me for because of the way I look. 'You're too regal for that.' People obviously perceive me like that, which is strange. It's not how I perceive myself."

Being misunderstood, or having others presume to know her, remains one of Paltrow's most gnawing peeves. "One of the things that goes along with my work life is this person, Gwyneth Paltrow, and people write all kinds of things about her and speculate, and say this and that. I don't read it, and I don't let it bother me. I don't engage in it. I don't empower it by getting upset about it, which would waste so much of my energy. And believe me, I used to get upset, but it's stupid.

"They don't know me. What they're writing about me, it's not me. I know who I am. Why should I make it my business to think about what strangers are writing about me, guessing about me or making up lies about me? It's really destructive, so I don't."

What everyone can agree on, though, is that right now, Paltrow pretty much has her choice of roles. Both the industry and her audiences see her as one of Hollywood's linchpins of the new millennium. In a poll of most bankable stars, Paltrow was the fourth highest ranked woman, behind Meg Ryan, Jodie Foster, and Sandra Bullock. And when Harlequin Enterprises asked lifestyle editors from 100 daily newspapers across North America who they thought were most likely to succeed Cary Grant and Marilyn Monroe as the quintessential Hollywood heartthrobs, the responses included Cameron Diaz, Uma Thurman, Neve Campbell, Matt Damon, Prince William, Brad Pitt, and Will Smith. Winning by a landslide, however, were Leonardo DiCaprio and Gwyneth Paltrow.

Many of Paltrow's peers would agree. Geoffrey Rush says Paltrow has a killer grin. "It's generous and humble and provocative and sexy and vulnerable, all at the same time," he gushes. Alfonso Cuarón, her *Great Expectations* director, concurs: "Cameras were invented to photograph Gwyneth. She turns to the camera and it's like, *Gulp*!" Of course some people *are* more biased than others. "She was beautiful from the beginning," says Arnold "Buster" Paltrow, Gwyneth's adoring grandfather.

Now, while it could be argued that DiCaprio has gotten an awful lot of mileage out of one or two high profile roles, Paltrow's reputation is based on her entire body of work, which keeps expanding at an amazing rate. One possible future project would have her playing Sylvia Plath, chronicling her love affair with Poet Laureate Ted Hughes and her subsequent suicide. Several attempts have been made to bring the story to celluloid, but now that Paltrow is interested and the movie is backed by Miramax, the odds are high that it will finally come to fruition. "I worked with Gwyneth on *Moonlight and Valentino* years ago," producer Alison Owen says, "and when I rang to ask her if she wanted to play Sylvia she said: *100,000 per cent — yes!*

"When we worked together on *Moonlight* there was a scene where a character says: 'I'm going to dress in black and read Sylvia Plath.' The director wanted to change the poet's name thinking no one would know who Plath was. Gwyneth made a two-hour impassioned case for keeping the Plath reference in. It worked. She also has the same intelligent East Coast background Plath had and she looks so much like her."

Although the part of Ted Hughes hadn't been cast as of autumn 1999, on Owen's wish list is Daniel Day-Lewis, and he is hoping that *Shakespeare in Love*'s John Madden will direct.

In the meantime, Paltrow continues learning how to live with her success and prioritize what's important to her. "I just go into everything with an open mind," Paltrow says. "I try to take everything as a learning experience and hope that I come out of it a better actress. I never have expectations, and I have to ignore the buzz. You can't take all that seriously."

Which is one reason why she prefers living in New York, where she says, "everybody does all different kinds of things. When you go out to LA, it's such an industry town. Everybody knows who everybody is, and everybody wants something. It's like you can't go anywhere. I would rather that teenagers come up to me, you know, by the Empire State Building, than these smarmy producers and managers who come up to you in LA. It's just like, 'Oh please leave me alone!' It's just a whole different energy.

"I like to visit LA, but I have difficulty connecting because the town is so propelled by show business," she explains. "In New York, when you go to a nice restaurant for lunch, there will be publishers, curators from MOMA, writers, and actors.

"You get to a point where you're thinking, where do I want to live, what kind of life do I want? One day I hope to have the power to determine my destiny." But at the same time, Paltrow realizes that life is not a series of connect the dots. "I just don't want to say, 'This is my plan. This is what I'm going to do.' It's not life."

She hopes to have children and do less jet-setting, perhaps settling down in Connecticut some day. "And you know what? That may happen and that may not. I love to work, but I don't have that something I recognize in other actresses. Winona Ryder doesn't have it, either. I don't feel 'I've got to do this . . . I've got to be number one.'"

Paltrow sounds sure of herself because she steadfastly maintains that acting is not her number one priority. "Family comes first. My mother could have had an incredible film career but she put it on hold to have my brother and me and to raise us. I think that's what I'll do when I decide to have children. I certainly won't keep up the schedule I have these past years. My children will have a different life from mine. My father always says when he was a kid you had Maine lobster in Maine. Now the world's homogenized. It's all in the mall."

When thinking about the future, one thing that seems to be a siren song is a sense of regaining control of a part of her life she feels has been compromised by her public success. "If my career just stopped, there is so much I could do. I'd get to go back to no one knowing who I was the way they do now."

But regardless of how her life proceeds from this moment, Paltrow takes comfort in an important realization: "I know myself better, so much better, and I realize that a lot of who I thought I was, well, I wasn't being fair. I'm a really nice person. I'm also complicated. But the biggest surprise is that I'm a much better person than most people bother to be. And I like that."

Filmography

1. *Shout* (1991)

Summary: Set in 1955, John Travolta stars as a teacher, Jack Cabe, who is hired at a home for wayward boys in Clarity, Texas. He turns to music to reach his wards, particularly the troubled Jesse. Heather Graham, in her film debut, costars as the daughter of the school's strict director who falls in love with Jesse.

Of Special Note: The week *Shout* opened, *The Fisher King* was number one at the box office, earning over $16 million. *Shout* debuted 9th, pulling in an anemic $1.6 million.

Awards, Accolades, and Insults: RAZZIE: Nomination, Worst Supporting Actor (John Travolta).

What the Critics Said:

"Bomb." — Leonard Maltin

"Dickens meets *Footloose*. Travolta, an actor who dances, does well enough, but his performance is nothing to *Shout* about." — Rita Kempley, *Washington Post*

Director: Jeffrey Hornaday

Writer: Joe Gaton

Cast:	John Travolta	Jack Cabe
	Jamie Walters	Jesse Tucker
	Heather Graham	Sara Benedict
	Linda Fiorentino	Molly
	Gwyneth Paltrow	Rebecca

2. *Hook* (1991)

Summary: Robin Williams answers the question of what would happen if Peter Pan grew up — he becomes a lawyer and is married to Wendy's granddaughter. But when Captain Hook kidnaps Peter's children, he returns to Never Never Land and enlists the aid of Tinkerbell and the Lost Boys to rescue them. But first, Peter has to remember how to be Peter Pan and recapture his youthful innocence in order to defeat Captain Hook one more time.

Of Special Note: *Hook* has many cameo appearances. Singer Jimmy Buffett plays one of the pirates who attempts to steal Peter's shoes when he first arrives in Never Never Land. The young Peter Pan is played by Dustin Hoffman's son. The pirate who is shot in the chest with the scorpion is played by Glenn Close.

Awards, Accolades, and Insults: RAZZIE: Nomination, Worst Supporting Actress (Julia Roberts); GOLDEN GLOBES: Best Performance by an Actor in a Motion Picture (Dustin Hoffman); ASC AWARD: Outstanding Achievement in Cinematography in Theatrical Releases; ACADEMY AWARDS: Best Art Direction — Set Decoration, Best Costume Design, Best Effects — Visual Effects, Best Makeup, Best Music, Best Song (Leslie Bricusse, lyrics, and John Williams, music, for "When You're Alone").

What the Critics Said:

"It's sort of like *Pirates of the Caribbean* and *It's a Small World* rolled into one. It's a helluva contraption, and certainly one to be marveled at. It gives a good ride. What it doesn't do, though, is instantly take a place in your heart. For all its pomp and color, for all the talent of its contributors, it's not a movie for which you can build a deep affection." — Hal Hinson

"The crucial failure in *Hook* is its inability to re-imagine the material, to find something new, fresh or urgent to do with the Peter Pan myth. Lacking that, Spielberg should simply have remade the original story, straight, for this generation." — Roger Ebert

Director: Steven Spielberg

Writers: Story by Jim V. Hart and Nick Castle; Malia Scotch Marmo

Producers: Gary Adelson, Craig Baumgarten, Bruce Cohen, Dodi Fayed, James V. Hart, Kathleen Kennedy, Malia Scotch Marmo, and Frank Marshall

Cast:		
	Dustin Hoffman	Captain Hook
	Robin Williams	Peter Banning
	Julia Roberts	Tinkerbell
	Bob Hoskins	Smee
	Maggie Smith	Granny Wendy
	Phil Collins	Inspector Good
	Gwyneth Paltrow	Young Wendy

3. *Cruel Doubt* (TV, 1992)

Summary: A true-crime story about the murder of North Carolina businessman Leith Von Stein, who was stabbed and bludgeoned to death in his bed. His wife, Bonnie, was also attacked but survived. When the investigation leads to the arrest of her disaffected, Dungeons and Dragons-addicted, drugged-out son, Chris Pritchard, Bonnie refuses to believe it. The motive for Chris wanting to kill his stepfather and his mother is a $2 million inheritance that he and his sister, Angela, would receive upon their deaths. A jury eventually finds Chris and two others guilty of murder. After his admission of guilt, Bonnie struggles to understand why her son would want to kill her.

Of Special Note: This was one of two movies made about the Von Stein murder case. The other, *Honor Thy Mother,* was based on Jerry Bledsoe's book, *Blood Games,* while *Cruel Doubt* was based on the book of the same name by Joe McGinniss.

Awards, Accolades, and Insults: CASTING SOCIETY OF AMERICA: Artios Award for Best Casting for TV Miniseries.

What the Critics Said:

"In the far smaller role of Chris's sister, Paltrow is a minor revelation. The actress, who happens to be the daughter of Danner and TV producer Bruce Paltrow (*St. Elsewhere*), summons up her own brand of sour-faced teen alienation, and does it so convincingly that when Angela briefly becomes a suspect, we feel it would be perfectly possible for this glowering girl to off her parents." — Ken Tucker, *Entertainment Weekly*

Director: Yves Simoneau

Writer: John Gay (based on the novel by Joe McGinniss)

Producer: Susan Baerwald

Cast:		
	Blythe Danner	Bonnie Von Stein
	Denis Arndt	Leith Von Stein
	Matt McGrath	Chris Pritchard
	Adam Baldwin	Detective John Taylor
	Gwyneth Paltrow	Angela Pritchard
	Edward Asner	Bill Osteen
	David Arquette	Josh Duggan

4. *Malice* (1993)

Summary: A surgeon rents a room from a college professor and his wife and turns their lives upside down.

What the Critics Said:

"Peering into the shadows of *Malice,* I was reminded of a remark at this year's Telluride Film Festival by John Alton, the 92-year-old cinematographer specialized in using shadows and darkness. 'If I'd used more lights,' he said, 'they would have been comedies.'" — Roger Ebert

"Every so often a movie comes along that isn't just swill but great swill — fast and stupid and proud. . . . Authentically bad, *Malice* is one of those rental treats that makes you realize you don't have to like a movie to enjoy it." — Ty Burr, *Entertainment Weekly*

Director: Harold Becker

Writers: Aaron Sorkin and Scott Frank; Story by Aaron Sorkin and James McCord

Producers: Harold Becker, Peter Brown, Michael Hirsh, and Patrick Loubert

Cast:	Alec Baldwin	Dr. Jed Hill
	Nicole Kidman	Tracy Kennsinger
	Bill Pullman	Andy Safian
	Bebe Neuwirth	Dana
	George C. Scott	Dr. Kessler
	Anne Bancroft	Mrs. Kennsinger
	Peter Gallagher	Dennis Riley
	Gwyneth Paltrow	Paula Bell

5. *Deadly Relations* (TV, 1993)

Summary: Another true-crime story, this telefilm tells the tale of Leonard Fagot, who takes out large life insurance policies on his daughters' husbands, who conveniently begin suffering freak accidents.

Of Special Note: The telefilm is based on a book written by two of Fagot's daughters after their father was convicted of murdering one of his sons-in-law.

What the Critics Said:

"Remember Mutual of Omaha's *Wild Kingdom*? In this dramatization, Robert Urich plays the type of animal that would appall *Wild Kingdom*'s phlegmatic host, Marlin Perkins." — David Hiltbrand, *People*

Director: Bill Condon

Writer: Dennis Nemec

Producer: Ed Milkovich

Cast:	Robert Urich	Leonard J. Fagot
	Shelley Fabares	Shirley Fagot
	Gwyneth Paltrow	Carol Fagot Holland
	Tony Higgins	Mike Holland
	Georgia Emelin	Joanne Fagot Westerfield
	Matthew Perry	George Westerfield

6. *Flesh and Bone* (1993)

Summary: A troubled young man must come to grips with sins from his past when he falls in love with a woman with whom he shares a haunting history.

What the Critics Said:

"Gwyneth Paltrow (Blythe Danner's real-life daughter) might have gotten a supporting-Oscar nomination had the film not flopped." — Mike Clark, *USA Today*

"The movie moseys along slower than an armadillo on Valium, and the grand finale will leave you humming, 'Is That All There Is?' as you exit." — Jim Byerley, *HBO*

"Paltrow, the daughter of Blythe Danner, is really something of an addendum as a punky young grifter apprenticed to Caan's chilling con man. It'll be nice for her résumé." — Rita Kempley, *Washington Post*

Director: Steven Kloves

Writer: Steven Kloves

Producers: G. Mac Brown and Sydney Pollack

Cast:		
	Dennis Quaid	Arlis Sweeney
	James Caan	Roy Sweeney
	Meg Ryan	Kay Davies
	Gwyneth Paltrow	Ginnie

7. *Mrs. Parker and the Vicious Circle* (1994)

Summary: A look at the complex life of Dorothy Parker, who will forever be known as the wittiest member of the Algonquin Round Table, a regular dinner attended by the best and brightest of the New York literary scene. Her ability with a quip was only matched by her string of failed relationships.

Of Special Note: The movie was also known as *Mrs. Parker and the Round Table.*

Awards, Accolades, and Insults: GOLDEN GLOBES: Nomination, Best Performance by an Actress in a Motion Picture (Jennifer Jason Leigh); INDEPENDENT SPIRIT AWARD: Nominations, Best Director (Alan Rudolph), Best Feature (Robert Altman), Best Female Lead (Jennifer Jason Leigh), Best Male Lead (Campbell Scott), Best Screenplay (Randy Sue Coburn and Alan Rudolph); NATIONAL SOCIETY OF FILM CRITICS AWARD: Best Actress (Jennifer Jason Leigh).

What the Critics Said:

"*Mrs. Parker* is a love story between two minds. It's also a vivid and melancholy demonstration that the world that nurtured them, warts and all, is gone." — John Hartl, *Film.com*

"After about two hours of watching *Mrs. Parker's* vicious circle, you start thinking about what kinds of doo-dads she would have written if they'd only had Prozac back then." — Zachary Woodruff, *Tucson Weekly*

Director: Alan Rudolph

Writers: Alan Rudolph and Randy Sue Coburn

Producers: Robert Altman, Scott Bushnell, and Ira Deutchman

Cast:

Jennifer Jason Leigh	Dorothy Parker
Campbell Scott	Robert Benchley
Matthew Broderick	Charles MacArthur
Peter Gallagher	Alan Campbell
Jennifer Beals	Gertrude Benchley
Andrew McCarthy	Eddie Parker
Wallace Shawn	Horatio Byrd
Martha Plimpton	Jane Grant
Sam Robards	Harold Ross
Lili Taylor	Edna Ferber
James LeGros	Deems Taylor
Gwyneth Paltrow	Paula Hunt
Nick Cassavetes	Robert Sherwood
David Thornton (I)	George S. Kaufman
Heather Graham	Mary Kennedy Taylor
Tom McGowan (II)	Alexander Woollcott
Chip Zien	Franklin P. Adams
Gary Basaraba	Heywood Broun
Jane Adams (II)	Ruth Hale
Stephen Baldwin	Roger Spalding
Matt Malloy (I)	Marc Connelly
Rebecca Miller	Neysa McMein
Jake Johannsen	John Peter Toohey
Amelia Campbell	Mary Brandon Sherwood
David Gow	Donald Ogden Stewart
Leni Parker	Beatrice Kaufman
J. M. Henry	Harpo Marx
Stanley Tucci	Fred Hunter
Mina Badie	Joanie Gerard
Randy Lowell	Alvan Barach
Keith Carradine	Will Rogers
Jon Favreau	Elmer Rice (as John Favreau)
Gabriel Gascon	Georges Attends

8. *Jefferson in Paris* (1995)

Summary: A fictional account of Jefferson's real-life romance with painter Maria Cosway, which is complicated by his reputed affair with Sally Hemmings. Set at the time when America's future founding father was living in Paris, pre-Revolution.

Awards, Accolades, and Insults: CANNES FILM FESTIVAL: Nomination, Golden Palm (James Ivory).

What the Critics Said:

"One of Hollywood's most untalented and unsightly performers, Gwyneth Paltrow (daughter of a famous actress and a successful producer) makes, as usual, an ass of herself as Patsy, as she mopes through the entire movie with the same sagging posture, her face in a single sullen, almost cretinous, expression." — John Simon, *National Review*

"Had the Merchant-Ivory team chosen to make that forbidden, mixed-race love their focus, and not gotten sidetracked with all of Jefferson's silly mooning over the pretentious Maria Cosway, then *Jefferson in Paris* might have come to life." — Edward Guthmann, *San Francisco Chronicle*

Director: James Ivory

Writer: Ruth Prawer Jhabvala

Producers: Humbert Balsan, Paul Bradley, Ismail Merchant, and Donald Rosenfeld

Cast:

Nick Nolte	Thomas Jefferson
Greta Scacchi	Maria Cosway
Simon Callow	Richard Cosway
Gwyneth Paltrow	Patsy Jefferson
Estelle Eonnet	Polly Jefferson
Thandie Newton	Sally Hemings

9. *Seven* (1995)

Summary: A serial killer wreaks retribution by killing seven people, each of whom have broken one of the seven deadly sins, in seven days.

Awards, Accolades, and Insults: ACADEMY AWARDS: Nomination, Best Film Editing; AMERICAN SOCIETY OF CINEMATOGRAPHERS: Nomination, Outstanding Achievement in Cinematography in Theatrical Releases; BRITISH ACADEMY AWARDS: BAFTA Film Award for Best Screenplay (Original); IMAGE AWARDS: Outstanding Lead Actor in a Motion Picture (Morgan Freeman); MTV MOVIE AWARDS: Best Movie, Best Villain (Kevin Spacey), Most Desirable Male (Brad Pitt); NATIONAL BOARD OF REVIEW: Best Supporting Actor (Kevin Spacey); NEW YORK FILM CRITICS AWARD: Best Supporting Actor (Kevin Spacey).

What the Critics Said:

"Gwyneth Paltrow plays the young cop's loving and oh-so-vulnerable wife. She's very good — a ray of sunshine breaking through a great deal of gloom. She also seems like a sacrificial lamb from the second she turns up on screen." — Carol Buckland, CNN *Showbiz*

"The actors, among them Gwyneth Paltrow as the young cop's wife (whom we immediately perceive as good, and therefore doomed), do their best to ground this twaddle in recognizable behavior. But it is very tiresome peering through the gloom, trying to catch a glimpse of something interesting, then having to avert one's eyes when it turns out to be just another brutally tormented body." — Richard Schickel, *Time*.

Director: David Fincher

Writer: Andrew Kevin Walker

Executive Producers: Dan Kolsrud, Anne Kopelson, Arnold Kopelson, and Gianni Nunnari

Cast:		
	Morgan Freeman	William Somerset
	Brad Pitt	David Mills
	Gwyneth Paltrow	Tracy Mills
	Kevin Spacey	John Doe

10. *Moonlight and Valentino* (1995)

Summary: Elizabeth Perkins, Whoopi Goldberg, Gwyneth Paltrow, and Kathleen Turner star in this sentimental story about a woman, Rebecca, who is coming to grips with the sudden death of her husband. Through the help of her friends and family, and a poetic housepainter, Rebecca learns to go on with life.

Of Special Note: Ellen Simon, Neil Simon's daughter, based the script, originally written as a stage play, on her own experience of losing her husband.

What the Critics Said:

"Perkins gives an outstanding performance." — Leonard Maltin

"Freud once asked, 'What does a woman want?' Having seen this movie, I believe that women want fewer movies like this." — Roger Ebert

"Perkins (of *Big* and *The Flintstones*) does a surprisingly decent job despite the material, and Paltrow (*Seven*) is adequate as the tense and troubled student." — Walter Addiego, *San Francisco Examiner*

"The film is . . . stolen by Gwyneth Paltrow as gawky Lucy. When she meets Rebecca's handsome pupil (Jeremy Sisto) and asks, 'Are we on a blind date?' or when she expresses her desire to have her older sister look at her naked body and, 'Tell me what you think,' she is enchanting. Paltrow is the perfect actress for the part." — Kirby Tepper, *Magill's Survey of Cinema*

Director: David Anspaugh

Writer: Ellen Simon (based on her stage play)

Producer: Tim Bevan

Cast:		
	Elizabeth Perkins	Rebecca Trager Lott
	Whoopi Goldberg	Sylvie Morrow
	Gwyneth Paltrow	Lucy Trager
	Kathleen Turner	Alberta Trager
	Jon Bon Jovi	The Painter

11. *Hard Eight* (1996)

Summary: A "noirish" character study about an older man, Sydney, his protégé and surrogate son, John, and John's girlfriend, Clementine — three castoffs eking out their lives in Reno.

Of Special Note: The film's original name was *Sydney*, but it was changed to *Hard Eight* for American distribution.

Awards, Accolades, and Insults: BOSTON SOCIETY OF FILM CRITICS: Best New Filmmaker (Paul Thomas Anderson); DEAUVILLE FILM FESTIVAL: Nomination, Grand Special Prize; INDEPENDENT SPIRIT AWARDS: Nominations, Best Cinematographer, Best First Feature, Best First Screenplay, Best Male Lead, Best Supporting Male.

What the Critics Said:

"Reilly and Ms. Paltrow play impulsive, not-very-bright people who are too buffeted by life to be able to plan ahead or even to think clearly in moments of crisis. But instead of telegraphing their characters' limitations, they allow us to discover them for ourselves." — Stephen Holden, *New York Times*

"It's startling, given her elegant turn in *Emma*, to see Paltrow so convincing as one so thoroughly unblessed with brains." — Mike Clark, *USA Today*

Director: Paul Thomas Anderson

Writer: Paul Thomas Anderson

Executive Producers: Hans Brockman, Francois Duplat, and Keith Samples

Cast:		
	Phillip Baker Hall	Sydney
	John C. Reilly	John
	Gwyneth Paltrow	Clementine
	Samuel L. Jackson	Jimmy
	F. William Parker	Hostage
	Philip Seymour Hoffman	Young Craps Player

12. *The Pallbearer* (1996)

Summary: *Friends* star David Schwimmer stars as Tom Thompson, a nebbish twenty-something who is asked to deliver the eulogy for a high school classmate he doesn't remember — even though the dead man's mother seems to believe he was her son's best friend. After meeting the mother, played by Barbara Hershey, Tom becomes sexually involved with her, although his heart is pining after the girl he had a secret crush on in high school, played by Paltrow.

Of Special Note: In Japan, the film's title was translated into *Happy Blue*.

What the Critics Said:

"A radiant Gwyneth Paltrow . . ." — Andy Jones, *Rough Cut*

"Ms. Paltrow makes Julie fetching enough to justify Tom's obsession, but her manner is as moony and helpless as his own." — Janet Maslin, *New York Times*

"Gwyneth Paltrow (*Seven*) gives a fine-tuned performance as one of those gorgeous, poor little rich waifs that are usually so annoying in such movies; she's a gift here, playing her turn straight with a deft lightness." — *Susan Lambert,* Boxoffice Magazine

Director: Matt Reeves

Writers: Jason Katims and Matt Reeves

Executive Producers: Jeffrey Abrams, Meryl Poster, and Bob and Harvey Weinstein

Cast:	David Schwimmer	Tom Thompson
	Gwyneth Paltrow	Julie DeMarco
	Michael Rapaport	Brad Schorr
	Toni Collette	Cynthia
	Carol Kane	Tom's Mom
	Barbara Hershey	Ruth Abernathy

13. *Emma* (1996)

Summary: A charming, witty adaptation of Jane Austen's comedy of manners about a headstrong young woman who makes a habit of playing matchmaker for others, but can't — or won't — recognize her own true feelings and is oblivious to the emotions of the men around her.

Of Special Note: Emma Thompson won an Oscar adapting another Austen novel, *Sense and Sensibility*, for the screen. In this film, there's also a Thompson presence, this time in the guise of Emma's sister, Sophie Thompson, and their mother, Phyllida Law.

Awards, Accolades, and Insults: ACADEMY AWARDS: Best Music — Original Musical or Comedy Score (Rachel Portman); Nomination, Best Costume Design; GOLDEN SATELLITE AWARD: Best Actress in a Motion Picture Comedy or Musical (Gwyneth Paltrow); WRITERS GUILD OF AMERICA: Nomination, Best Screenplay Based on Material Previously Produced or Published.

What the Critics Said:

"After standing out in *Seven* and in box-office failures from *Flesh and Bone* through *The Pallbearer*, it was only a matter of time until Paltrow exploded on screen. She does so here, and in a role that really needs her, for truth to tell, Emma's a potential pain. Never once, thanks to Paltrow, do we want to wring her neck (which, by the way, is lovely)." — Mike Clark, *USA Today*

"Gwyneth Paltrow delivers a star-making performance as the title character." — Jack Garner, Gannett News Service

"Gwyneth Paltrow gives a riveting performance as the ardent matchmaker Emma Woodhouse in this cheerfully glib adaptation by Douglas McGrath." — Jack Matthews, *Newsday*

Director: Douglas McGrath

Writer: Douglas McGrath (based on the novel by Jane Austen)

Executive Producers: Patrick Cassavetti, Donna Gigliotti, Bob and Harvey Weinstein

Cast:		
	Gwyneth Paltrow	Emma Woodhouse
	James Cosmo	Mr. Weston
	Greta Scacchi	Mrs. Weston
	Alan Cumming	Rev. Elton
	Denys Hawthorne	Mr. Woodhouse
	Sophie Thompson	Miss Bates
	Jeremy Northam	Mr. Knightley
	Toni Collette	Harriet Smith
	Kathleen Byron	Mrs. Goddard
	Phyllida Law	Mrs. Bates
	Edward Woodall	Mr. Martin
	Brett Miley	Little Boy
	Brian Capron	John Knightley
	Karen Westwood	Isabella
	Paul Williamson (I)	Footman
	Polly Walker (II)	Jane Fairfax
	Rebecca Craig	Miss Martin
	Ewan McGregor	Frank Churchill
	Angela Down	Mrs. Martin
	John Franklyn-Robbins	Mr. Cole
	Juliet Stevenson	Mrs. Elton
	Ruth Jones	Bates Maid

14. *Sliding Doors* (1998)

Summary: An imaginative film that explores two different courses a young woman's life would take depending on whether she makes it in time to get into a subway train or the doors close before she gets there. In the first scenario, she meets a man on the train, but when she arrives at home, she unexpectedly finds her boyfriend in bed with another woman. In the alternate reality, she misses the train, gets mugged, and by the time she gets home, simply finds her boyfriend in the shower. From there, the dual lives are shown moving ahead in tandem.

Awards, Accolades, and Insults: BRITISH ACADEMY AWARDS: Nomination, Alexander Korda Award for Best British Film; EUROPEAN FILM AWARD: Best Writing (Peter Howitt); FLORIDA FILM CRITICS CIRCLE: Best Actress (Gwyneth Paltrow).

What the Critics Said:

"*Sliding Doors* is way too strained, in narrative logic and in performance, to work. Paltrow either whines or twinkles." — Richard Corliss, *Time*

"*Sliding Doors*, a lightly engaging British comedy, offers the thoroughly absorbing spectacle of Gwyneth Paltrow making her way through not one but two romances." — Shawn Levy, *Portland Oregonian*

Director: Peter Howitt

Writer: Peter Howitt

Executive Producers: Guy East and Nigel Sinclair

Cast:		
	Gwyneth Paltrow	Helen Quilley
	John Hannah	James
	John Lynch	Gerry
	Jeanne Tripplehorn	Lydia

14. *Shakespeare in Love* (1998)

Summary: A fanciful telling of the writing and premiere of Shakespeare's masterpiece, *Romeo and Juliet.* Suffering from writer's block, and in desperate need of a hit, the young Shakespeare finds his muse when he falls in love with a woman betrothed to another but desperate to act.

Of Special Note: Rupert Everett appears in the uncredited role of Christopher Marlowe.

Trivia: At one point in preproduction, Julia Roberts was very close to being signed to play Viola.

Awards, Accolades, and Insults: WRITERS GUILD OF AMERICA: Best Screenplay Written Directly for the Screen (Marc Norman and Tom Stoppard); SCREEN ACTORS GUILD: Outstanding Performance by a Cast (Ben Affleck, Simon Callow, Jim Carter, Martin Clunes, Judi Dench, Joseph Fiennes,

Colin Firth, Gwyneth Paltrow, Geoffrey Rush, Antony Sher, Imelda Staunton, Tom Wilkinson, and Mark Williams), Outstanding Performance by a Female Actor in a Leading Role (Gwyneth Paltrow); Nominations, Outstanding Performance by a Female Actor in a Supporting Role, Outstanding Performance by a Male Actor in a Leading Role, Outstanding Performance by a Male Actor in a Supporting Role; NEW YORK FILM CRITICS CIRCLE: Best Screenplay (Marc Norman and Tom Stoppard); NATIONAL SOCIETY OF FILM CRITICS: Best Supporting Actress (Judi Dench); MTV MOVIE AWARDS: Best Kiss (Joseph Fiennes and Gwyneth Paltrow); GOLDEN GLOBES: Best Screenplay — Motion Picture (Marc Norman and Tom Stoppard), Best Performance by an Actress in a Motion Picture Comedy or Musical (Gwyneth Paltrow), Best Motion Picture Comedy or Musical; BRITISH ACADEMY AWARDS: Best Performance by an Actress in a Supporting Role (Judi Dench), Best Film (Donna Gigliotti, Marc Norman, David Parfitt, Harvey Weinstein, and Edward Zwick); BLOCKBUSTER ENTERTAINMENT AWARDS: Favorite Male Newcomer (Joseph Fiennes); ACADEMY AWARDS: Best Writing — Screenplay Written Directly for the Screen (Marc Norman and Tom Stoppard), Best Supporting Actress (Judi Dench), Best Music — Original Musical or Comedy Score (Stephen Warbeck), Best Costume Design (Sandy Powell), Best Art Direction — Set Decoration (Martin Childs and Jill Quertier), Best Actress (Gwyneth Paltrow), Best Picture (Donna Gigliotti, Marc Norman, David Parfitt, Harvey Weinstein, and Edward Zwick).

What the Critics Said:

"After *Sliding Doors* and now this, Paltrow has to be hailed as one of the most versatile female stars in the world." — Bruce Kirkland, *Ottawa Sun*

"Paltrow, every bit the perfect match for Fiennes, gives us a reason to pay attention to her again after rather routine turns in *A Perfect Murder* and *Sliding Doors*." — Philip Booth, *Orlando Weekly*

"Paltrow's performance almost allows us to overlook her eccentric facial accessories. She has an arch comic approach, and charming spontaneity; she steals every scene from the dully-handsome Joseph Fiennes. Paltrow also knows how to speak Shakespeare's prose; an important requisite, one would think, for a work about Shakespeare." — Bjorn Thomson, *Savoy*

"Gwyneth Paltrow, in her first great, fully realized starring performance, makes a heroine so breathtaking that she seems utterly plausible as the playwright's guiding light. In a film steamy enough to start a sonnet craze, her Viola de Lesseps really does seem to warrant the most timeless love poems, and to speak Shakespeare's own elegant language with astonishing ease. *Shakespeare in Love* itself seems as smitten with her as the poet is, and as alight with the same love of language and beauty." — Janet Maslin, *New York Times*

Director: John Madden

Writers: Marc Norman and Tom Stoppard (with the help of William Shakespeare)

Executive Producers: Donna Gigliotti, Marc Norman, David Parfitt, Harvey Weinstein, and Edward Zwick

Cast:

Joseph Fiennes	Will Shakespeare
Gwyneth Paltrow	Viola de Lesseps
Judi Dench	Queen Elizabeth
Ben Affleck	Ned Alleyn
Colin Firth	Lord Wessex
Simon Callow	Tilney, Master of the Revels
Geoffrey Rush	Philip Henslowe
Martin Clunes	Richard Burbage
Sandra Reinton	Rosaline
Imelda Staunton	Nurse

15. *Out of the Past* (1998)

Summary: An award-winning documentary spotlighting key but nearly forgotten historical figures who played a prominent role in the struggle for gay rights. Using the Ken Burns tried-and-true method of presenting period photos and having actors such as Gwyneth Paltrow and Edward Norton reading from personal journals, director Jeffrey Dupre presents a vivid picture of gay-movement leaders such as Michael Wigglesworth, a Puritan cleric, lesbian novelist Sarah Orne Jewett, and Henry Gerber, an early twentieth-century gay activist.

Awards, Accolades, and Insults: GLADD: Outstanding Film Documentary; SUNDANCE FILM FESTIVAL: Audience Award Documentary (Jeffrey Dupre); Nomination, Grand Jury Prize Documentary; LA OUTFEST: Outstanding Documentary Feature (Jeffrey Dupre).

What the Critics Said:

"What *Out of the Past* reminds us of is the ways that America, despite its declared belief in tolerance and equality, has frequently overlooked and ghettoized the immeasurable social and artistic contributions of millions of its citizens, based on sexual taboos and prejudices. It's a legacy of oppression which, as this detailed and quietly passionate movie assures us, we simply must, and therefore shall, overcome." — Ray Greene, *Boxoffice Magazine*

"Dupre and his collaborators have produced a very polished and engaging documentary that moves with great facility between the hidden past and the current visibility of the Gay Rights movement." — Randy Pitman, *Video Librarian*

"Jeff Dupre makes the powerful, simple point that you need a past history to establish a present, and one of the more insidious side effects of homophobia has been to erase that past." — John Anderson, *Newsday*

Director: Jeffrey Dupre

Writer: Michelle Ferrari

Producers: Eliza Byard, Andrew Tobias, Jeffrey Dupre, and Michelle Ferrari

Voice-Over Cast:

Linda Hunt	Narrator
Stephen Spinella	Michael Wigglesworth
Gwyneth Paltrow	Sarah Orne Jewett
Cherry Jones	Annie Adams Fields
Edward Norton	Henry Gerber
Leland Gantt	Bayard Rustin

16. *Great Expectations* (1998)

Summary: An updated remake of the Dickens classic in which a young boy, Finn, from a poor family falls in love with Estella, the daughter of wealthy parents. When Estella is old enough, she moves away, leaving Finn despondent and unable to pursue his talent in art. Years later, Finn moves to New York where he meets up with Estella, although his dreams of being with the love of his life don't work out the way he had hoped.

What the Critics Said:

"Paltrow's is also a performance lacking in dimension." — Kenneth Turan, *Los Angeles Times*

"As Paltrow struts her ermine-like, barely clad body and Hawke sketches and salivates, you're seeing (as Estella might put it) the movie's prime *raison d'etre*. There's nothing wrong, nor particularly right about the experience. It just sits there, like a Nike ad." — Desson Howe, *Washington Post*

Director: Alfonso Cuarón

Writer: Mitch Glazer (based on the novel by Charles Dickens)

Producers: Deborah Lee and Art Linson

Cast:

Ethan Hawke	Finnegan Bell
Gwyneth Paltrow	Estella
Hank Azaria	Walter Plane
Chris Cooper	Uncle Joe
Anne Bancroft	Ms. Nora Diggers Dinsmoor
Robert De Niro	Prisoner — Lustig

17. *Hush* (1998)

Summary: Jessica Lange plays a mother-in-law from hell and Paltrow the object of her contempt. Typically, the son is completely oblivious to his mother's murderous designs until it is way too late.

Awards, Accolades, and Insults: RAZZIE: Nomination, Worst Actress (Jessica Lange).

What the Critics Said:

"*Hush* is an absurdly bad mixture of *Rosemary's Baby* and any Bette Davis movie from the 1960s." — Barbara Schulgasser, *San Francisco Examiner*

"Schaech and Paltrow make a pretty pair, but this silly show is all Lange's." — Peter Keough, *Boston Phoenix*

"Lange, Paltrow and Schaech (who was in *That Thing You Do!*) should blame co-writer/director Jonathan Darby. Darby has no one to blame but himself." — *E-Online*

Director: Jonathan Darby

Writers: Jonathan Darby and Jane Rusconi; Story by Jonathan Darby

Producers: Helen Whitfield and Douglas Wick

Cast:

Jessica Lange	Martha Baring
Gwyneth Paltrow	Helen
Johnathon Schaech	Jackson Baring
Debi Mazar	Lisa

18. A *Perfect Murder* (1998)

Summary: A remake of the Hitchcock classic, *Dial M for Murder*. This time around, Michael Douglas stars as the older husband facing financial ruin who blackmails a struggling artist to kill his wife in order to collect the money from her trust fund. Only this time, the hitman happens to be the wife's secret but not-so-secret lover.

Of Special Note: The Japanese release was titled *Dial M*.

Awards, Accolades, and Insults: BLOCKBUSTER ENTERTAINMENT AWARDS: Favorite Actress — Suspense (Gwyneth Paltrow); Nominations, Favorite Actor — Suspense, Favorite Supporting Actor — Suspense.

What the Critics Said:

"[Paltrow]'s such a doltish colt that some of the more cynical among us may actually root for her demise. (Especially if they sat through *Hush* and saw what can happen to a movie when she survives a murder plot.)" — Susan Wloszczyna, *USA Today*

"Gwyneth Paltrow, an uneven but promising actress, has nothing to do in Andrew Davis's snoozy, slack thriller *A Perfect Murder* — but, oh, her clothes! Or, specifically, the way Paltrow wears them" — Stephanie Zacharek, *Salon*

Director: Andrew Davis

Writer: Patrick Smith Kelly (based on the stage play *Dial M for Murder* by Frederick Knott)

Producers: Stephen Brown, Anne Kopelson, Arnold Kopelson, Christopher Mankiewicz, and Peter MacGregor-Scott

Cast:	Michael Douglas	Steven Taylor
	Gwyneth Paltrow	Emily Bradford Taylor
	Viggo Mortensen	David Shaw

19. *Duets* (1999)

Summary: A road movie revolving around the sometimes-obsessive world of karaoke. Converging on Omaha, where a national karaoke competition is taking place, are an assortment of characters, including a struggling singer hoping the competition will be his big break, a down-on-his-luck salesman, a con artist, and an escaped convict.

Of Special Note: *Duets* was originally supposed to star Brad Pitt, until he and Paltrow called off their engagement.

Director: Bruce Paltrow

Writer: John Byrum

Executive Producers: Neil Canton, Tony Ludwig, Lee R. Mayes, and Alan Riche

Cast:	Maria Bello	Suzi
	André Braugher	Reggie
	Paul Giamatti	Todd
	Huey Lewis	Ricky Dean
	Steve Oatway	Ralph Beckerman
	Gwyneth Paltrow	Liv
	Scott Speedman	Billy

20. *The Talented Mr. Ripley* (1999)

Summary: Ripley is sent to Europe to bring home a spoiled, rich millionaire playboy. But as he watches his quarry, Ripley becomes obsessed with him. Instead of bringing him back, Ripley kills the playboy and assumes his life.

Of Special Note: Paltrow's castmate, Cate Blanchett, was also nominated for the 1998 Best Actress Oscar for her performance in *Elizabeth*.

Awards, Accolades, and Insults: NATIONAL BOARD OF REVIEW: Best Supporting Actor (Philip Seymour Hoffman); GOLDEN GLOBES: Nominations, Best Performance by an Actor in a Supporting Role, Best Performance by an Actor in a Motion Picture — Drama, Best Director — Motion Picture, Best Original Score — Motion Picture, Best Motion Picture — Drama; BRITISH ACADEMY AWARDS: Best Performance by an Actor in a Supporting Role (Jude Law); Nominations, Best Film, Best Adapted Screenplay, Best Performance by an Actress in a Supporting Role, The David Lean Award for Best Achievement in Direction; ACADEMY AWARDS: Nominations, Best Actor in a

Supporting Role, Best Screenplay — Adaptation, Best Original Score, Best Art Direction, Best Costume Design.

What the Critics Said:

"The Best Alfred Hitchcock movie made since Alfred Hitchcock died." — Tom Block, culturevulture.net

"The movie gives us enticing sights and sounds, brilliant scenes, gifted actors and artists and at least part of one of the all-time great nerve-jangling thriller plots." — Michael Wilmington, *Chicago Tribune*

"Gwyneth Paltrow is more tiresome than usual indulging her specialty of scrunch-faced tearless crying." — Amy Taubin, *Village Voice*

Director: Anthony Minghella

Writer: Anthony Minghella (based on the novel by Patricia Highsmith)

Producers: William Horberg, Sydney Pollack, and Tom Sternberg

Cast:

Matt Damon	Tom Ripley
Gwyneth Paltrow	Marge Sherwood
Jude Law	Dickie Greenleaf
Cate Blanchett	Meredith Logue
Philip Seymour Hoffman	Freddie Miles

21. *Bounce* (2000)

Summary: Buddy Amaral, a free-living advertising executive, becomes emotionally unglued after a plane he was supposed to be on crashes, killing all on board. His guilt stems from his decision to let a man he just met, Greg Janello, take his seat. In the aftermath of the crash, Buddy's despair leads him to alcoholism, depression, and, finally, rehab. Once out, Buddy tracks down Greg's widow, Abby, as part of his therapy. The situation becomes complicated when Buddy finds himself falling in love with Abby, who knows nothing about his connection to Greg's death.

Director: Don Roos

Writer: Don Roos

Cast:
Jennifer Grey
Ben Affleck
Gwyneth Paltrow

Works Consulted

The primary source materials utilized in the preparation of this book were film press production notes, television transcripts, press conference interviews, film reviews, backstage award-show interviews, on-line interviews, and a number of newspaper and magazine articles.

Affleck, Ben. Interview. By Evgenia Peretz. *Vanity Fair* Oct. 1999.

Barnes, Harper. "Basinger and Baldwin Can't Pull This One Off." Rev. of *The Getaway*. Dir. Roger Donaldson. *St. Louis Post-Dispatch* 11 Feb.1994.

——. "A Stark Story of Secret Lives." Rev. of *Flesh and Bone*. Dir. Steve Kloves. *St. Louis Post-Dispatch* 5 Nov. 1993.

Bellafante, Ginia. "People: Heaviness Lite." *Time* 15 Nov. 1993.

Carr, Jay. "The Natural." *Minneapolis Star Tribune* 9 Aug. 1996.

Clark, John. "Daughter. Then Somebody's Girlfriend. With *Emma*, Gwyneth Paltrow Is Finally, Triumphantly, Somebody." *Newsday* 4 Aug. 1996.

Clark, Mike. "*Emma* and Paltrow: A Sublime Match." Rev. of *Emma*. Dir. Douglas McGrath. *USA Today* 2 Aug. 1996.

——. Rev. of *Flesh and Bone*. Dir. Steve Kloves. *USA Today* 22 Apr. 1994.

Connelly, Sherryl. "Fame's Not the Name of the Game for Gwyneth Paltrow." *New York Daily News* 29 Apr. 1998.

Corliss, Richard. "A Touch of Class." *Time* 29 July 1996.

Danner, Blythe. Interview. *Entertainment Tonight*. 19 Dec. 1996.

Denerstein, Robert. "Romeo and Gwyneth in *Shakespeare*: Paltrow Plays Muse to the Bard." *Denver Rocky Mountain News* 29 Dec. 1998.

Ebert, Roger. Rev. of *Emma*. Dir. Douglas McGrath. *Chicago Sun-Times* July 1996

——. Rev. of *Flesh and Bone*. Dir. Steve Kloves. *Chicago Sun-Times* 5 Nov. 1993.

——. Rev. of *Hook*. Dir. Steven Spielberg. *Chicago Sun-Times* 11 Dec. 1991.

——. Rev. of *Hush*. Dir. Jonathan Darby. *Chicago Sun-Times* Mar. 1998.

——. Rev. of *Malice*. Dir. Harold Becker. *Chicago Sun-Times* 1 Oct. 1993.

——. Rev. of *The Pallbearer*. Dir. Matt Reeves. *Chicago Sun-Times* May 1996.

——. Rev. of *A Perfect Murder*. Dir. Andrew Davis. *Chicago Sun-Times* 5 June 1998.

—. Rev. of *Seven*. Dir. David Fincher. *Chicago Sun-Times* 22 Sept. 1995.

Fierman, Daniel. "The Talented Mr. Hoffman." *Entertainment Weekly* 19 Nov. 1999.

Gliatto, Tom. "Love Lost as a Couple, Brad Pitt & Gwyneth Paltrow Appeared to Have It All . . ." *People* 30 June 1997.

Gleiberman, Owen. Rev. of *Jefferson in Paris*. Dir. James Ivory. *Entertainment Weekly* 7 Apr. 1995.

Highsmith, Patricia. *The Talented Mr. Ripley*. 1955. New York: Knopf, 1999.

Hinson, Hal. Rev. of *Hook*. Dir. Steven Spielberg. *Washington Post* 11 Dec. 1991.

Hobson, Louis B. "It's a Fiennes Line: Youngest Sibling, Joseph, Becoming a Hot Commodity." *Sun* [Edmonton, AB] 23 Dec. 1998.

—. "One of the Boys: Gwyneth Paltrow Romps in Elizabethan Romantic Comedy." *Sun* [Edmonton, AB] 23 Dec. 1998.

Hochman, David. "'Love's' Lady Talks." *Entertainment Weekly* 8 Jan. 1999.

—. "A Star Is Born." *US* Aug. 1996.

Howe, Desson. Rev. of *Flesh and Bone*. Dir. Steve Kloves. *Washington Post* 5 Nov. 1993.

Jewel, Dan, et al. "Blast Off His Career and Love Life (with Gwyneth Paltrow) in Orbit, Ben Affleck Knows Just One Direction: Straight Up." *People* 20 July 1998.

Kempley, Rita. Rev. of *Shout*. Dir. Jeffrey Hornaday. *Washington Post* 4 Oct. 1991.

Lee, Luaine. "Actress Paltrow Braves Life in the Spotlight." *Denver Rocky Mountain News* 9 Mar. 1997.

—. "Empty Nester Danner Eyes Return." *Denver Rocky Mountain News* 30 Aug. 1997.

Lloyd, Emily. Interview. "Britain's Emily Lloyd Breaks Hearts and Kayos the Critics in *Wish You Were Here*." By John Stark. *People* 31 Aug. 1987.

Luscombe, Belinda. "Matt Damon Acts Out." *Time* 27 Dec. 1999.

Maltin, Leonard. *Leonard Maltin's Movie & Video Guide*. New York: Plume, 1991-93.

Mattheou, Demetrios. "The Double Life of Gwyneth." *Independent on Sunday* [London, Eng.] 26 Apr. 1998.

Mooney, Josh. "Brad Pitt: Thief of Hearts." *Cosmopolitan* 1 Nov. 1995.

"Movies: Now Playing." Rev. of *Shout*. Dir. Jeffrey Hornaday. *Entertainment Weekly* 18 Oct. 1991.

Mungo, Paul. "A Natural Porn Director." *Independent on Sunday* [London, Eng.] 11 Jan. 1998.

Murray, Steve. "Gwyneth Paltrow Puts the Accent on Acting." *Atlanta Journal and Constitution* 24 Apr. 1998.

Nashawaty, Chris. "Ripley Believe It or Not With *The Talented Mr. Ripley*." *Entertainment Weekly* 17 Dec. 1999.

O'Farrell, Maggie. "My Name Is Joe and I'm an Actor." *Independent on Sunday* [London, Eng.] 17 Jan. 1999.

Paltrow, Gwyneth. "Castaway." *Marie Clarie* Jan. 1998.

——. Interview. "Gwyneth Paltrow — Fashion Superstar." By Merle Ginsberg. W Dec. 1998.
——. Interview. By Michael Szymanski. Mr. Showbiz. *mrshowbiz.com* 14 Mar. 1999.
——. Interview. Mr. Showbiz. *mrshowbiz.com* 1997.
——. Interview. "Perfectly Paltrow." By Jesse Kornbluth. *Buzz* 37 (1995).
——. Interview. By Reggie Nadelson. *Tattler* 8 Jan. 1999.
——. Interview. By Robert Paltrow. *Miami Herald* 15 Feb. 1998.
——. Interview. *Seventeen* Jan. 1997.
——. Interview. "*Shakespeare in Love*: Interview with Gwyneth Paltrow." By Prairie Miller. 1 Jan. 1998.
——. Interview. "With a Nod to Jane Austen, Paltrow Dishes." By Jack Garner. Gannett News Service. 14 Aug. 1996.
Pearlman, Cindy. "How the Stars Beat the Blues." *Ladies Home Journal* 1 Nov. 1996.
Persico, Joyce J. "Pitt and the Pendulum." *Minneapolis Star Tribune* 27 Sept. 1995.
Pierson, Melissa. Rev. of *Shout*. Dir. Jeffrey Hornaday. *Entertainment Weekly* 4 Apr. 1997.
Pitt, Brad. Interview. By Diane Sawyer. *Primetime Live*. ABC. 31 Dec. 1997.
——. Interview. "Hurricane Brad." By Bronwen Hruska. *Newsday* 17 Sept. 1995.
Puig, Claudia. "Plain Expectations: Stardom Sneaked Up on Gwyneth Paltrow." *USA Today* 20 Feb. 1998.
Ragan, David. "Star Bright, Star Bite! The Terrible Things Celebs Say About One Another." *Cosmopolitan* 1 Apr. 1996.
——. "Superstar Daughters on Their Mom Memories." *Cosmopolitan* 1 May 1997.
Rozen, Leah. Rev. of *Flesh and Bone*. Dir. Steve Kloves. *People* 15 Nov. 1993.
Rubenstein, Hal. "Gwyneth When She Glitters." *In Style* 1 Jan. 1999.
Schickel, Richard. Rev. of *Mrs. Parker and the Vicious Circle*. Dir. Alan Rudolph. *Time* 12 Dec. 1994.
Schneider, Karen S. "Look Who Bagged Brad the Down Lone Heartthrob . . ." *People* 26 Aug. 1996.
Schulgasser, Barbara. Rev. of *Hush*. Dir. Jonathan Darby. *San Francisco Examiner* 6 Mar. 1998.
——. Rev. of *Jefferson in Paris*. Dir. James Ivory. *San Francisco Examiner* 7 Apr. 1995.
Simon, Ellen. Interview. "A Script for Healing." By Jane Wollman Rusoff. *Good Housekeeping* 1 Nov. 1995.
Slotek, Jim. "Paltrow Born Bard to the Bone: *Shakespeare in Love* Actress Weaned on Playwright Will Right from the Womb." *Toronto Sun* 17 Dec. 1998.
Spitz, David. "People" *Time* 14 June 1999.
Stuart, Jan. "Meet Joe Fiennes." *Newsday* 9 Dec. 1998.
Tepper, Kirby. Rev. of *Moonlight and Valentino*. Dir. David Anspaugh. *Magill's Survey of Cinema* 15 June 1995.